Data Science for Marketing Analytics

Achieve your marketing goals with the data analytics power of Python

Tommy Blanchard

Debasish Behera

Pranshu Bhatnagar

Data Science for Marketing Analytics

Authors: Tommy Blanchard, Debasish Behera, Pranshu Bhatnagar

Technical Reviewer: Dipankar Nath

Managing Editor: Neha Nair

Acquisitions Editor: Kunal Sawant

Production Editor: Samita Warang

Editorial Board: David Barnes, Ewan Buckingham, Shivangi Chatterji, Simon Cox, Manasa Kumar, Alex Mazonowicz, Douglas Paterson, Dominic Pereira, Shiny Poojary, Saman Siddiqui, Erol Staveley, Ankita Thakur, and Mohita Vyas

First Published: March 2019

Production Reference: 1290319

ISBN: 978-1-78995-941-3

Published by Packt Publishing Ltd.

Livery Place, 35 Livery Street

Birmingham B3 2PB, UK

Table of Contents

Data Exploration and Visualization   49

Unsupervised Learning: Customer Segmentation   93

Choosing the Best Segmentation Approach   121

Predicting Customer Revenue Using Linear Regression   155

Other Regression Techniques and Tools for Evaluation   181

Supervised Learning: Predicting Customer Churn   207

Preface

About the Book

Data Science for Marketing Analytics covers every stage of data analytics, from working with a raw dataset to segmenting a population and modeling different parts of it based on the segments.

The book starts by teaching you how to use Python libraries, such as pandas and Matplotlib, to read data from Python, manipulate it, and create plots using both categorical and continuous variables. Then, you'll learn how to segment a population into groups and use different clustering techniques to evaluate customer segmentation. As you make your way through the chapters, you'll explore ways to evaluate and select the best segmentation approach, and go on to create a linear regression model on customer value data to predict lifetime value. In the concluding chapters, you'll gain an understanding of regression techniques and tools for evaluating regression models, and explore ways to predict customer choice using classification algorithms. Finally, you'll apply these techniques to create a churn model for modeling customer product choices.

By the end of this book, you will be able to build your own marketing reporting and interactive dashboard solutions.

About the Authors

Tommy Blanchard earned his PhD from the University of Rochester and did his postdoctoral training at Harvard. Now, he leads the data science team at Fresenius Medical Care North America. His team performs advanced analytics and creates predictive models to solve a wide variety of problems across the company.

Debasish Behera works as a data scientist for a large Japanese corporate bank, where he applies machine learning/AI to solve complex problems. He has worked on multiple use cases involving AML, predictive analytics, customer segmentation, chat bots, and natural language processing. He currently lives in Singapore and holds a Master's in Business Analytics (MITB) from the Singapore Management University.

Pranshu Bhatnagar works as a data scientist in the telematics, insurance, and mobile software space. He has previously worked as a quantitative analyst in the FinTech industry and often writes about algorithms, time series analysis in Python, and similar topics. He graduated with honors from the Chennai Mathematical Institute with a degree in Mathematics and Computer Science and has completed certification books in Machine Learning and Artificial Intelligence from the International Institute of Information Technology, Hyderabad. He is based in Bangalore, India.

Objectives

- Analyze and visualize data in Python using pandas and Matplotlib
- Study clustering techniques, such as hierarchical and k-means clustering
- Create customer segments based on manipulated data
- Predict customer lifetime value using linear regression
- Use classification algorithms to understand customer choice
- Optimize classification algorithms to extract maximal information

Audience

Data Science for Marketing Analytics is designed for developers and marketing analysts looking to use new, more sophisticated tools in their marketing analytics efforts. It'll help if you have prior experience of coding in Python and knowledge of high school level mathematics. Some experience with databases, Excel, statistics, or Tableau is useful but not necessary.

Approach

Data Science for Marketing Analytics takes a hands-on approach to the practical aspects of using Python data analytics libraries to ease marketing analytics efforts. It contains multiple activities that use real-life business scenarios for you to practice and apply your new skills in a highly relevant context.

Minimum Hardware Requirements

For an optimal student experience, we recommend the following hardware configuration:

- Processor: Dual Core or better
- Memory: 4 GB RAM
- Storage: 10 GB available space

Software Requirements

You'll also need the following software installed in advance:

- Any of the following operating systems: Windows 7 SP1 32/64-bit, Windows 8.1 32/64-bit, or Windows 10 32/64-bit, Ubuntu 14.04 or later, or macOS Sierra or later.

- Browser: Google Chrome or Mozilla Firefox

- Conda

- Python 3.x

Conventions

Code words in text, database table names, folder names, filenames, file extensions, pathnames, dummy URLs, user input, and Twitter handles are shown as follows: "Import the **cluster** module from the **sklearn** package."

A block of code is set as follows:

```
plt.xlabel('Income')
plt.ylabel('Age')
plt.show()
```

New terms and important words are shown in bold. Words that you see on the screen, for example, in menus or dialog boxes, appear in the text like this: "The **Year** column appears to have matched to the right values, but the **line** column does not seem to make much sense."

Installation and Setup

We recommend installing Python using the Anaconda distribution, available here: https://www.anaconda.com/distribution/.

It contains most of the modules that will be used. Additional Python modules can be installed using the methods here: https://docs.python.org/3/installing/index. html. There is only one module that is used that is not part of the standard Anaconda distribution; use one of the methods in the linked page to install it:

- **kmodes**

If you do not use the Anaconda distribution, make sure you have the following modules installed:

- `jupyter`
- `pandas`
- `sklearn`
- `numpy`
- `scipy`
- `seaborn`
- `statsmodels`

Installing the Code Bundle

Copy the code bundle for the class to the `C:/Code` folder.

Additional Resources

The code bundle for this book is also hosted on GitHub at: https://github.com/TrainingByPackt/Data-Science-for-Marketing-Analytics.

We also have other code bundles from our rich catalog of books and videos available at https://github.com/PacktPublishing/. Check them out!

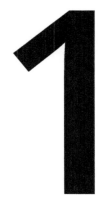

Data Preparation and Cleaning

Learning Objectives

By the end of this chapter, you will be able to:

- Create pandas DataFrames in Python
- Read and write data into different file formats
- Slice, aggregate, filter, and apply functions (built-in and custom) to DataFrames
- Join DataFrames, handle missing values, and combine different data sources

This chapter covers basic data preparation and manipulation techniques in Python, which is the foundation of data science.

Introduction

The way we make decisions in today's world is changing. A very large proportion of our decisions—from choosing which movie to watch, which song to listen to, which item to buy, or which restaurant to visit—all rely upon recommendations and ratings generated by analytics. As decision makers continue to use more of such analytics to make decisions, they themselves become data points for further improvements, and as their own custom needs for decision making continue to be met, they also keep using these analytical models frequently.

The change in consumer behavior has also influenced the way companies develop strategies to target consumers. With the increased digitization of data, greater availability of data sources, and lower storage and processing costs, firms can now crunch large volumes of increasingly granular data with the help of various data science techniques and leverage it to create complex models, perform sophisticated tasks, and derive valuable consumer insights with higher accuracy. It is because of this dramatic increase in data and computing power, and the advancement in techniques to use this data through data science algorithms, that the McKinsey Global Institute calls our age the **Age of Analytics**.

Several industry leaders are already using data science to make better decisions and to improve their marketing analytics. Google and Amazon have been making targeted recommendations catering to the preferences of their users from their very early years. Predictive data science algorithms tasked with generating leads from marketing campaigns at Dell reportedly converted 50% of the final leads, whereas those generated through traditional methods had a conversion rate of only 17%. Price surges on Uber for non-pass holders during rush hour also reportedly had massive positive effects on the company's profits. In fact, it was recently discovered that price management initiatives based on an evaluation of customer lifetime value tended to increase business margins by 2%–7% over a 12-month period and resulted in a 200%–350% ROI in general.

Although using data science principles in marketing analytics is a proven cost-effective, efficient way for a lot of companies to observe a customer's journey and provide a more customized experience, multiple reports suggest that it is not being used to its full potential. There is a wide gap between the possible and actual usage of these techniques by firms. This book aims to bridge that gap, and covers an array of useful techniques involving everything data science can do in terms of marketing strategies and decision-making in marketing. By the end of the book, you should be able to successfully create and manage an end-to-end marketing analytics pipeline in Python, segment customers based on the data provided, predict their lifetime value, and model their decision-making behavior on your own using data science techniques.

This chapter introduces you to cleaning and preparing data—the first step in any data-centric pipeline. Raw data coming from external sources cannot generally be used directly; it needs to be structured, filtered, combined, analyzed, and observed before it can be used for any further analyses. In this chapter, we will explore how to get the right data in the right attributes, manipulate rows and columns, and apply transformations to data. This is essential because, otherwise, we will be passing incorrect data to the pipeline, thereby making it a classic example of garbage in, garbage out.

Data Models and Structured Data

When we build an analytics pipeline, the first thing that we need to do is to build a **data model**. A data model is an overview of the data sources that we will be using, their relationships with other data sources, where exactly the data from a specific source is going to enter the pipeline, and in what form (such as an Excel file, a database, or a JSON from an internet source). The data model for the pipeline evolves over time as data sources and processes change. A data model can contain data of the following three types:

- **Structured Data**: This is also known as *completely structured* or *well-structured data*. This is the simplest way to manage information. The data is arranged in a flat tabular form with the correct value corresponding to the correct attribute. There is a unique column, known as an **index**, for easy and quick access to the data, and there are no duplicate columns. Data can be queried exactly through SQL queries, for example, data in relational databases, MySQL, Amazon Redshift, and so on.

- **Semi-structured data**: This refers to data that may be of variable lengths and that may contain different data types (such as numerical or categorical) in the same column. Such data may be arranged in a nested or hierarchical tabular structure, but it still follows a fixed schema. There are no duplicate columns (attributes), but there may be duplicate rows (observations). Also, each row might not contain values for every attribute, that is, there may be missing values. Semi-structured data can be stored accurately in NoSQL databases, Apache Parquet files, JSON files, and so on.

- **Unstructured data**: Data that is unstructured may not be tabular, and even if it is tabular, the number of attributes or columns per observation may be completely arbitrary. The same data could be represented in different ways, and the attributes might not match each other, with values leaking into other parts. Unstructured data can be stored as text files, CSV files, Excel files, images, audio clips, and so on.

Marketing data, traditionally, comprises data of all three types. Initially, most data points originated from different (possibly manual) data sources, so the values for a field could be of different lengths, the value for one field would not match that of other fields because of different field names, some rows containing data from even the same sources could also have missing values for some of the fields, and so on. But now, because of digitization, structured and semi-structured data is also available and is increasingly being used to perform analytics. The following figure illustrates the data model of traditional marketing analytics comprising all kinds of data: structured data such as databases (top), semi-structured data such as JSONs (middle), and unstructured data such as Excel files (bottom):

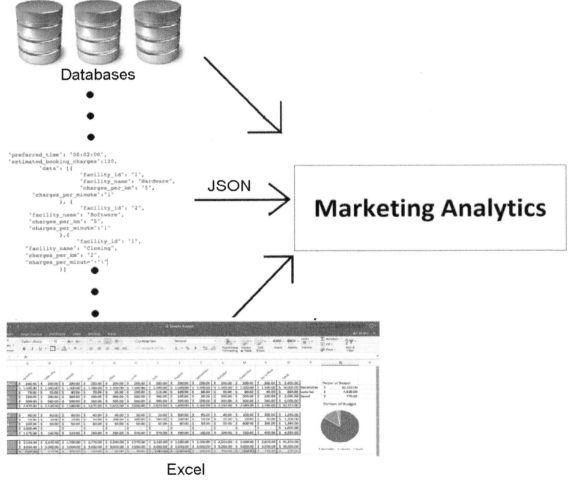

Figure 1.1: Data model of traditional marketing analytics

A data model with all these different kinds of data is prone to errors and is very risky to use. If we somehow get a garbage value into one of the attributes, our entire analysis will go awry. Most of the times, the data we need is of a certain kind and if we don't get that type of data, we might run into a bug or problem that would need to be investigated. Therefore, if we can enforce some checks to ensure that the data being passed to our model is almost always of the same kind, we can easily improve the quality of data from unstructured to at least semi-structured.

This is where programming languages such as Python come into play. Python is an all-purpose general programming language that not only makes writing structure-enforcing scripts easy, but also integrates with almost every platform and automates data production, analysis, and analytics into a more reliable and predictable pipeline. Apart from understanding patterns and giving at least a basic structure to data, Python forces intelligent pipelines to accept the right value for the right attribute. The majority of analytics pipelines are exactly of this kind. The following figure illustrates how most marketing analytics today structure different kinds of data by passing it through scripts to make it at least semi-structured:

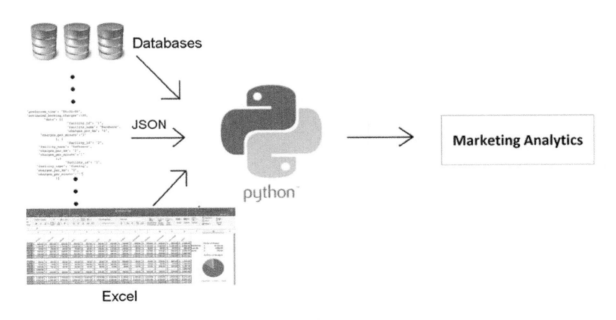

Figure 1.2: Data model of most marketing analytics that use Python

By making use of such structure-enforcing scripts, we will have a pipeline of semi-structured data coming in with expected values in the right fields; however, the data is not yet in the best possible format to perform analytics. If we can completely structure our data (that is, arrange it in flat tables, with the right value pointing to the right attribute with no nesting or hierarchy), it will be easy for us to see how every data point individually compares to other points being considered in the common fields, and would also make the pipeline scalable. We can easily get a feel of the data–that is, see in what range most values lie, identify the clear outliers, and so on–by simply scrolling through the data.

While there are a lot of tools that can be used to convert data from an unstructured/semi-structured format to a fully structured format (for example, Spark, STATA, and SAS), the tool that is most commonly used for data science, can be integrated with practically any framework, has rich functionalities, minimal costs, and is easy-to-use for our use case, is **pandas**. The following figure illustrates how a data model structures different kinds of data from being possibly unstructured to semi-structured (using Python), to completely structured (using pandas):

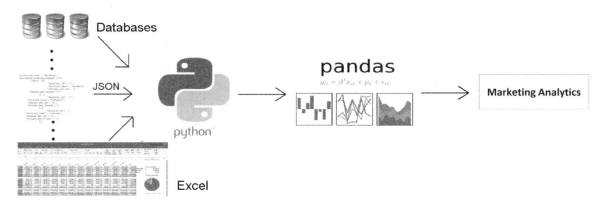

Figure 1.3: Data model to structure the different kinds of data

> Note
>
> For the purpose of this book, we will assume that you are more or less comfortable with NumPy.

pandas

pandas is a software library written in Python and is the basis for data manipulation and analysis in the language. Its name comes from "panel data," an econometrics term for datasets that include observations over multiple time periods for the same individuals.

pandas offers a collection of high-performance, easy-to-use, and intuitive data structures and analysis tools that are of great use to marketing analysts and data scientists alike. It has the following two primary object types:

- **DataFrame**: This is the fundamental tabular relationship object that stores data in rows and columns (like a spreadsheet). To perform data analysis, functions and operations can be directly applied to DataFrames.

- **Series**: This refers to a single column of the DataFrame. The value can be accessed through its index. As Series automatically infers a type, it automatically makes all DataFrames well-structured.

The following figure illustrates a pandas DataFrame with an automatic integer index (0, 1, 2, 3...):

	Year	Product	line	Product.1	type	Product.2	Order	method	type.1	Retailer	...	Quantity	Unit
0	2004	Camping	Equipment	Cooking	Gear	TrailChef	Water	Bag	Telephone	United	...	6.59	156672.570
1	2004	Camping	Equipment	Cooking	Gear	TrailChef	Water	Bag	Telephone	Canada	...	7145.88	6.190
2	2004	Camping	Equipment	Cooking	Gear	TrailChef	Water	Bag	Telephone	Mexico	...	NaN	NaN
3	2004	Camping	Equipment	Cooking	Gear	TrailChef	Water	Bag	Telephone	Brazil	...	NaN	NaN
4	2004	Camping	Equipment	Cooking	Gear	TrailChef	Water	Bag	Telephone	Japan	...	91707.18	5.488

5 rows × 26 columns

Figure 1.4: A sample pandas DataFrame

Now that we understand what pandas objects are and how they can be used to automatically get structured data, let's take a look at some of the functions we can use to import and export data in pandas and see if the data we passed is ready to be used for further analyses.

Importing and Exporting Data With pandas DataFrames

Every team in a marketing group can have its own preferred data type for their specific use case. Those who have to deal with a lot more text than numbers might prefer using JSON or XML, while others may prefer CSV, XLS, or even Python objects. pandas has a lot of simple **APIs (application program interfaces)** that allow it to read a large variety of data directly into DataFrames. Some of the main ones are shown here:

Data Source Type	Read Function	Write Function	Format Type
CSV	read_csv	to_csv	Text
JSON	read_json	to_json	Text
HTML	read_html	to_html	Text
XML	read_xml	to_xml	Text
Excel	read_excel	to_excel	Binary
Stata	read_stata	to_stata	Binary
SAS	read_sas	to_sas	Binary
Clipboard	read_clipboard	to_clipboard	Text
Python Pickle File Format	read_pickle	to_pickle	Binary

Figure 1.5: Ways to import and export different types of data with pandas DataFrames

Note

Remember that a well-structured DataFrame does not have hierarchical or nested data. The **read_xml**, **read_json()**, and **read_html()** functions (and others) cause the data to lose its hierarchical datatypes/nested structure and convert it into flattened objects such as lists and lists of lists. Pandas, however, does support hierarchical data for data analysis. You can save and load such data by pickling from your session and maintaining the hierarchy in such cases. When working with data pipelines, it's advised to split nested data into separate streams to maintain the structure.

When loading data, pandas provides us with additional parameters that we can pass to **read** functions, so that we can load the data differently. Some additional parameters that are used commonly when importing data into pandas are given here:

- **skiprows = k**: This skips the first *k* rows.

- **nrows = k**: This parses only the first *k* rows.

- **names = [col1, col2...]**: This lists the column names to be used in the parsed DataFrame.

- **header = k**: This applies the column names corresponding to the *kth* row as the header for the DataFrame. *k* can also be **None**.

- **index_col = col**: This sets **col** as the index of the DataFrame being used. This can also be a list of column names (used to create a *MultiIndex*) or **None**.

- **usecols = [l1, l2...]**: This provides either integer positional indices in the document columns or strings that correspond to column names in the DataFrame to be read. For example, [0, 1, 2] or ['foo', 'bar', 'baz'].

> **Note**
>
> There are similar specific parameters for almost every in-built function in pandas. You can find details about them with the documentation for pandas available at the following link: https://pandas.pydata.org/pandas-docs/stable/.

Viewing and Inspecting Data in DataFrames

Once you've read the DataFrame using the API, as explained earlier, you'll notice that, unless there is something grossly wrong with the data, the API generally never fails, and we always get a DataFrame object after the call. However, we need to inspect the data ourselves to check whether the right attribute has received the right data, for which we can use several in-built functions that pandas provides. Assume that we have stored the DataFrame in a variable called **df** then:

- **df.head(n)** will return the first **n** rows of the DataFrame. If no **n** is passed, by default, the function considers **n** to be 5.

- **df.tail(n)** will return the last **n** rows of the DataFrame. If no **n** is passed, by default, the function considers **n** to be 5.

- **df.shape** will return a tuple of the type (number of rows, number of columns).

- **df.dtypes** will return the type of data in each column of the pandas DataFrame (such as **float**, **char**, and so on).

- **df.info()** will summarize the DataFrame and print its size, type of values, and the count of non-null values.

Exercise 1: Importing JSON Files into pandas

For this exercise, you need to use the **user_info.json** file provided to you in the **Lesson01** folder. The file contains some anonymous personal user information collected from six customers through a web-based form in JSON format. You need to open a Jupyter Notebook, import the JSON file into the console as a pandas DataFrame, and see whether it has loaded correctly, with the right values being passed to the right attribute.

> **Note**
>
> All the exercises and activities in this chapter can be done in both the Jupyter Notebook and Python shell. While we can do them in the shell for now, it is highly recommended to use the Jupyter Notebook. To learn how to install Jupyter and set up the Jupyter Notebook, check https://jupyter.readthedocs.io/en/latest/install.html. It will be assumed that you are using a Jupyter Notebook from the next chapter onward.

1. Open a Jupyter Notebook to implement this exercise. Once you are in the console, import the pandas library using the **import** command, as follows:

   ```
   import pandas as pd
   ```

2. Read the **user_info.json** JSON file into the **user_info** DataFrame:

   ```
   user_info = pd.read_json("user_info.json")
   ```

3. Check the first few values in the DataFrame using the **head** command:

   ```
   user_info.head()
   ```

You should see the following output:

	_id	about	address	age	balance	company	email	eyeColor	favoriteFruit	friends	...	
0	5c0a28d7a647437fd3d3a6aa	Nostrud consectetur elit occaecat dolore incid...	698 Kansas Place, Bethpage, Louisiana, 7695	20	$3,806.93	RODEMCO	graceberry@rodemco.com	green	strawberry	[{u'id': 0, u'name': u'Small Pena'}, {u'id': 1...		832f1af4 4ba8- f4cbf34:
1	5c0a28d780f6278b11586ab1	Sunt id ipsum velit voluptate. Ullamco non non...	309 Kingsway Place, Kilbourne, New York, 3771	22	$3,330.01	VIAGRAND	hilarysellers@viagrand.com	brown	apple	[{u'id': 0, u'name': u'Spears Smith'}, {u'id'...		4306 9506- e69a063!
2	5c0a28d722e2e29d9bce2b64	Laborum ad excepteur amet sunt aliqua veniam c...	347 Seeley Street, Witmer, Kansas, 9369	40	$1,619.46	EQUITOX	sherrigilbert@equitox.com	green	apple	[{u'id': 0, u'name': u'Sexton Watts'}, {u'id'...		5019 7cc4- 3483131
3	5c0a28d76b5e8859a754cb4f	Eu amet aliqua magna ipsum quis et ut reprehen...	178 Stewart Street, Ferney, Wyoming, 9118	29	$3,334.12	ANARCO	caldwellpatterson@anarco.com	blue	strawberry	[{u'id': 0, u'name': u'Anne Holcomb'}, {u'id'...		d2c4 2974- d1dae5d
4	5c0a28d7ebb99c08e2288c76	Sunt amet exercitation aliqua cillum commodo o...	189 Rogers Avenue, Lindisfarne, Mississippi, 1961	33	$1,368.48	MEGALL	headmcconnell@megall.com	brown	strawberry	[{u'id': 0, u'name': u'Elnora Peck'}, {u'id' ...		df0b 2e81 16f138e:

5 rows × 22 columns

Figure 1.6: Viewing the first few rows of user_info.json

4. As we can see, the data makes sense superficially. Let's see if the data types match too. Type in the following command:

```
user_info.info()
```

You should get the following output:

```
<class 'pandas.core.frame.DataFrame'>
RangeIndex: 6 entries, 0 to 5
Data columns (total 22 columns):
_id              6 non-null object
about            6 non-null object
address          6 non-null object
age              6 non-null int64
balance          6 non-null object
company          6 non-null object
email            6 non-null object
eyeColor         6 non-null object
favoriteFruit    6 non-null object
friends          6 non-null object
gender           6 non-null object
greeting         6 non-null object
guid             6 non-null object
index            6 non-null int64
isActive         6 non-null bool
latitude         6 non-null float64
longitude        6 non-null float64
name             6 non-null object
phone            6 non-null object
picture          6 non-null object
registered       6 non-null object
tags             6 non-null object
dtypes: bool(1), float64(2), int64(2), object(17)
memory usage: 1.1+ KB
```

Figure 1.7: Information about the data in user_info

From the preceding figure, notice that the **isActive** column is Boolean, the **age** and **index** columns are integers, whereas the **latitude** and **longitude** columns are floats. The rest of the elements are Python objects, most likely to be strings. Looking at the names, they match our intuition. So, the data types seem to match. Also, the number of observations seems to be the same for all fields, which implies that there has been no data loss.

Note

The **64** displayed with the type above is an indicator of precision and varies on different platforms.

5. Let's also see the number of rows and columns in the DataFrame using the shape attribute of the DataFrame:

    ```
    user_info.shape
    ```

    This will give you (6, 22) as the output, indicating that the DataFrame created by the JSON has 6 rows and 22 columns.

Congratulations! You have loaded the data correctly, with the right attributes corresponding to the right columns and with no missing values. Since the data was already structured, it is now ready to be put into the pipeline to be used for further analysis.

Exercise 2: Identifying Semi-Structured and Unstructured Data

In this exercise, you will be using the **data.csv** and **sales.xlsx** files provided to you in the **Lesson01** folder. The **data.csv** file contains the views and likes of 100 different posts on Facebook in a marketing campaign, and **sales.xlsx** contains some historical sales data recorded in MS Excel about different customer purchases in stores in the past few years. We want to read the files into pandas DataFrames and check whether the output is ready to be added into the analytics pipeline. Let's first work with the **data.csv** file:

1. Import pandas into the console, as follows:

    ```
    import pandas as pd
    ```

2. Use the **read_csv** method to read the **data.csv** CSV file into a **campaign_data** DataFrame:

    ```
    campaign_data = pd.read_csv("data.csv")
    ```

3. Look at the current state of the DataFrame using the **head** function:

    ```
    campaign_data.head()
    ```

Your output should look as follows:

Campaign Data	
views	likes
90006	402
101141	389
97297	403
117182	397

Figure 1.8: Viewing raw campaign_data

From the preceding output, we can observe that the first column has an issue; we want to have "views" and "likes" as the column names and for the DataFrame to have numeric values.

4. We will read the data into **campaign_data** again, but this time making sure that we use the first row to get the column names using the **header** parameter, as follows:

```
campaign_data = pd.read_csv("data.csv", header = 1)
```

5. Let's now view **campaign_data** again, and see whether the attributes are okay now:

```
campaign_data.head()
```

Your DataFrame should now appear as follows:

	views	likes
0	90006	402
1	101141	389
2	97297	403
3	117182	397
4	99637	404

Figure 1.9: campaign_data after being read with the header parameter

6. The values seem to make sense—with the views being far more than the likes—when we look at the first few rows, but because of some misalignment or missing values, the last few rows might be different. So, let's have a look at it:

    ```
    campaign_data.tail()
    ```

    You will get the following output:

	views	likes
95	100464	391
96	96382	387
97	94971	389
98	103070	410
99	110387	411

    Figure 1.10: The last few rows of campaign_data

7. There doesn't seem to be any misalignment of data or missing values at the end. However, although we have seen the last few rows, we still can't be sure that all values in the middle (hidden) part of the DataFrame are okay too. We can check the datatypes of the DataFrame to be sure:

    ```
    campaign_data.info()
    ```

    You should get the following output:

    ```
    <class 'pandas.core.frame.DataFrame'>
    RangeIndex: 100 entries, 0 to 99
    Data columns (total 2 columns):
    views    100 non-null int64
    likes    100 non-null int64
    dtypes: int64(2)
    memory usage: 1.6 KB
    ```

    Figure 1.11: info() of campaign_data

8. We also need to ensure that we have not lost some observations because of our cleaning. We use the **shape** function for that:

```
campaign_data.shape
```

You will get an output of (100, 2), indicating that we still have 100 observations with 2 columns. The dataset is now completely structured and can easily be a part of any further analysis or pipeline.

9. Let's now analyze the **sales.xlsx** file. Use the **read_excel** function to read the file in a DataFrame called **sales**:

```
sales = pd.read_excel("sales.xlsx")
```

10. Look at the first few rows of the **sales** DataFrame:

```
sales.head()
```

Your output should look as follows:

	Year	Product	line	Product.1	type	Product.2	Order	method	type.1	Retailer	...	Quantity	Unit
0	2004	Camping	Equipment	Cooking	Gear	TrailChef	Water	Bag	Telephone	United	...	6.59	156672.570
1	2004	Camping	Equipment	Cooking	Gear	TrailChef	Water	Bag	Telephone	Canada	...	7145.88	6.190
2	2004	Camping	Equipment	Cooking	Gear	TrailChef	Water	Bag	Telephone	Mexico	...	NaN	NaN
3	2004	Camping	Equipment	Cooking	Gear	TrailChef	Water	Bag	Telephone	Brazil	...	NaN	NaN
4	2004	Camping	Equipment	Cooking	Gear	TrailChef	Water	Bag	Telephone	Japan	...	91707.18	5.488

5 rows × 26 columns

Figure 1.12: First few rows of sales.xlsx

From the preceding figure, the **Year** column appears to have matched to the right values, but the **line** column does not seem to make much sense. The **Product.1**, **Product.2**, columns imply that there are multiple columns with the same name! Even the values of the **Order** and **method** columns being **Water** and **Bag**, respectively, make us feel as though something is wrong.

11. Let's look at gathering some more information, such as null values and the data types of the columns, and see if we can make more sense of the data:

```
sales.info()
```

Your output will look as follows:

```
<class 'pandas.core.frame.DataFrame'>
RangeIndex: 65535 entries, 0 to 65534
Data columns (total 26 columns):
Year          65535 non-null int64
Product       65535 non-null object
line          65535 non-null object
Product.1     65535 non-null object
type          65535 non-null object
Product.2     65535 non-null object
Order         65535 non-null object
method        61083 non-null object
type.1        46709 non-null object
Retailer      32525 non-null object
country       24135 non-null object
Revenue       21494 non-null object
Planned       20925 non-null object
revenue       20645 non-null object
Product.3     20588 non-null object
cost          19224 non-null float64
Quantity      13663 non-null float64
Unit          7046 non-null float64
cost.1        2403 non-null float64
Unit.1        650 non-null float64
price         233 non-null float64
Gross         46 non-null float64
profit        4 non-null float64
Unit.2        0 non-null float64
sale          0 non-null float64
price.1       0 non-null float64
dtypes: float64(11), int64(1), object(14)
memory usage: 13.0+ MB
```

Figure 1.13: Output of sales.info()

As there are some columns with no non-null values, the column names seem to have broken up incorrectly. This is probably why the output of **info** showed a column such as **revenue** as having an arbitrary data type such as **object** (usually used to refer to columns containing strings). It makes sense if the actual column names start with a capital letter and the remaining columns are created as a result of data spilling from the preceding columns.

12. Let's try to read the file with just the new, correct column names and see whether we get anything. Use the following code:

```
sales = pd.read_excel("sales.xlsx", names = ["Year", "Product line",
"Product type", "Product", "Order method type", "Retailer Country",
"Revenue", "Planned revenue", "Product cost", "Quantity", "Unit cost",
"Unit price", "Gross Profit", "Unit sale price"])
```

You get the following output:

```
-----------------------------------------------------------------
ValueError                          Traceback (most recent call last)
<ipython-input-12-bd2f1651eb25> in <module>()
      1 sales = pd.read_excel("sales.xlsx", names = ["Year", "Product line", "Product type", "Product", "Order method type",
      2                                           "Retailer Country", "Revenue", "Planned revenue", "Product cost", "Quantit
y",
----> 3                                           "Unit cost", "Unit price", "Gross Profit", "Unit sale price"])

/home/poseidon/.local/lib/python2.7/site-packages/pandas/util/_decorators.pyc in wrapper(*args, **kwargs)
    176                 else:
    177                     kwargs[new_arg_name] = new_arg_value
--> 178             return func(*args, **kwargs)
    179         return wrapper
    180     return _deprecate_kwarg

/home/poseidon/.local/lib/python2.7/site-packages/pandas/util/_decorators.pyc in wrapper(*args, **kwargs)
    176                 else:
    177                     kwargs[new_arg_name] = new_arg_value
--> 178             return func(*args, **kwargs)
    179         return wrapper
    180     return _deprecate_kwarg

/home/poseidon/.local/lib/python2.7/site-packages/pandas/io/excel.pyc in read_excel(io, sheet_name, header, names, index_col, u
secols, squeeze, dtype, engine, converters, true_values, false_values, skiprows, nrows, na_values, parse_dates, date_parser, th
ousands, comment, skipfooter, convert_float, **kwds)
    327             skipfooter=skipfooter,
```

Figure 1.14: Attempting to structure sales.xlsx

Unfortunately, the issue is not just with the columns, but with the underlying values too. The value of one column is leaking into another and thus ruining the structure. Understandably, the code fails because of length mismatch. Therefore, we can conclude that the **sales.xlsx** data is very unstructured.

With the use of the API and what we know up till this point, we can't directly get this data to be structured. To understand how to approach structuring this kind of data, we need to dive deep into the internal structure of pandas objects and understand how data is actually stored in pandas, which we will do in the following sections. We will come back to preparing this data for further analysis in a later section.

Structure of a pandas Series

Let's say you want to store some values from a data store in a data structure. It is not necessary for every element of the data to have values, so your structure should be able to handle that. It is also a very common scenario where there is some discrepancy between two data sources on how to identify a data point. So, instead of using default numerical indices (such as 0-100) or user-given names to access it, like in a dictionary, you would like to access every value by a name that comes from within the data source. This is achieved in pandas using a **pandas Series**.

A pandas Series is nothing but an indexed NumPy array. To make a pandas Series, all you need to do is create an array and give it an index. If you create a Series without an index, it will create a default numeric index that starts from 0 and goes on for the length of the Series, as shown in the following figure:

Figure 1.15: Sample pandas Series

> **Note**
>
> As a Series is still a NumPy array, all functions that work on a NumPy array, work the same way on a pandas Series too.

Once you've created a number of Series, you might want to access the values associated with some specific indices all at once to perform an operation. This is just aggregating the Series with a specific value of the index. It is here that pandas DataFrames come into the picture. A pandas DataFrame is just a dictionary with the column names as keys and values as different pandas Series, joined together by the index:

	age		balance		_id	about	address	age	balance	company
0	20	0	$3,806.93	0	5c0a28d7a647437fd3d3a6aa	Nostrud consectetur elit occaecat dolore incid...	698 Kansas Place, Bethpage, Louisiana, 7695	20	$3,806.93	RODEMCO
1	22	1	$3,330.01	1	5c0a28d780f6278b11586ab1	Sunt id ipsum velit voluptate. Ullamco non non...	309 Kingsway Place, Kilbourne, New York, 3771	22	$3,330.01	VIAGRAND
2	40	2	$1,619.46	2	5c0a28d722e2e29d9bce2b64	Laborum ad excepteur amet sunt aliqua veniam c...	347 Seeley Street, Witmer, Kansas, 9369	40	$1,619.46	EQUITOX
3	29	3	$3,334.12	3	5c0a28d76b5e8859a754cb4f	Eu amet aliqua magna ipsum quis et ut reprehen...	178 Stewart Street, Ferney, Wyoming, 9118	29	$3,334.12	ANARCO
4	33	4	$1,368.48	4	5c0a28d7ebb99c08e2288c76	Sunt amet exercitation aliqua cillum commodo o...	189 Rogers Avenue, Lindisfarne, Mississippi, 1961	33	$1,368.48	MEGALL

Figure 1.16: Series joined together by the same index create a pandas Dataframe

This way of storing data makes it very easy to perform the operations we need on the data we want. We can easily choose the Series we want to modify by picking a column and directly slicing off indices based on the value in that column. We can also group indices with similar values in one column together and see how the values change in other columns.

Other than this one-dimensional Series structure to access the DataFrame, pandas also has the concept of axes, where an operation can be applied to both rows (or indices) and columns. You can choose which one to apply it to by specifying the axis, 0 referring to rows and 1 referring to columns, thereby making it very easy to access the underlying headers and the values associated with them:

	_id	about	address	age	balance	company	email	eyeColor	favoriteFruit	friends	...
0	5c0a28d7a647437fd3d3a6aa	Nostrud consectetur elit occaecat dolore incid...	698 Kansas Place, Bethpage, Louisiana, 7695	20	$3,806.93	RODEMCO	graceberry@rodemco.com	green	strawberry	[{'id': 0, 'name': 'Small Pena'}, {'id': 1, 'n...	832f1af4-4ba8-f4cbf34...
1	5c0a28d780f6278b11586ab1	Sunt id ipsum velit voluptate. Ullamco non non...	309 Kingsway Place, Kilbourne, New York, 3771	22	$3,330.01	VIAGRAND	hilarysellers@viagrand.com	brown	apple	[{'id': 0, 'name': 'Spears Smith'}, {'id': 1, ...	4306 9506-e69a063...
2	5c0a28d722e2e29d9bce2b64	Laborum ad excepteur amet sunt aliqua veniam c...	347 Seeley Street, Witmer, Kansas, 9369	40	$1,619.46	EQUITOX	sherrigilbert@equitox.com	green	apple	[{'id': 0, 'name': 'Sexton Watts'}, {'id': 1, ...	5019 7cc4-3483131
3	5c0a28d76b5e8859a754cb4f	Eu amet aliqua magna ipsum quis et ut reprehen...	178 Stewart Street, Ferney, Wyoming, 9118	29	$3,334.12	ANARCO	caldwellpatterson@anarco.com	blue	strawberry	[{'id': 0, 'name': 'Anne Holcomb'}, {'id': 1, ...	d2c4 2974-d1dae5d...
4	5c0a28d7ebb99c08e2288c76	Sunt amet exercitation aliqua cillum commodo o...	189 Rogers Avenue, Lindisfarne, Mississippi, 1961	33	$1,368.48	MEGALL	headmcconnell@megall.com	brown	strawberry	[{'id': 0, 'name': 'Elnora Peck'}, {'id': 1, '...	df0b 2e81-16f138e...

(axis = 1 or axis = 'columns'; axis = 0 or axis = 'index')

Figure 1.17: Understanding axis = 0 and axis = 1 in pandas

Data Manipulation

Now that we have deconstructed the structure of the pandas DataFrame down to its basics, the rest of the wrangling tasks, that is, creating new DataFrames, selecting or slicing a DataFrame into its parts, filtering DataFrames for some values, joining different DataFrames, and so on, will become very intuitive.

Selecting and Filtering in pandas

It is standard convention in spreadsheets to address a cell by (column name, row name). Since data is stored in pandas in a similar manner, this is also the way to address a cell in a pandas DataFrame: the column name acts as a key to give you the pandas Series, and the row name gives you the value on that index of the DataFrame.

But if you need to access more than a single cell, such as a subset of some rows and columns from the DataFrame, or change the order of display of some columns on the DataFrame, you can make use of the syntax listed in the following table:

Operation	Syntax	Result
Select a column	df[col]	Series
Select multiple columns	df[[col1, col2..]]	DataFrame
Select a row by label	df.loc[label]	Series
Select a row by integer location	df.iloc[loc]	Series
Slice rows	df[start_idx: end_idx]	DataFrame
Select multiple rows by Boolean vector	df[bool_vec]	DataFrame

Figure 1.18: A table listing the syntax used for different operations on a pandas DataFrame

Creating Test DataFrames in Python

We frequently need to create test objects while building a data pipeline in pandas. Test objects give us a reference point to figure out what we have been able to do up till that point and make it easier to debug our scripts. Generally, test DataFrames are small in size, so that the output of every process is quick and easy to compute. There are two ways to create test DataFrames—by creating completely new DataFrames, or by duplicating or taking a slice of a previously existing DataFrame:

- **Creating new DataFrames**: We typically use the **DataFrame** method to create a completely new DataFrame. The function directly converts a Python object into a pandas DataFrame. The **DataFrame** function will, in general, work with any iterable collection of data (such as **dict**, **list**, and so on). We can also pass an empty collection or a singleton collection to the function.

  For example, we will get the same DataFrame through either of the following lines of code:

  ```
  pd.DataFrame({'category': pd.Series([1, 2, 3])}
  pd.DataFrame([1, 2, 3], columns=['category'])
  pd.DataFrame.from_dict({'category': [1, 2, 3]})
  ```

The following figure shows the outputs received each time:

	category
0	1
1	2
2	3

Figure 1.19: Output generated by all three ways to create a DataFrame

A DataFrame can also be built by passing any pandas objects to the **DataFrame** function. The following line of code gives the same output as the preceding figure:

```
pd.DataFrame(pd.Series([1,2,3]), columns=["category"])
```

- **Duplicating or slicing a previously existing DataFrame**: The second way to create a test DataFrame is by copying a previously existing DataFrame. Python, and therefore, pandas, has shallow references. When we say **obj1 = obj2**, the objects share the location or the reference to the same object in memory. So, if we change **obj2**, **obj1** also gets modified, and vice versa. This is tackled in the standard library with the **deepcopy** function in the copy module. The **deepcopy** function allows the user to recursively go through the objects being pointed to by the references and create entirely new objects.

So, when you want to copy a previously existing DataFrame and don't want the previous DataFrame to be affected by modifications in the current DataFrame, you need to use the **deepcopy** function. You can also slice the previously existing DataFrame and pass it to the function, and it will be considered a new DataFrame. For example, the following code snippet will recursively copy everything in **df1** and not have any references to it when you make changes to **df**:

```
import pandas
import copy
df = copy.deepcopy(df1)
```

Adding and Removing Attributes and Observations

pandas provides the following functions to add and delete rows (observations) and columns (attributes):

- `df['col'] = s`: This adds a new column, **col**, to the DataFrame, **df**, with the Series, **s**.

- `df.assign(c1 = s1, c2 = s2...)`: This adds new columns, **c1**, **c2**, and so on, with series, **s1**, **s2**, and so on, to the **df** DataFrame in one go.

- `df.append(df2 / d2, ignore_index)`: This adds values from the **df2** DataFrame to the bottom of the **df** DataFrame wherever the columns of **df2** match those of **df**. Alternatively, it also accepts dict and **d2**, and if `ignore_index = True`, it does not use index labels.

- `df.drop(labels, axis)`: This remove the rows or columns specified by the labels and corresponding axis, or those specified by the index or column names directly.

- `df.dropna(axis, how)`: Depending on the parameter passed to **how**, this decides whether to drop rows (or columns if `axis = 1`) with missing values in any of the fields or in all of the fields. If no parameter is passed, the default value of **how** is **any** and the default value of **axis** is 0.

- `df.drop_duplicates(keep)`: This removes rows with duplicate values in the DataFrame, and keeps the first (`keep = 'first'`), last (`keep = 'last'`), or no occurrence (`keep = False`) in the data.

We can also combine different pandas DataFrames sequentially with the **concat** function, as follows:

- `pd.concat([df1,df2..])`: This creates a new DataFrame with **df1**, **df2**, and all other DataFrames combined sequentially. It will automatically combine columns having the same names in the combined DataFrames.

Exercise 3: Creating and Modifying Test DataFrames

This exercise aims to test the understanding of the students about creating and modifying DataFrames in pandas. We will create a test DataFrame from scratch and add and remove rows/columns to it by making use of the functions and concepts described so far:

1. Import pandas and copy libraries that we will need for this task (the **copy** module in this case):

    ```
    import pandas as pd
    import copy
    ```

2. Create a DataFrame, **df1**, and use the **head** method to see the first few rows of the DataFrame. Use the following code:

```
df1 = pd.DataFrame({'category': pd.Series([1, 2, 3])})
df1.head()
```

Your output should be as follows:

	category
0	1
1	2
2	3

Figure 1.20: The first few rows of df1

3. Create a test DataFrame, **df**, by duplicating **df1**. Use the **deepcopy** function:

```
df = copy.deepcopy(df1)
df.head()
```

You should get the following output:

	category
0	1
1	2
2	3

Figure 1.21: The first few rows of df

4. Add a new column, **cities**, containing different kinds of city groups to the test DataFrame using the following code and take a look at the DataFrame again:

```
df['cities'] = pd.Series([['Delhi', 'Mumbai'], ['Lucknow', 'Bhopal'],
['Chennai', 'Bangalore']])
df.head()
```

You should get the following output:

	category	cities
0	1	[Delhi, Mumbai]
1	2	[Lucknow, Bhopal]
2	3	[Chennai, Bangalore]

Figure 1.22: Adding a row to df

5. Now, add multiple columns pertaining to the user viewership using the **assign** function and again look at the data. Use the following code:

```
df.assign(
    young_viewers = pd.Series([2000000, 3000000, 1500000]),
    adult_viewers = pd.Series([2500000, 3500000, 1600000]),
    aged_viewers = pd.Series([2300000, 2800000, 2000000])
)
df.head()
```

Your DataFrame will now appear as follows:

	category	cities	adult_viewers	aged_viewers	young_viewers
0	1	[Delhi, Mumbai]	2500000	2300000	2000000
1	2	[Lucknow, Bhopal]	3500000	2800000	3000000
2	3	[Chennai, Bangalore]	1600000	2000000	1500000

Figure 1.23: Adding multiple columns to df

6. Use the **append** function to add a new row to the DataFrame. As we know that the new row contains partial information, we will pass the **ignore_index** parameter as **True**:

```
df.append({'cities': ["Kolkata", "Hyderabad"], 'adult_viewers': 2000000,
    'aged_viewers': 2000000, 'young_viewers': 1500000}, ignore_index =
True)
df.head()
```

Your DataFrame should now look as follows:

	category	cities	adult_viewers	aged_viewers	young_viewers
0	1.0	[Delhi, Mumbai]	2500000	2300000	2000000
1	2.0	[Lucknow, Bhopal]	3500000	2800000	3000000
2	3.0	[Chennai, Bangalore]	1600000	2000000	1500000
3	NaN	[Kolkata, Hyderabad]	2000000	2000000	1500000

Figure 1.24: Adding another row by using the append function on df

7. Now, use the **concat** function to duplicate the test DataFrame and save it as **df2**. Take a look at the new DataFrame:

```
df2 = pd.concat([df, df], sort = False)
df2
```

df2 will show duplicate entries of **df1**, as shown here:

	category	cities	adult_viewers	aged_viewers	young_viewers
0	1.0	[Delhi, Mumbai]	2500000	2300000	2000000
1	2.0	[Lucknow, Bhopal]	3500000	2800000	3000000
2	3.0	[Chennai, Bangalore]	1600000	2000000	1500000
3	NaN	[Kolkata, Hyderabad]	2000000	2000000	1500000
0	1.0	[Delhi, Mumbai]	2500000	2300000	2000000
1	2.0	[Lucknow, Bhopal]	3500000	2800000	3000000
2	3.0	[Chennai, Bangalore]	1600000	2000000	1500000
3	NaN	[Kolkata, Hyderabad]	2000000	2000000	1500000

Figure 1.25: Using the concat function to duplicate a DataFrame, df2, in pandas

8. To delete a row from the **df** DataFrame, we will now pass the index of the row we want to delete—in this case, the third row—to the **drop** function, as follows:

```
df.drop([3])
```

You will get the following output:

	category	cities	adult_viewers	aged_viewers	young_viewers
0	1.0	[Delhi, Mumbai]	2500000	2300000	2000000
1	2.0	[Lucknow, Bhopal]	3500000	2800000	3000000
2	3.0	[Chennai, Bangalore]	1600000	2000000	1500000

Figure 1.26: Using the drop function to delete a row

9. Similarly, let's delete the **aged_viewers** column from the DataFrame. We will pass the column name as the parameter to the **drop** function and specify the axis as 1:

```
df.drop(['aged_viewers'])
```

Your output will be as follows:

	category	cities	adult_viewers	young_viewers
0	1.0	[Delhi, Mumbai]	2500000	2000000
1	2.0	[Lucknow, Bhopal]	3500000	3000000
2	3.0	[Chennai, Bangalore]	1600000	1500000
3	NaN	[Kolkata, Hyderabad]	2000000	1500000

Figure 1.27: Dropping the aged_viewers column in the DataFrame

10. Note that, as the result of the **drop** function is also a DataFrame, we can chain another function on it too. So, we drop the **cities** field from **df2** and remove the duplicates in it as well:

```
df2.drop('cities', axis = 1).drop_duplicates()
```

The **df2** DataFrame will now look as follows:

	category	adult_viewers	aged_viewers	young_viewers
0	1.0	2500000	2300000	2000000
1	2.0	3500000	2800000	3000000
2	3.0	1600000	2000000	1500000
3	NaN	2000000	2000000	1500000

Figure 1.28: Dropping the cities field and then removing duplicates in df2

Congratulations! You've successfully performed some basic operations on a DataFrame. You now know how to add rows and columns to DataFrames and how to concatenate multiple DataFrames together in a big DataFrame.

In the next section, you will learn how to combine multiple data sources into the same DataFrame. When combining data sources, we need to make sure to include common columns from both sources but make sure that no duplication occurs. We would also need to make sure that, unlike the **concat** function, the combined DataFrame is smart about the index and does not duplicate rows that already exist. This feature is also covered in the next section.

Combining Data

Once the data is prepared from multiple sources in separate pandas DataFrames, we can use the **pd.merge** function to combine them into the same DataFrame based on a relevant key passed through the **on** parameter. It is possible that the joining key is named differently in the different DataFrames that are being joined. So, while calling **pd.merge(df, df1)**, we can provide a **left_on** parameter to specify the column to be merged from **df** and a **right_on** parameter to specify the index in **df1**.

pandas provides four ways of combining DataFrames through the **how** parameter. All values of these are different **joins** by themselves and are described as follows:

How to Join	Syntax	Description
Inner Join	pd.merge(df, df1, how = 'inner')	Joins the rows that have the key(s) present in both the DataFrames.
Outer Join	pd.merge(df, df1, how = 'outer')	Joins the rows that have the key(s) present in any of the DataFrames.
Left Join	pd.merge(df, df1, how = 'left')	Joins the rows that have the key(s) present in the first DataFrame.
Right Join	pd.merge(df, df1, how = 'right')	Joins the rows that have the key(s) present in the second DataFrame.

Figure 1.29: Table describing different joins

The following figure shows two sample DataFrames, **df1** and **df2**, and the results of the various joins performed on these DataFrames:

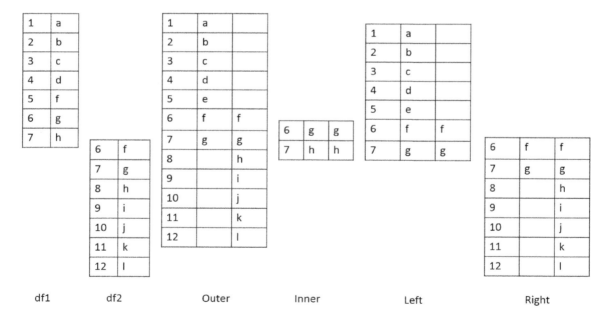

Figure 1.30: Table showing two DataFrames and the outcomes of different joins on them

For example, we can perform a right and outer join on the DataFrames of the previous exercise using the following code:

```
pd.merge(df, df1, how = 'right')
pd.merge(df, df1, how = 'outer')
```

The following will be the output of the preceding two joins:

```
pd.merge(df, df1, how = 'right')
```

	category	cities	adult_viewers	aged_viewers	young_viewers
0	1.0	[Delhi, Mumbai]	2500000	2300000	2000000
1	2.0	[Lucknow, Bhopal]	3500000	2800000	3000000
2	3.0	[Chennai, Bangalore]	1600000	2000000	1500000

```
df = pd.merge(df, df1, how = 'outer')
df.head()
```

	category	cities	adult_viewers	aged_viewers	young_viewers
0	1.0	[Delhi, Mumbai]	2500000	2300000	2000000
1	2.0	[Lucknow, Bhopal]	3500000	2800000	3000000
2	3.0	[Chennai, Bangalore]	1600000	2000000	1500000
3	NaN	[Kolkata, Hyderabad]	2000000	2000000	1500000

Figure 1.31: Examples of the different types of merges in pandas

Handling Missing Data

Once we have joined two datasets, it is easy to see what happens to an index present in one of the tables but not in the other. The other columns of that index get the **np.nan** value, which is pandas' way of telling us that data is missing in that column. Depending on where and how the values are going to be used, missing values can be treated differently. The following are various ways of treating missing values:

- We can get rid of missing values completely using **df.dropna**, as explained in the *Adding and Removing Attributes and Observations* section.

- We can also replace all the missing values at once using **df.fillna()**. The value we want to fill in will depend heavily on the context and the use case for the data. For example, we can replace all missing values with the mean or median of the data, or even some easy to filter values, such as −1 using **df.fillna(df.mean())**,**df.fillna(df.median)**, or **df.fillna(-1)**, as shown here:

```
df.fillna(df.mean())
```

	category	cities	adult_viewers	aged_viewers	young_viewers
0	1.0	[Delhi, Mumbai]	2500000	2300000	2000000
1	2.0	[Lucknow, Bhopal]	3500000	2800000	3000000
2	3.0	[Chennai, Bangalore]	1600000	2000000	1500000
3	2.0	[Kolkata, Hyderabad]	2000000	2000000	1500000

```
df.fillna(df.median())
```

	category	cities	adult_viewers	aged_viewers	young_viewers
0	1.0	[Delhi, Mumbai]	2500000	2300000	2000000
1	2.0	[Lucknow, Bhopal]	3500000	2800000	3000000
2	3.0	[Chennai, Bangalore]	1600000	2000000	1500000
3	2.0	[Kolkata, Hyderabad]	2000000	2000000	1500000

```
df.fillna(-1)
```

	category	cities	adult_viewers	aged_viewers	young_viewers
0	1.0	[Delhi, Mumbai]	2500000	2300000	2000000
1	2.0	[Lucknow, Bhopal]	3500000	2800000	3000000
2	3.0	[Chennai, Bangalore]	1600000	2000000	1500000
3	-1.0	[Kolkata, Hyderabad]	2000000	2000000	1500000

Figure 1.32: Using the df.fillna function

- We can interpolate missing values using the **interpolate** function:

```
df.interpolate()
```

	category	cities	adult_viewers	aged_viewers	young_viewers
0	1.0	[Delhi, Mumbai]	2500000	2300000	2000000
1	2.0	[Lucknow, Bhopal]	3500000	2800000	3000000
2	3.0	[Chennai, Bangalore]	1600000	2000000	1500000
3	3.0	[Kolkata, Hyderabad]	2000000	2000000	1500000

Figure 1.33: Using the interpolate function to predict category

Other than using in-built operations, we can also perform different operations on DataFrames by filtering out rows with missing values in the following ways:

- We can check for slices containing missing values using the **pd.isnull()** function, or those without it using the **pd.isnotnull()** function, respectively:

```
df.isnull()
```

You should get the following output:

	category	cities	adult_viewers	aged_viewers	young_viewers
0	False	False	False	False	False
1	False	False	False	False	False
2	False	False	False	False	False
3	True	False	False	False	False

Figure 1.34: Using the .isnull function

- We can check whether individual elements are **NA** using the **isna** function:

```
df[['category']].isna
```

This will give you the following output:

	category
0	False
1	False
2	False
3	True

Figure 1.35: Using the isna function

This describes missing values only in pandas. You might come across different types of missing values in your pandas DataFrame if it gets data from different sources, for example, **None** in databases. You'll have to filter them out separately, as described in previous sections, and proceed.

Exercise 4: Combining DataFrames and Handling Missing Values

The aim of this exercise is to get you used to combining different DataFrames and handling missing values in different contexts, as well as to revisit how to create DataFrames. The context is to get user information about users definitely watching a certain webcast on a website so that we can recognize patterns in their behavior:

1. Import the **numpy** and **pandas** modules, which we'll be using:

```
importnumpy as np
import pandas as pd
```

2. Create two empty DataFrames, **df1** and **df2**:

```
df1 = pd.DataFrame()
df2 = pd.DataFrame()
```

3. We will now add dummy information about the viewers of the webcast in a column named **viewers** in **df1**, and the people using the website in a column named **users** in **df2**. Use the following code:

```
df1['viewers'] = ["Sushmita", "Aditya", "Bala", "Anurag"]
df2['users'] = ["Aditya", "Anurag", "Bala", "Sushmita", "Apoorva"]
```

4. We will also add a couple of additional columns to each DataFrame. The values for these can be added manually or sampled from a distribution, such as normal distribution through NumPy:

```
np.random.seed(1729)
df1 = df1.assign(views = np.random.normal(100, 100, 4))
df2 = df2.assign(cost = [20, np.nan, 15, 2, 7])
```

5. View the first few rows of both DataFrames, still using the **head** method:

```
df1.head()
df2.head()
```

You should get the following outputs for both **df1** and **df2**:

	viewers	views			users	cost
				0	Aditya	20.0
0	Sushmita	31.266056		1	Anurag	NaN
1	Aditya	17.900529		2	Bala	15.0
2	Bala	265.236086		3	Sushmita	2.0
3	Anurag	42.470696		4	Apoorva	7.0

df1   df2

Figure 1.36: Contents of df1 and df2

6. Do a left join of **df1** with **df2** and store the output in a DataFrame, **df**, because we only want the user stats in **df2** of those users who are viewing the webcast in **df1**. Therefore, we also specify the joining key as **"viewers"** in **df1** and **"users"** in **df2**:

```
df = df1.merge(df2, left_on="viewers", right_on="users", how="left")
df.head()
```

Your output should now look as follows:

	viewers	views	users	cost
0	Sushmita	31.266056	Sushmita	2.0
1	Aditya	17.900529	Aditya	20.0
2	Bala	265.236086	Bala	15.0
3	Anurag	42.470696	Anurag	NaN

Figure 1.37: Using the merge and fillna functions

7. You'll observe some missing values (**NaN**) in the preceding output. We will handle these values in the DataFrame by replacing them with the mean values in that column. Use the following code:

```
df.fillna(df.mean())
```

Your output will now look as follows:

	viewers	views	users	cost
0	Sushmita	31.266056	Sushmita	2.000000
1	Aditya	17.900529	Aditya	20.000000
2	Bala	265.236086	Bala	15.000000
3	Anurag	42.470696	Anurag	12.333333

Figure 1.38: Imputing missing values with the mean through fillna

Congratulations! You have successfully wrangled with data in data pipelines and transformed attributes externally. But to handle the **sales.xlsx** file that we saw previously, this is still not enough. We need to apply functions and operations on the data inside the DataFrame too. Let's learn how to do that and more in the next section.

Applying Functions and Operations on DataFrames

By default, operations on all pandas objects are element-wise and return the same type of pandas objects. For instance, look at the following code:

```
df['viewers'] = df['adult_viewers']+df['aged_viewers']+df['young_viewers']
```

This will add a **viewers** column to the DataFrame with the value for each observation being equal to the sum of the values in the **adult_viewers**, **aged_viewers**, and **young_viewers** columns.

Similarly, the following code will multiply every numerical value in the **viewers** column of the DataFrame by 0.03 or whatever you want to keep as your target CTR (click-through rate):

```
df['expected clicks'] = 0.03*df['viewers']
```

Hence, your DataFrame will look as follows once these operations are performed:

	category	cities	adult_viewers	aged_viewers	young_viewers	viewers	expected clicks
0	1.0	[Delhi, Mumbai]	2500000	2300000	2000000	6800000	204000.0
1	2.0	[Lucknow, Bhopal]	3500000	2800000	3000000	9300000	279000.0
2	3.0	[Chennai, Bangalore]	1600000	2000000	1500000	5100000	153000.0
3	NaN	[Kolkata, Hyderabad]	2000000	2000000	1500000	5500000	165000.0

Figure 1.39: Operations on pandas DataFrames

Pandas also supports several out-of-the-box built-in functions on pandas objects. These are listed in the following table:

Function Name	Description
sum	Compute sum of elements
prod	Compute product of elements
mean	Compute mean of elements
std	Compute standard deviation
var	Compute variance
min	Find minimum value
max	Find maximum value
median	Compute median of elements
any	Evaluate whether any elements passed to the collection are true
all	Evaluate whether all elements passed to the collection are true

Figure 1.40: Built-in functions used in pandas

Note

Remember that pandas objects are Python objects too. Therefore, we can write our own custom functions to perform specific tasks on them.

We can iterate through the rows and columns of pandas objects using **itertuples** or **iteritems**. Consider the following DataFrame, named **df**:

	category	cities	adult_viewers	aged_viewers	young_viewers	viewers	expected clicks
0	1.0	[Delhi, Mumbai]	2500000	2300000	2000000	6800000	204000.0
1	2.0	[Lucknow, Bhopal]	3500000	2800000	3000000	9300000	279000.0
2	3.0	[Chennai, Bangalore]	1600000	2000000	1500000	5100000	153000.0
3	NaN	[Kolkata, Hyderabad]	2000000	2000000	1500000	5500000	165000.0

Figure 1.41: DataFrame df

The following methods can be performed on this DataFrame:

- **itertuples**: This method iterates over the rows of the DataFrame in the form of named tuples. By setting the index parameter to **False**, we can remove the index as the first element of the tuple and set a custom name for the yielded named tuples by setting it in the name parameter. The following screenshot illustrates this over the DataFrame shown in the preceding figure:

```
for row in df.itertuples(index = False):
    print(row)

Pandas(category=1.0, cities=['Delhi', 'Mumbai'], adult_viewers=2500000, aged_viewers=2300000, young_viewers=2000000, viewers=68
00000, _6=204000.0)
Pandas(category=2.0, cities=['Lucknow', 'Bhopal'], adult_viewers=3500000, aged_viewers=2800000, young_viewers=3000000, viewers=
9300000, _6=279000.0)
Pandas(category=3.0, cities=['Chennai', 'Bangalore'], adult_viewers=1600000, aged_viewers=2000000, young_viewers=1500000, viewe
rs=5100000, _6=153000.0)
Pandas(category=nan, cities=['Kolkata', 'Hyderabad'], adult_viewers=2000000, aged_viewers=2000000, young_viewers=1500000, viewe
rs=5500000, _6=165000.0)
```

```
for row in df.itertuples(name = "Monthly"):
    print(row)

Monthly(Index=0, category=1.0, cities=['Delhi', 'Mumbai'], adult_viewers=2500000, aged_viewers=2300000, young_viewers=2000000,
viewers=6800000, _7=204000.0)
Monthly(Index=1, category=2.0, cities=['Lucknow', 'Bhopal'], adult_viewers=3500000, aged_viewers=2800000, young_viewers=300000
0, viewers=9300000, _7=279000.0)
Monthly(Index=2, category=3.0, cities=['Chennai', 'Bangalore'], adult_viewers=1600000, aged_viewers=2000000, young_viewers=1500
000, viewers=5100000, _7=153000.0)
Monthly(Index=3, category=nan, cities=['Kolkata', 'Hyderabad'], adult_viewers=2000000, aged_viewers=2000000, young_viewers=1500
000, viewers=5500000, _7=165000.0)
```

Figure 1.42: Testing itertuples

- **iterrows**: This method iterates over the rows of the DataFrame in tuples of the type **(label, content)**, where **label** is the index of the row and **content** is a pandas Series containing every item in the row. The following screenshot illustrates this:

```
for label, content in df.iterrows():
    print(label, content['viewers'], getattr(content, 'expected clicks'))
```
```
(0, 6800000, 204000.0)
(1, 9300000, 279000.0)
(2, 5100000, 153000.0)
(0, 5500000, 165000.0)
```

Figure 1.43: Testing iterrows

- **iteritems**: This method iterates over the columns of the DataFrame in tuples of the type **(label,content)**, where **label** is the name of the column and **content** is the content in the column in the form of a pandas Series. The following screenshot shows how this is performed:

```
for label, content in df.iteritems():
    print(label, content[2])
```
```
('category', 3)
('cities', ['Chennai', 'Bangalore'])
('adult_viewers', 1600000)
('aged_viewers', 2000000)
('young_viewers', 1500000)
('viewers', 5100000)
('expected clicks', 153000.0)
```

Figure 1.44: Checking out iteritems

To apply built-in or custom functions to pandas, we can make use of the **map** and **apply** functions. We can pass any built-in, NumPy, or custom functions as parameters to these functions, and they will be applied to all elements in the column:

- **map**: This returns an object of the same kind as that was passed to it. A dictionary can also be passed as input to it, as shown here:

```
df['category'].map({1:'a',2:'b',3:'c',4:'d'})
```

```
0       a
1       b
2       c
3     NaN
Name: category, dtype: object
```

Figure 1.45: Using the map function

- **apply**: This applies the function to the object passed and returns a DataFrame. It can easily take multiple columns as input. It also accepts the **axis** parameter, depending on how the function is to be applied, as shown:

```
df[['young_viewers', 'viewers']].apply(lambda x: (x[0]*1.0)/x[1], axis = 1)
```

```
0    0.294118
1    0.322581
2    0.294118
3    0.272727
dtype: float64
```

Figure 1.46: Using the apply function

Other than working on just DataFrames and Series, functions can also be applied to pandas GroupBy objects. Let's see how that works.

Grouping Data

Suppose you want to apply a function differently on some rows of a DataFrame, depending on the values in a particular column in that row. You can slice the DataFrame on the key(s) you want to aggregate on and then apply your function to that group, store the values, and move on to the next group.

pandas provides a much better way to do this, using the **groupby** function, where you can pass keys for groups as a parameter. The output of this function is a **DataFrameGroupBy** object that holds groups containing values of all the rows in that group. We can select the new column we would like to apply a function to, and pandas will automatically aggregate the outputs on the level of different values on its keys and return the final DataFrame with the functions applied to individual rows.

For example, the following will collect the rows that have the same number of **aged_viewers** together, take their values in the **expected clicks** column, and add them together:

```
df.groupby('aged_viewers')['expected clicks'].sum()

aged_viewers
2000000     318000.0
2300000     204000.0
2800000     279000.0
Name: expected clicks, dtype: float64
```

Figure 1.47: Using the groupby function on a Series

Instead, if we were to pass **[['series']]** to the GroupBy object, we would have gotten a DataFrame back, as shown:

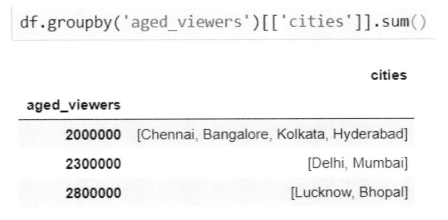

```
df.groupby('aged_viewers')[['cities']].sum()
```

aged_viewers	cities
2000000	[Chennai, Bangalore, Kolkata, Hyderabad]
2300000	[Delhi, Mumbai]
2800000	[Lucknow, Bhopal]

Figure 1.48: Using the groupby function on a DataFrame

Exercise 5: Applying Data Transformations

The aim of this exercise is to get you used to performing regular and **groupby** operations on DataFrames and applying functions to them. You will use the **user_info.json** file in the **Lesson02** folder on GitHub, which contains information about six customers.

1. Import the **pandas** module that we'll be using:

    ```
    import pandas as pd
    ```

2. Read the **user_info.json** file into a pandas DataFrame, **user_info**, and look at the first few rows of the DataFrame:

    ```
    user_info = pd.read_json('user_info.json')
    user_info.head()
    ```

    You will get the following output:

	_id	about	address	age	balance	company	email	eyeColor	favoriteFruit	friends	...	
0	5c0a28d7a647437fd3d3a6aa	Nostrud consectetur elit occaecat dolore incid...	698 Kansas Place, Bethpage, Louisiana, 7695	20	$3,806.93	RODEMCO	graceberry@rodemco.com	green	strawberry	[{u'id': 0, u'name': u'Small Pena'), {u'id': 1...	...	832f1af4 4ba8- f4cbf34:
1	5c0a28d780f6278b11586ab1	Sunt id ipsum velit voluptate. Ullamco non non...	309 Kingsway Place, Kilbourne, New York, 3771	22	$3,330.01	VIAGRAND	hilarysellers@viagrand.com	brown	apple	[{u'id': 0, u'name': u'Spears Smith'), {u'id':...	...	4306 9506- e69a063!
2	5c0a28d722e2e29d9bce2b64	Laborum ad excepteur amet sunt aliqua veniam c...	347 Seeley Street, Witmer, Kansas, 9369	40	$1,619.46	EQUITOX	sherrigilbert@equitox.com	green	apple	[{u'id': 0, u'name': u'Sexton Watts'), {u'id':...	...	5019 7cc4- 3483131
3	5c0a28d76b5e8859a754cb4f	Eu amet aliqua magna ipsum quis et ut reprehen...	178 Stewart Street, Ferney, Wyoming, 9118	29	$3,334.12	ANARCO	caldwellpatterson@anarco.com	blue	strawberry	[{u'id': 0, u'name': u'Anne Holcomb'), {u'id':...	...	d2c4 2974- d1dae5d
4	5c0a28d7ebb99c08e2288c76	Sunt amet exercitation aliqua cillum commodo o...	189 Rogers Avenue, Lindisfarne, Mississippi, 1961	33	$1,368.48	MEGALL	headmcconnell@megall.com	brown	strawberry	[{u'id': 0, u'name': u'Elnora Peck'), {u'id':...	...	df0b 2e81 16f138e:

5 rows × 22 columns

Figure 1.49: Output of the head function on user_info

3. Now, look at the attributes and the data inside them:

```
user_info.info()
```

You will get the following output:

```
<class 'pandas.core.frame.DataFrame'>
RangeIndex: 6 entries, 0 to 5
Data columns (total 22 columns):
_id             6 non-null object
about           6 non-null object
address         6 non-null object
age             6 non-null int64
balance         6 non-null object
company         6 non-null object
email           6 non-null object
eyeColor        6 non-null object
favoriteFruit   6 non-null object
friends         6 non-null object
gender          6 non-null object
greeting        6 non-null object
guid            6 non-null object
index           6 non-null int64
isActive        6 non-null bool
latitude        6 non-null float64
longitude       6 non-null float64
name            6 non-null object
phone           6 non-null object
picture         6 non-null object
registered      6 non-null object
tags            6 non-null object
dtypes: bool(1), float64(2), int64(2), object(17)
memory usage: 1.1+ KB
```

Figure 1.50: Output of the info function on user_info

4. Let's make use of the **map** function to see how many friends each user in the data has. Use the following code:

```
user_info['friends'].map(lambda x: len(x))
```

You will get the following output:

```
0    3
1    3
2    3
3    3
4    3
5    3
Name: friends, dtype: int64
```

Figure 1.51: Using the map function on user_info

5. We use the **apply** function to get a grip on the data within each column individually and apply regular Python functions to it. Let's convert all the values in the **tags** column of the DataFrame to capital letters using the **upper** function for strings in Python, as follows:

```
user_info['tags'].apply(lambda x: [t.upper() for t in x])
```

You should get the following output:

```
0    [EU, ID, FUGIAT, DESERUNT, NULLA, PROIDENT, LA...
1    [DESERUNT, DO, ADIPISICING, IN, ALIQUA, DUIS, ...
2    [ADIPISICING, CILLUM, DESERUNT, AUTE, IPSUM, C...
3    [ADIPISICING, VENIAM, DOLOR, DUIS, AUTE, TEMPO...
4    [QUI, AUTE, VOLUPTATE, EIUSMOD, EST, EST, CUPI...
5    [DOLORE, EIUSMOD, LABORUM, DOLORE, ALIQUIP, AL...
Name: tags, dtype: object
```

Figure 1.52: Converting values in tags

6. Use the **groupby** function to get the different values obtained by a certain attribute. We can use the **count** function on each such mini pandas DataFrame generated. We'll do this first for the eye color:

```
user_info.groupby('eyeColor')['_id'].count()
```

Your output should now look as follows:

```
eyeColor
blue     1
brown    2
green    3
Name: _id, dtype: int64
```

Figure 1.53: Checking distribution of eyeColor

7. Similarly, let's look at the distribution of another variable, `favoriteFruit`, in the data too:

```
user_info.groupby('favoriteFruit')['_id'].count()
```

```
favoriteFruit
apple          3
strawberry     3
Name: _id, dtype: int64
```

Figure 1.54: Seeing the distribution in use_info

We are now sufficiently prepared to handle any sort of problem we might face when trying to structure even unstructured data into a structured format. Let's do that in the activity here.

Activity 1: Addressing Data Spilling

We will now solve the problem that we encountered in Exercise 1. We start by loading `sales.xlsx`, which contains some historical sales data, recorded in MS Excel, about different customer purchases in stores in the past few years. Your current team is only interested in the following product types: **Climbing Accessories**, **Cooking Gear**, **First Aid**, **Golf Accessories**, **Insect Repellents**, and **Sleeping Bags**. You need to read the files into pandas DataFrames and prepare the output so that it can be added into your analytics pipeline. Follow the steps given here:

1. Open the Python console and import **pandas** and the **copy** module.

2. Load the data from **sales.xlsx** into a separate DataFrame, named **sales**, and look at the first few rows of the generated DataFrame. You will get the following output:

	Year	Product	line	Product.1	type	Product.2	Order	method	type.1	Retailer	...	Quantity	Unit
0	2004	Camping	Equipment	Cooking	Gear	TrailChef	Water	Bag	Telephone	United	...	6.59	156672.570
1	2004	Camping	Equipment	Cooking	Gear	TrailChef	Water	Bag	Telephone	Canada	...	7145.88	6.190
2	2004	Camping	Equipment	Cooking	Gear	TrailChef	Water	Bag	Telephone	Mexico	...	NaN	NaN
3	2004	Camping	Equipment	Cooking	Gear	TrailChef	Water	Bag	Telephone	Brazil	...	NaN	NaN
4	2004	Camping	Equipment	Cooking	Gear	TrailChef	Water	Bag	Telephone	Japan	...	91707.18	5.488

5 rows × 26 columns

Figure 1.55: Output of the head function on sales.xlsx

3. Analyze the datatype of the fields and get hold of prepared values.

4. Get the column names right. In this case, every new column starts with a capital case.

5. Look at the first column, if the value in the column matches the expected values, just correct the column name and move on to the next column.

6. Take the first column with values leaking into other columns and look at the distribution of its values. Add the values from the next column and go on to as many columns as required to get to the right values for that column.

7. Slice out the portion of the DataFrame that has the largest number of columns required to cover the value for the right column and structure the values for that column correctly in a new column with the right attribute name.

8. You can now drop all the columns from the slice that are no longer required once the field has the right values and move on to the next column.

9. Repeat 4–7 multiple times, until you have gotten a slice of the DataFrame completely structured with all the values correct and pointing to the intended column. Save this DataFrame slice. Your final structured DataFrame should appear as follows:

	Year	Product line	Product type	Product	Order method type	Retailer country	Revenue	Planned revenue	Product cost	Quantity	Unit cost	Unit price	Gross profit	Unit sale price
0	2004	Golf Equipment	Golf Accessories	Course Pro Golf and Tee Set	Sales visit	United States	5819.70	6586.16	1733.2	619.0	2.8	10.64	4086.50	5.105
1	2004	Golf Equipment	Golf Accessories	Course Pro Golf and Tee Set	Sales visit	United Kingdom	NaN	NaN	NaN	NaN	NaN	NaN	NaN	NaN
2	2005	Golf Equipment	Golf Accessories	Course Pro Golf and Tee Set	Sales visit	United States	10904.28	11363.52	2990.4	1068.0	2.8	10.64	7913.88	10.210
3	2005	Golf Equipment	Golf Accessories	Course Pro Golf and Tee Set	Sales visit	United Kingdom	27987.84	28855.68	7593.6	2712.0	2.8	10.64	20394.24	10.320
4	2006	Golf Equipment	Golf Accessories	Course Pro Golf and Tee Set	Sales visit	United States	NaN	NaN	NaN	NaN	NaN	NaN	NaN	NaN

Figure 1.56: First few rows of the structured DataFrame

Note

The solution for this activity can be found on page 316.

Summary

Data processing and wrangling is the initial, and a very important, part of the data science pipeline. It is generally helpful if people preparing data have some domain knowledge about the data, since that will help them stop at the right processing point and use their intuition to build the pipeline better and more quickly. Data processing also requires coming up with innovative solutions and hacks.

In this chapter, you learned how to structure large datasets by arranging them in a tabular form. Then, we got this tabular data into pandas and distributed it between the right columns. Once we were sure that our data was arranged correctly, we combined it with other data sources. We also got rid of duplicates and needless columns, and finally, dealt with missing data. After performing these steps, our data was made ready for analysis and could be put into a data science pipeline directly.

In the next chapter, we will deepen our understanding of pandas and talk about reshaping and analyzing DataFrames for better visualizations and summarizing data. We will also see how to directly solve generic business-critical problems efficiently.

Data Exploration and Visualization

Learning Objectives

By the end of this chapter, you will be able to:

- Create summaries, aggregations, and descriptive statistics from your data

- Reshape pandas DataFrames to detect relationships in data

- Build pivot tables and perform comparative analysis and tests

- Create effective visualizations through Matplotlib and seaborn

This chapter explains how to derive various descriptive statistics and generate insights and visualizations from your data.

Introduction

In the previous chapter, we saw how to transform data and attributes obtained from raw sources into expected attributes and values through pandas. After structuring data into a tabular form, with each field containing the expected (correct and clean) values, we can say that this data is prepared for further analysis, which involves utilizing the prepared data to solve business problems. To ensure the best outcomes for a project, we need to be clear about the scope of the data, the questions we can address with it, and what problems we can solve with it before we can make any useful inference from the data.

To do that, not only do we need to understand the kind of data we have, but also the way some attributes are related to other attributes, what attributes are useful for us, and how they vary in the data provided. Performing this analysis on data and exploring ways we can use it, is not a straightforward task. We have to perform several initial exploratory tests on our data. Then, we need to interpret their results and possibly create and analyze more statistics and visualizations before we make a statement about the scope or analysis of the dataset. In data science pipelines, this process is referred to as **Exploratory Data Analysis**.

In this chapter, we will go through techniques to explore and analyze data by means of solving some problems critical for businesses, such as identifying attributes useful for marketing, analyzing key performance indicators, performing comparative analyses, and generating insights and visualizations. We will use the pandas, Matplotlib, and seaborn libraries in Python to solve these problems.

Identifying the Right Attributes

Given a structured marketing dataset, the first thing you should do is to try and build intuition for the data and create insights. It is also possible to make a call on whether a certain attribute is required for the analysis or not. The insights generated should instinctively agree with the values and there should be no doubts about the quality of the data, its interpretation, or its application for solving the business problems we are interested in. If some values don't make intuitive sense, we must dig deeper into the data, remove outliers, and understand why the attribute has those values. This is important in order to avoid inaccurate model creation, building a model on the wrong data, or the inefficient use of resources.

Before we start with the model creation, we should summarize the attributes in our data and objectively compare them with our business expectations. To quantify business expectations, we generally have target metrics whose relationships we want to analyze with the attributes in our data. These metrics may depend on domain knowledge and business acumen and are known as **Key Performance Indicators** (**KPIs**).

Assuming that the data is stored in pandas DataFrames, this analysis can be performed using pandas itself, as pandas supports many functions and collections useful for generating insights and summaries. Most of the time, the result of these operations are other pandas DataFrames or Series, so it is also possible to chain multiple functions on top of each other in one go. Some of the most commonly used functions are as follows:

- `info()`: This function returns the index, datatype, and memory information of the DataFrame.

- `describe()`: This function gives descriptive summary statistics for numerical columns in the DataFrame.

- `columns`: This function returns all of the column names of the DataFrame as an index.

- `head(n)`: This function returns `n` values in the DataFrame from the top. `n` is equal to 5 by default.

- `tail(n)`: This function returns `n` values in the DataFrame from the bottom. `n` is equal to 5 by default.

- `groupby(col)[cols].agg_func`: This function collects rows with similar values to `col` and applies `agg_func` to `cols`.

Other than these functions, we also have functions meant for pandas Series. When applied to DataFrames, the functions are applied to every column of the DataFrame as an individual series:

- `unique()`:This function returns the list of unique values in a Series.

- `count()`:This function returns the total number of non-null and non-NA values.

- `min()`:This function returns the minimum value in the Series.

- `max()`:This function returns the maximum value in the Series.

- `mean()`:This function returns the mean of all non-null and non-NA values in the Series.

- `median()`:This function returns the median of all non-null and non-NA values in the Series.

- **mode()**:This function returns the most frequently occurring value in the Series.

- **quantile(x)**: This function returns the value at the xth quantile in the Series (where, x<=1). **x** can be passed as an array of fractions to get values at multiple quantiles.

> **Note**
>
> The **value_counts(dropna=False)** function is also a commonly used function, which shows the unique values and counts of categorical values. It works only on pandas Series and cannot be applied to DataFrames.

Once we have identified the attributes that we are interested in analyzing, we can see how these attributes vary in the dataset individually. If the number of unique values in a field is small, we can consider them to be categorical and obtain some groups in our data based on the values of these attributes directly and understand some naive relationships between them. If the number of unique values of an attribute is large, we consider the data to be continuous and analyze it in a more subjective way through visualizations.

Exercise 6: Exploring the Attributes in Sales Data

The sales of some products in your company in the past few years have been increasing and the company wants to build a marketing strategy for them. Read the **sales.csv** file provided within the **Lesson02** folder on GitHub (this is the cleaned data we prepared in the last chapter) and identify the KPIs for this analysis. Also, generate some insights with the data by using the correct attributes for each analysis:

1. Import **pandas** into the console and read the **sales.csv** file into a pandas DataFrame named **sales**, as shown:

```
import pandas as pd
sales = pd.read_csv('sales.csv')
sales.head()
```

Your output will look as follows:

	Year	Product line	Product type	Product	Order method type	Retailer country	Revenue	Planned revenue	Product cost	Quantity	Unit cost	Unit price	Gross profit	Unit sale price
0	2004	Golf Equipment	Golf Accessories	Course Pro Golf and Tee Set	Sales visit	United States	5819.70	6586.16	1733.2	619.0	2.8	10.64	4086.50	5.105
1	2004	Golf Equipment	Golf Accessories	Course Pro Golf and Tee Set	Sales visit	United Kingdom	NaN	NaN	NaN	NaN	NaN	NaN	NaN	NaN
2	2005	Golf Equipment	Golf Accessories	Course Pro Golf and Tee Set	Sales visit	United States	10904.28	11363.52	2990.4	1068.0	2.8	10.64	7913.88	10.210
3	2005	Golf Equipment	Golf Accessories	Course Pro Golf and Tee Set	Sales visit	United Kingdom	27987.84	28855.68	7593.6	2712.0	2.8	10.64	20394.24	10.320
4	2006	Golf Equipment	Golf Accessories	Course Pro Golf and Tee Set	Sales visit	United States	NaN	NaN	NaN	NaN	NaN	NaN	NaN	NaN

Figure 2.1: The first five rows of sales.csv

2. Now look only at the columns and their contents using the following code to ascertain their relevance in further analysis:

```
sales.columns
```

This gives you the following output:

```
Index([u'Year', u'Product line', u'Product type', u'Product',
       u'Order method type', u'Retailer country', u'Revenue',
       u'Planned revenue', u'Product cost', u'Quantity', u'Unit cost',
       u'Unit price', u'Gross profit', u'Unit sale price'],
       dtype='object')
```

Figure 2.2: The columns in sales.csv

Also, use the **info** function:

```
sales.info()
```

This gives you the following output:

```
<class 'pandas.core.frame.DataFrame'>
RangeIndex: 17823 entries, 0 to 17822
Data columns (total 14 columns):
Year                17823 non-null int64
Product line        17823 non-null object
Product type        17823 non-null object
Product             17823 non-null object
Order method type   17823 non-null object
Retailer country    17823 non-null object
Revenue              6045 non-null float64
Planned revenue      6045 non-null float64
Product cost         6045 non-null float64
Quantity             5860 non-null float64
Unit cost            6045 non-null float64
Unit price           6045 non-null float64
Gross profit         6045 non-null float64
Unit sale price      6045 non-null float64
dtypes: float64(8), int64(1), object(5)
memory usage: 1.9+ MB
```

Figure 2.3: Information about the sales DataFrame

3. Identify the categorical fields and their distribution using the **unique()** function, as shown:

    First check the **Year** column:

    ```
    sales['Year'].unique()
    ```

    You will get the following output:

    ```
    array([2004, 2005, 2006, 2007])
    ```

    Figure 2.4: The number of years the data is spread over

    Then check the **Product line** column:

    ```
    sales['Product line'].unique()
    ```

You will get the following output:

```
array(['Golf Equipment', 'Camping Equipment', 'Outdoor Protection',
       'Mountaineering Equipment'], dtype=object)
```

Figure 2.5: The different product lines the data covers

Then check the **Product type** column:

```
sales['Product type'].unique()
```

You will get the following output:

```
array(['Golf Accessories', 'Sleeping Bags', 'Cooking Gear', 'First Aid',
       'Insect Repellents', 'Climbing Accessories'], dtype=object)
```

Figure 2.6: The different types of products the data covers

Check the **Product** column:

```
sales['Product'].unique()
```

You will get the following output:

```
array(['Course Pro Golf and Tee Set', 'Hibernator Self - Inflating Mat',
       'TrailChef Deluxe Cook Set', 'Deluxe Family Relief Kit',
       'Course Pro Golf Bag', 'TrailChef Water Bag',
       'TrailChef Kitchen Kit', 'TrailChef Cook Set',
       'TrailChef Single Flame', 'TrailChef Double Flame',
       'Hibernator Camp Cot', 'BugShield Lotion Lite',
       'Compact Relief Kit', 'Insect Bite Relief', 'Course Pro Umbrella',
       'Course Pro Gloves', 'Firefly Climbing Lamp',
       'Firefly Rechargeable Battery', 'Granite Chalk Bag',
       'TrailChef Canteen', 'TrailChef Cup', 'TrailChef Kettle',
       'TrailChef Utensils', 'Hibernator Lite', 'Hibernator Extreme',
       'Hibernator Pad', 'Hibernator Pillow', 'BugShield Natural',
       'BugShield Spray', 'BugShield Lotion', 'BugShield Extreme',
       'Calamine Relief', 'Aloe Relief', 'Granite Carabiner',
       'Granite Belay', 'Granite Pulley', 'Firefly Charger', 'Hibernator'],
      dtype=object)
```

Figure 2.7: Different products covered in the dataset

Check the **Order method type** column:

```
sales['Order method type'].unique()
```

You will get the following output:

```
array(['Sales visit', 'Telephone', 'Web', 'Special', 'Mail', 'E-mail',
       'Fax'], dtype=object)
```

Figure 2.8: Different ways in which people making purchases have ordered

Finally, check the **Retailer country** column:

```
sales['Retailer country'].unique()
```

You will get the following output:

```
array(['United States', 'United Kingdom', 'Canada', 'Mexico', 'Brazil',
       'Japan', 'Korea', 'China', 'Singapore', 'Australia', 'Netherlands',
       'Sweden', 'Finland', 'Denmark', 'France', 'Germany', 'Belgium',
       'Switzerland', 'Austria', 'Italy', 'Spain'], dtype=object)
```

Figure 2.9: The countries in which products have been sold

4. Now that we have analyzed the categorical values, let's get a quick summary of the numerical fields, using the **describe** function to make sure that they are relevant for further analysis:

```
sales.describe()
```

This gives the following output:

	Year	Revenue	Planned revenue	Product cost	Quantity	Unit cost	Unit price	Gross profit	Unit sale price
count	17823.000000	6.045000e+03	6.045000e+03	6.045000e+03	5860.000000	6045.000000	6045.000000	6.045000e+03	6045.000000
mean	2005.164955	1.038455e+05	1.058923e+05	5.701932e+04	4691.273549	58.882618	48.900855	4.336203e+04	44.795072
std	0.956260	1.836042e+05	1.881274e+05	1.117846e+05	8950.955313	348.369401	62.814500	7.185831e+04	58.399255
min	2004.000000	0.000000e+00	0.000000e+00	3.360000e+01	5.000000	0.850000	3.660000	-1.336560e+04	0.000000
25%	2004.000000	1.364924e+04	1.383736e+04	5.759760e+03	625.000000	2.760000	7.000000	7.009650e+03	6.580000
50%	2005.000000	4.154119e+04	4.189571e+04	1.906720e+04	1695.000000	9.000000	18.000000	1.894653e+04	17.650000
75%	2006.000000	1.120026e+05	1.144758e+05	5.796000e+04	4858.000000	34.970000	66.770000	5.002308e+04	62.760000
max	2007.000000	3.644349e+06	3.477910e+06	2.061750e+06	164142.000000	7833.000000	265.140000	1.416160e+06	265.140000

Figure 2.10: Description of the numerical columns in sales.csv

As all the values show considerable variation in the data, we will keep all of them for further analysis.

5. Now that we have shortlisted the categorical fields that we are interested in, let's analyze their spread in the data and see if we need to do any filtering. Do this first for the **Year** column:

```
sales['Year'].value_counts()
```

This gives the following output:

```
2006    5451
2005    5451
2004    5451
2007    1470
Name: Year, dtype: int64
```

Figure 2.11: Frequency table of the Year column

Repeat this for the **Product line** column:

```
sales['Product line'].value_counts()
```

This gives the following output:

```
Camping Equipment           8562
Outdoor Protection          4410
Mountaineering Equipment    3087
Golf Equipment              1764
Name: Product line, dtype: int64
```

Figure 2.12: Frequency table of the Product line column

Then check for the **Product type** column:

```
sales['Product type'].value_counts()
```

This gives the following output:

```
Cooking Gear           5880
Climbing Accessories   3087
Sleeping Bags          2682
Insect Repellents      2205
First Aid              2205
Golf Accessories       1764
Name: Product type, dtype: int64
```

Figure 2.13: Frequency table of the Product line column

Check for the **Order method type** column:

```
sales['Order method type'].value_counts()
```

This gives the following output:

```
Special      2547
Fax          2547
E-mail       2547
Web          2547
Mail         2547
Telephone    2547
Sales visit  2541
Name: Order method type, dtype: int64
```

Figure 2.14: Frequency table of the Product line column

Finally, check for the **Retailer country** column:

```
sales['Retailer country'].value_counts()
```

You should get the following output:

```
United Kingdom   865
United States    865
Switzerland      847
Brazil           847
Korea            847
Finland          847
Australia        847
Denmark          847
Mexico           847
Spain            847
China            847
Belgium          847
Japan            847
Germany          847
Netherlands      847
France           847
Italy            847
Singapore        847
Sweden           847
Austria          847
Canada           847
Name: Retailer country, dtype: int64
```

Figure 2.15: Frequency table of the Product line column

As all columns occur reasonably frequently, and there are no unexplained values in the data so far, we can proceed without filtering the data for now.

6. Now that we have understood the spread in the categorical fields, we should also dig deeper into the spread of the numerical fields in the data and check whether we need to filter some values. We will do this by checking the quantiles of each categorical field:

```
sales.quantile([0.1, 0.2, 0.3, 0.4, 0.5, 0.6, 0.7, 0.8, 0.9, 1.0])
```

This gives the following output:

	Year	Revenue	Planned revenue	Product cost	Quantity	Unit cost	Unit price	Gross profit	Unit sale price
0.1	2004.0	4500.000	4677.456	1685.988	259.0	1.880000	6.00	2500.320	5.490000
0.2	2004.0	10184.888	10384.020	3993.504	495.0	2.420000	6.59	5342.104	6.000000
0.3	2004.0	17967.612	18210.880	7540.816	781.0	2.800000	8.00	8732.020	7.000000
0.4	2005.0	28502.354	28774.800	12444.132	1151.0	5.600000	12.81	13380.776	11.304500
0.5	2005.0	41541.190	41895.710	19067.200	1695.0	9.000000	18.00	18946.530	17.650000
0.6	2005.0	59452.444	61323.904	29127.864	2571.8	15.930000	35.00	27107.838	24.390000
0.7	2006.0	90163.784	91491.844	44843.860	3891.0	32.951029	54.93	40633.834	49.414263
0.8	2006.0	145288.136	146890.684	75031.920	6311.2	60.000000	90.09	62452.036	83.780000
0.9	2006.0	262308.196	265536.964	145997.700	11524.7	79.560000	129.72	107435.346	123.230000
1.0	2007.0	3644349.300	3477909.780	2061750.000	164142.0	7833.000000	265.14	1416159.780	265.140000

Figure 2.16: Spread of the numerical columns in sales.csv

7. Let's use qualitative reasoning to create some quick insights for country-wide statistics now. We will first take the sum across different countries by selecting attributes that give an idea of overall values, such as revenue, product cost, quantity, gross profit, and so on, instead of unit values such as Unit cost or Unit sale price. Use the following code:

```
sales.groupby('Retailer country')['Revenue','Planned revenue','Product cost','Quantity','Gross profit'].sum()
```

You should get the following output:

Retailer country	Revenue	Planned revenue	Product cost	Quantity	Gross profit
Australia	1.526422e+07	1.552855e+07	8367046.10	649467.0	6384806.59
Austria	1.631419e+07	1.663918e+07	8923176.61	719084.0	6871597.34
Belgium	1.415299e+07	1.434713e+07	7695759.79	622150.0	5964513.37
Brazil	1.686686e+07	1.718625e+07	9210809.34	744353.0	7092849.29
Canada	3.918371e+07	3.975547e+07	21435997.54	1701123.0	16670505.63
China	4.350234e+07	4.432347e+07	23925152.71	1935454.0	18003637.37
Denmark	8.455457e+06	8.657223e+06	4695594.80	368479.0	3496915.24
Finland	2.714528e+07	2.768705e+07	14879340.33	1207265.0	11335187.27
France	3.595367e+07	3.640336e+07	19646425.37	1620252.0	14968952.89
Germany	3.509449e+07	3.565769e+07	19213400.37	1576459.0	14637047.69
Italy	2.601864e+07	2.649849e+07	14223866.13	1142868.0	10910074.30
Japan	4.603330e+07	4.691096e+07	25256321.68	2047615.0	19208447.45
Korea	3.174933e+07	3.226426e+07	17388109.35	1432122.0	13189782.95
Mexico	2.660842e+07	2.720830e+07	14559723.33	1173878.0	11175487.89
Netherlands	2.506122e+07	2.554392e+07	13716572.61	1121981.0	10464386.40
Singapore	2.886032e+07	2.945750e+07	15901641.50	1270886.0	11959852.99
Spain	2.367628e+07	2.415171e+07	12929558.31	1052358.0	9962395.94
Sweden	9.718640e+06	9.804136e+06	5258635.87	432962.0	4079646.04
Switzerland	1.065317e+07	1.079256e+07	5785329.90	465683.0	4489793.93
United Kingdom	3.988824e+07	4.081019e+07	22100106.53	1656837.0	16542988.78
United States	1.075452e+08	1.104916e+08	59569196.14	4549587.0	44714622.05

Figure 2.17: Total revenue, cost, quantities sold, and profit in each country in the past four years

From the preceding figure, we can infer that Denmark made the least sales and the US made the most sales in the past four years. Most countries generated revenue of around 20,000,000 USD and almost reached their planned revenue targets.

8. Let's now take the mean across different countries by using attributes that give an idea of the individual value of the product, such as unit sale price, unit cost, quantity, and so on. Use the following code:

```
sales.groupby('Retailer country')['Revenue','Planned revenue','Product
cost','Quantity','Unit cost','Unit price','Gross profit','Unit sale
price'].mean()
```

You should get the following output:

Retailer country	Revenue	Planned revenue	Product cost	Quantity	Unit cost	Unit price	Gross profit	Unit sale price
Australia	65794.049353	66933.410603	36064.853879	2873.747788	46.569968	46.828448	27520.718060	43.073775
Austria	63727.294570	64996.808203	34856.158633	2887.887550	53.321432	50.122734	26842.177109	45.285907
Belgium	58970.775000	59779.727417	32065.665792	2681.681034	48.276413	48.253708	24852.139042	44.445764
Brazil	106752.290633	108773.738987	58296.261646	4865.052288	79.542414	46.980759	44891.451203	43.213174
Canada	97959.284950	99388.685350	53589.993850	4395.666667	69.936654	47.781300	41676.264075	44.512998
China	192488.245442	196121.556814	105863.507566	8878.229358	110.158067	53.785133	79662.112257	49.097133
Denmark	41448.317206	42437.366471	23017.621569	1870.451777	41.523586	51.148088	17141.741373	46.517176
Finland	130506.174038	133110.827644	71535.290048	5976.559406	83.147766	47.003173	54496.092644	43.090212
France	89436.994279	90555.617189	48871.704900	4154.492308	59.163594	47.227438	37236.201219	43.252405
Germany	88399.215718	89817.861788	48396.474484	4084.090674	62.195636	50.447154	36869.137758	46.217439
Italy	85307.013082	86880.299279	46635.626656	3874.128814	60.447363	48.496754	35770.735410	44.434877
Japan	118034.096308	120284.509077	64759.799179	5416.970899	83.429044	47.312692	49252.429359	42.988547
Korea	123538.232763	125541.879144	67658.013035	5705.665339	68.223581	48.365798	51322.112646	44.200622
Mexico	96407.300906	98580.800616	52752.620761	4380.141791	54.945672	46.842319	40490.898152	42.961267
Netherlands	79559.427175	81091.815937	43544.674952	3678.626230	58.807858	49.378000	33220.274286	44.626565
Singapore	99176.345945	101228.521924	54644.816151	4522.725979	69.325948	49.999931	41099.151168	45.866685
Spain	79718.122424	81318.879529	43533.866364	3654.020833	61.862859	46.400303	33543.420673	42.942191
Sweden	40494.333792	40850.566583	21910.982792	1858.206009	47.705907	53.585125	16998.525167	49.215721
Switzerland	58533.873736	59299.777143	31787.526923	2616.196629	42.835353	46.807912	24669.197418	42.730779
United Kingdom	140947.836996	144205.602968	78092.249223	6046.850365	25.784710	49.579470	58455.790742	45.249123
United States	221286.423807	227349.010638	122570.362428	9700.611940	26.623756	50.446646	92005.395165	46.354537

Figure 2.18: The average revenue, cost, quantity, and so on for each country

From the preceding figure, you will observe that the US, China, the UK, Finland, Japan, and some other countries made the highest revenue on average. Also, the average cost of the product is about 43 USD across all countries.

9. Let's look at what countries were affected the worst when sales dipped. Were there some countries for which sales never dipped? Use the following code to group data by **Retailer country**:

```
sales.dropna().groupby('Retailer country')['Revenue','Planned
revenue','Product cost','Quantity','Unit cost','Unit price','Gross
profit','Unit sale price'].min()
```

You should get the following output:

Retailer country	Revenue	Planned revenue	Product cost	Quantity	Unit cost	Unit price	Gross profit	Unit sale price
Australia	0.0	294.00	120.78	49.0	0.85	3.66	-558.00	0.000000
Austria	0.0	0.00	33.60	5.0	0.85	3.66	-360.00	0.000000
Belgium	0.0	0.00	70.18	6.0	0.85	3.66	-280.72	0.000000
Brazil	966.0	966.00	455.63	138.0	0.85	3.66	510.37	3.192857
Canada	198.0	198.00	93.39	33.0	0.85	3.66	53.40	2.875000
China	0.0	618.00	291.49	103.0	0.85	3.66	-840.00	0.000000
Denmark	0.0	738.00	312.96	40.0	0.85	3.66	-2561.74	0.000000
Finland	486.0	486.00	223.56	81.0	0.85	3.66	262.44	3.141429
France	0.0	230.12	90.24	43.0	0.85	3.66	-190.40	0.000000
Germany	234.0	0.00	110.37	32.0	0.85	3.66	-1119.04	0.000000
Italy	0.0	330.00	154.56	55.0	0.85	3.66	-224.00	0.000000
Japan	0.0	0.00	67.20	22.0	0.85	3.66	-1225.18	0.000000
Korea	276.0	276.00	130.18	46.0	0.85	3.66	-3831.84	3.137143
Mexico	432.0	432.00	203.76	51.0	0.85	3.66	-542.00	2.615000
Netherlands	0.0	308.57	113.28	40.0	0.85	3.66	-13365.60	0.000000
Singapore	576.0	576.00	271.68	32.0	0.85	3.66	1.28	3.142857
Spain	348.0	348.00	160.08	40.0	0.85	3.66	103.68	2.200000
Sweden	0.0	0.00	67.76	23.0	0.85	3.66	-1438.56	0.000000
Switzerland	0.0	162.00	74.52	27.0	0.85	3.66	-2790.00	0.000000
United Kingdom	0.0	264.00	124.52	44.0	0.85	3.66	-4009.68	0.000000
United States	0.0	156.90	57.60	24.0	0.85	3.66	-186.00	0.000000

Figure 2.19: The lowest price, quantity, cost prices, and so on for each country

From the preceding figure, you can infer that almost every product has at some point made a loss in most countries. Brazil, Spain, and Canada are some good exceptions.

10. Similarly, let's now generate statistics with respect to other categorical variables, such as **Year**, **Product line**, **Product type**, and **Product**. Use the following code for the **Year** variable:

```
sales.groupby('Year')['Revenue','Planned revenue','Product
cost','Quantity','Unit cost','Unit price','Gross profit','Unit sale
price'].sum()
```

This gives the following output:

Year	Revenue	Planned revenue	Product cost	Quantity	Unit cost	Unit price	Gross profit	Unit sale price
2004	1.528977e+08	1.567331e+08	8.538058e+07	7318558.0	97750.174438	92781.46	62482134.57	84841.786496
2005	1.908502e+08	1.947044e+08	1.029861e+08	8453776.0	113381.098628	103147.42	81126260.32	93071.003707
2006	2.228721e+08	2.270020e+08	1.209524e+08	8786835.0	134772.241249	82126.84	95563977.64	76786.074337
2007	6.112591e+07	6.167953e+07	3.536268e+07	2931694.0	10041.912620	17549.95	22951118.87	16087.343791

Figure 2.20: Total revenue, cost, quantities, and so on sold every year

From the above figure, it appears that revenue, profits, and quantities have dipped in the year 2007. However, we have seen previously that more than 90% of the data is from before 2007, so we should not be alarmed by this. There is considerable progress every year here.

11. Use the following code for the **Product line** variable:

```
sales.groupby('Product line')['Revenue','Planned revenue','Product
cost','Quantity','Unit cost','Unit price','Gross profit','Unit sale
price'].sum()
```

You should get the following output:

Product line	Revenue	Planned revenue	Product cost	Quantity	Unit cost	Unit price	Gross profit	Unit sale price
Camping Equipment	4.860065e+08	4.966410e+08	2.862390e+08	15200145.0	323199.354903	214876.61	1.825174e+08	195361.436414
Golf Equipment	4.205702e+07	4.235803e+07	1.525444e+07	2367637.0	14195.740000	39488.03	2.483757e+07	36115.529168
Mountaineering Equipment	5.254793e+07	5.293751e+07	2.522232e+07	3672582.0	11540.322032	24108.88	2.639106e+07	23103.209617
Outdoor Protection	4.713449e+07	4.818252e+07	1.796598e+07	6250499.0	7010.010000	17132.15	2.837751e+07	16206.033132

Figure 2.21: Total revenue, cost, quantities, and so on, generated by each product division

The preceding figure indicates that the sale of **Camping Equipment** is the bread and butter of the company.

12. Use the following code for the **Product type** variable:

```
sales.groupby('Product type')['Revenue','Planned revenue','Product
cost','Quantity','Unit cost','Unit price','Gross profit','Unit sale
price'].sum()
```

You should get the following output:

Product type	Revenue	Planned revenue	Product cost	Quantity	Unit cost	Unit price	Gross profit	Unit sale price
Climbing Accessories	5.254793e+07	5.293751e+07	2.522232e+07	3672582.0	11540.322032	24108.88	2.639106e+07	23103.209617
Cooking Gear	2.859992e+08	2.888950e+08	1.671281e+08	13390271.0	57293.698207	100202.17	1.057078e+08	89698.697296
First Aid	1.175132e+07	1.230833e+07	6.032276e+06	770426.0	5358.250000	11885.57	5.550439e+06	11231.226854
Golf Accessories	4.205702e+07	4.235803e+07	1.525444e+07	2367637.0	14195.740000	39488.03	2.483757e+07	36115.529168
Insect Repellents	3.538318e+07	3.587419e+07	1.193371e+07	5480073.0	1651.760000	5246.58	2.282707e+07	4974.806279
Sleeping Bags	2.000073e+08	2.077460e+08	1.191109e+08	1809874.0	265905.656696	114674.44	7.680951e+07	105662.739118

Figure 2.22: Total revenue, cost, quantities, and so on generated by each product type

You will observe that **Sleeping Bags** are a major source of revenue for the company because the unit cost of sleeping bags is the highest. Also, the number of **Sleeping Bags** sold is the second lowest across all types.

13. Use the following code for the **Product** variable:

```
sales.groupby('Product')['Revenue','Planned revenue','Product
cost','Quantity','Unit cost','Unit price','Gross profit','Unit sale
price'].mean()
```

You should get the following output:

Order method type	Revenue	Planned revenue	Product cost	Quantity	Gross profit
E-mail	3.238293e+07	3.301196e+07	1.768881e+07	1503654.0	1.352462e+07
Fax	1.376507e+07	1.399805e+07	7.399451e+06	653190.0	5.993243e+06
Mail	9.749679e+06	9.942812e+06	5.211545e+06	483151.0	4.175907e+06
Sales visit	6.946909e+07	7.141927e+07	3.870416e+07	3084491.0	2.890578e+07
Special	6.642340e+06	6.618693e+06	3.550795e+06	324760.0	2.824776e+06
Telephone	7.056328e+07	7.230265e+07	3.889483e+07	3200421.0	2.907046e+07
Web	4.251736e+08	4.328256e+08	2.332322e+08	18241196.0	1.776287e+08

Figure 2.23: Average revenue, cost, quantities, and so on generated by each method of ordering

Observe that most sales were generated through the internet (more than all the other sources combined).

14. Finally, you need to identify the KPIs. Looking at the previous insights and stats generated, it would make sense to target **Revenue** as one of the KPIs for further analysis.

Congratulations! You have successfully explored the attributes in a dataset and identified the KPIs for further analysis. In the next section, we will learn how to generate targeted insights from the prepared data.

Generating Targeted Insights

Once we have identified the KPIs for our analysis, we can proceed to make insights with respect to only those variables that affect the bottom line of the KPIs.

Selecting and Renaming Attributes

After we have explored our attributes, we might feel like the variation in the data for a certain attribute could be understood more clearly if it were focused on individually. As explained in detail in the previous chapter, we can select parts of data in pandas through the following methods:

- **[cols]**: This method selects the columns to be displayed.

- **loc[label]**: This method selects rows by label or Boolean condition.

- **loc[row_labels, cols]**: This method selects rows in **row_labels** and their values in the **cols** columns.

- **iloc[location]**: This method selects rows by integer location. It can be used to pass a list of row indices, slices, and so on.

For example, we can select **Revenue**, **Quantity**, and **Gross Profit** columns from the **United States** in the **sales** DataFrame, as follows:

```
sales.loc[sales['Retailer country']=='United States', ['Revenue', 'Quantity',
'Gross profit']].head()
```

This should get you the following output:

	Revenue	Quantity	Gross profit
0	5819.70	619.0	4086.50
2	10904.28	1068.0	7913.88
4	NaN	NaN	NaN
63	159492.97	16137.0	114309.37
65	159040.72	15773.0	114876.32

Figure 2.24: Sub-selecting observations and attributes in pandas

Sometimes, the insight we want to deliver might not be captured in the way we want even after selecting it. For example, the attribute might be named differently from what we have seen, making the analysis harder to interpret. It is possible to rename columns and indexes in pandas by using the **rename** function.

The **rename** function takes a dictionary as an input, which contains the current column name as a key and the desired renamed attribute name as value. It also takes the **axis** as a parameter, which denotes whether the index or the column has to be renamed. It takes the index as the default. The following code renames the **Revenue** column to **Earnings**:

```
sales.rename({'Revenue':'Earnings'}, axis = 'columns').head()
```

The DataFrame will now appear as follows:

	Year	Product line	Product type	Product	Order method type	Retailer country	Earnings	Planned revenue	Product cost	Quantity	Unit cost	Unit price	Gross profit	Unit sale price
0	2004	Golf Equipment	Golf Accessories	Course Pro Golf and Tee Set	Sales visit	United States	5819.70	6586.16	1733.2	619.0	2.8	10.64	4086.50	5.105
1	2004	Golf Equipment	Golf Accessories	Course Pro Golf and Tee Set	Sales visit	United Kingdom	NaN	NaN	NaN	NaN	NaN	NaN	NaN	NaN
2	2005	Golf Equipment	Golf Accessories	Course Pro Golf and Tee Set	Sales visit	United States	10904.28	11363.52	2990.4	1068.0	2.8	10.64	7913.88	10.210
3	2005	Golf Equipment	Golf Accessories	Course Pro Golf and Tee Set	Sales visit	United Kingdom	27987.84	28855.68	7593.6	2712.0	2.8	10.64	20394.24	10.320
4	2006	Golf Equipment	Golf Accessories	Course Pro Golf and Tee Set	Sales visit	United States	NaN	NaN	NaN	NaN	NaN	NaN	NaN	NaN

Figure 2.25: Output after using the rename function on sales

Transforming Values

Even after sub-selecting the right features in the DataFrame and renaming them, we can sometimes still get lost in unnecessary details such as floating-point precision, instead of looking at the bigger picture. To avoid that, we can transform numerical data to categorical data, and vice versa, in order to make the understanding clearer.

For example, consider the **Unit cost** field in **sales.csv** and check the spread of data in that column:

```
sales['Unit cost'].quantile([0.0, 0.25,0.5,0.75,1])
```

On using the above code, we get the following output:

```
0.00        0.85
0.25        2.76
0.50        9.00
0.75       34.97
1.00     7833.00
Name: Unit cost, dtype: float64
```

Figure 2.26: The default spread in columns across the Unit cost field

The **astype()** function provides an API to coerce a pandas DataFrame column to a certain type:

```
sales['Unit cost'] = sales['Unit cost'].astype('category')

sales.dtypes
```

The above snippet results in the following output:

```
Year                     int64
Product line            object
Product type            object
Product                 object
Order method type       object
Retailer country        object
Revenue                float64
Planned revenue        float64
Product cost           float64
Quantity               float64
Unit cost             category
Unit price             float64
Gross profit           float64
Unit sale price        float64
dtype: object
```

Figure 2.27: Changing the datatype of a pandas column by coercion

We can also change the actual values of the data with something else through a custom transformation, and again use the **map** and **apply** functions on the DataFrame to encode the label into a different type of data. For instance, we can write a custom function in Python to transform the numeric **Unit cost** attribute into a categorical column:

```
def cat_gen(x):
    if pd.isnull(x):
        return np.nan
    elif x<=2.76:
        return "cheap"
    elif 2.76<x<=9.0:
        return "medium"
    elif 9.0<x<=34.97:
        return "moderate"
    else:
        return "expensive"


sales['Cost category'] = sales['Unit cost'].map(cat_gen)
sales['Cost category'].value_counts(dropna = True)
```

This will give us the following output:

```
cheap        1644
medium       1520
expensive    1503
moderate     1378
Name: Cost category, dtype: int64
```

Figure 2.28: Converting numerical data to categorical data using custom transformations

Exercise 7: Targeting Insights for Specific Use Cases

A newspaper company has given you their rates for putting up advertisements in cities P, Q, and R. You need to compare the advertisement rates across the cities and figure out the cost of displaying advertisements on every day of the week in all three cities, and the mean advertisement prices for each day in those three cities. Let's revisit the methods we used in the previous chapter and use it to solve this problem:

1. Read the **newpaper_prices.csv** CSV file and look at it:

    ```
    df = pd.read_csv('newspaper_prices.csv', index_col = 'Day')
    df
    ```

    You should get the following output:

Day	P Cost	P Views	Q Cost	Q Views	R Cost	R Views
Monday	50	20000	150	200000	50	10000
Tuesday	50	15000	150	210000	50	20000
Wednesday	50	23000	150	175000	50	20000
Thursday	50	20000	150	230000	50	14000
Friday	75	19000	200	150000	75	23000
Saturday	100	30000	300	500000	100	22000
Sunday	100	40000	300	450000	100	25000

Figure 2.29: The first few rows of newspaper_prices.csv

2. Apply the **sum** function on the DataFrame to get the sum across different observations:

    ```
    df.sum()
    ```

    You should get the following output:

    ```
    P Cost          475
    P Views      167000
    Q Cost         1400
    Q Views     1915000
    R Cost          475
    R Views      134000
    dtype: int64
    ```

Figure 2.30: The sum of values in each column

You will observe that Q provides the highest number of views but is also the most expensive.

3. Now select the columns we want and apply the **mean** function to them:

```
df[['P Cost', 'Q Cost', 'R Cost']].mean(axis = 1)
```

This should give you the following output:

```
Day
Monday       83.333333
Tuesday      83.333333
Wednesday    83.333333
Thursday     83.333333
Friday      116.666667
Saturday    166.666667
Sunday      166.666667
dtype: float64
```

Figure 2.31: Applying a function on a different axis

As we have taken the mean across different cities, we have received the average cost for each day in different cities. We can infer that the average cost of newspapers on Fridays, Saturdays, and Sundays is more than on Mondays, Tuesdays, and Wednesdays.

Reshaping the Data

Other than just focusing on the relevant parts of the data, we can also extract a lot more information from a dataset by changing how the attributes and observations are arranged. These reshaped datasets represent different indices, fields, and so on for the same data, but by analyzing them, we can understand the relationships in our data clearly and we can easily see what kind of values occur together in the same location and how. Let's consider the data in **CTA_comparison.csv** in the **Lesson02** folder, stored in a DataFrame **cta** as follows:

```
cta = pd.read_csv('CTA_comparison.csv')

cta
```

The DataFrame should appear as follows:

	time	CTA Variant	views	sales
0	12:30:00	A	500	100
1	13:30:00	B	800	50
2	14:30:00	C	300	14
3	15:30:00	A	700	94
4	16:30:00	C	300	20
5	17:30:00	B	800	45
6	18:30:00	B	800	56
7	19:30:00	C	250	18
8	20:30:00	A	500	125

Figure 2. 32: The entire data in CTA_comparison.csv

We can reshape the DataFrame by just changing the index of the DataFrame through the **set_index** function in pandas. For example, we can set the index of the **CTA_comparison.csv** data to **CTA Variant** using the following code:

```
cta.set_index('CTA Variant')
```

The DataFrame will now appear as follows:

CTA Variant	time	views	sales
A	12:30:00	500	100
B	13:30:00	800	50
C	14:30:00	300	14
A	15:30:00	700	94
C	16:30:00	300	20
B	17:30:00	800	45
B	18:30:00	800	56
C	19:30:00	250	18
A	20:30:00	500	125

Figure 2.33: Changing the index with the help of set_index

You can also reshape data by creating a hierarchy. This can be done in pandas easily, by passing multiple columns to the **set_index** function. For instance, we can set the **CTA Variant** and **views** as the index of the DataFrame using the **set_index** method as follows:

```
cta.set_index(['CTA Variant', 'views'])
```

The DataFrame will now appear as follows:

CTA Variant	views	time	sales
A	500	12:30:00	100
B	800	13:30:00	50
C	300	14:30:00	14
A	700	15:30:00	94
C	300	16:30:00	20
B	800	17:30:00	45
	800	18:30:00	56
C	250	19:30:00	18
A	500	20:30:00	125

Figure 2.34: Hierarchical Data in pandas through set_index

The same hierarchy can also be created more clearly, by passing multiple columns to the **groupby** function:

```
cta_views = cta.groupby(['CTA Variant', 'views']).count()
cta_views
```

This gives the following output:

CTA Variant	views	time	sales
A	500	2	2
	700	1	1
B	800	3	3
C	250	1	1
	300	2	2

Figure 2.35: Grouping by multiple columns to generate hierarchies

Using this hierarchy, we can easily have a look at groups that occur only in some scenarios and not in others. For instance, CTA Variant B only gets 800 views in all 3 cases, whereas variants A and C get only these two kinds of views.

It is possible to reshape this dataset further too. We can switch the indices from rows to columns and vice versa. This basic reshape transformation is achieved in pandas by using the **unstack** and **stack** functions, explained here:

- **unstack(level)**: This function moves the row index with the name or integral location **level** to the innermost column index. By default, it moves the innermost row:

```
h1 = cta_views.unstack(level = 'CTA Variant')
h1
```

This gives the following output:

	time			sales		
CTA Variant	A	B	C	A	B	C
views						
250	NaN	NaN	1.0	NaN	NaN	1.0
300	NaN	NaN	2.0	NaN	NaN	2.0
500	2.0	NaN	NaN	2.0	NaN	NaN
700	1.0	NaN	NaN	1.0	NaN	NaN
800	NaN	3.0	NaN	NaN	3.0	NaN

Figure 2.36: Example of unstacking DataFrames

We can see that the row index has changed to only **views** while the column has got the additional **CTA Variant** attribute as an index along with the regular **time** and **sales** columns.

- **stack(level)**: This function moves the column index with the name or integral location **level** to the innermost row index. By default, it moves the innermost column:

```
h1.stack(0)
```

This gives the following output:

CTA Variant		A	B	C
views				
250	sales	NaN	NaN	1.0
	time	NaN	NaN	1.0
300	sales	NaN	NaN	2.0
	time	NaN	NaN	2.0
500	sales	2.0	NaN	NaN
	time	2.0	NaN	NaN
700	sales	1.0	NaN	NaN
	time	1.0	NaN	NaN
800	sales	NaN	3.0	NaN
	time	NaN	3.0	NaN

Figure 2.37: Example of stacking a DataFrame

Now the stack function has taken the other **sales** and **time** column values to the row index and only the **CTA Variant** feature has become the column index.

Exercise 8: Understanding Stacking and Unstacking

You are the owner of a website that randomly shows advertisements A or B to users each time a page is loaded. If an advertisement succeeds in getting a user to click on it, the converted field gets the value 1, otherwise it gets 0. The data for this is present in the **conversion_rates.csv** file in the **Lesson02** folder, and you need to use pandas to find relationships, if any, between the variables in the dataset. Create a DataFrame, **df**, that can access the conversion ratio of advertisement A as **df['A']['conversion_ratio']**.

Your visualization code requires the number of advertisements viewed, converted, and the **conversion_ratio** to be in the row indices and both the variants to be in the columns. Create a DataFrame to work in that scenario:

1. Import pandas into the console and read the **conversion_rates.csv** file into a pandas DataFrame called **data**, as shown here:

```
import pandas as pd
data = pd.read_csv('conversion_rates.csv')
```

2. Look at the first few rows of the DataFrame using the **head** method:

```
data.head()
```

You should get the following output:

	converted	group
0	0	B
1	0	B
2	0	A
3	0	B
4	0	A

Figure 2.38: The first few rows of conversion_rates.csv

3. Group the data and count the number of conversions, storing the result in a DataFrame named **converted**:

```
converted = data.groupby('group').sum()
converted
```

You will get the following output:

	converted
group	
A	90
B	21

Figure 2.39: Count of converted displays

4. Group the data and count the number of times each advertisement was displayed. Store this in a DataFrame named **viewed** and rename the column name to **viewed**:

```
viewed = data.groupby('group').count().rename({'converted':'viewed'}, axis
= 'columns')
viewed
```

You will get the following output:

	viewed
group	
A	1030
B	970

Figure 2.40: Count of number of views

5. Combine the converted and viewed datasets in a new DataFrame, named **stats**, as shown here:

```
stats = converted.merge(viewed, on = 'group')
stats
```

This gives the following output:

	converted	viewed
group		
A	90	1030
B	21	970

Figure 2.41: Combined dataset

6. Create a new column called **conversion_ratio** to get the ratio of converted ads to the number of times the ads were displayed:

```
stats['conversion_ratio'] = stats['converted_x']/stats['converted_y']
stats
```

This gives the following output:

	converted	viewed	conversion_ratio
group			
A	90	1030	0.087379
B	21	970	0.021649

Figure 2.42: Adding an additional column to stats

7. Create a DataFrame where group A's conversion rate is accessed as **df['A']**
['conversion_rate']. Use the **stack** function for this operation:

```
df = stats.stack()
df
```

This gives the following output:

```
group
A        converted               90.000000
         viewed                1030.000000
         conversion_ratio         0.087379
B        converted               21.000000
         viewed                 970.000000
         conversion_ratio         0.021649
dtype: float64
```

Figure 2.43: Understanding the different levels of your dataset

8. Check whether you're able to access the desired value using the following code:

```
df['A']['conversion_rate']
```

You should get a value close to 0.08737.

9. Reverse the rows with the columns in the stats DataFrame with the **unstack()**
function twice:

```
stats.unstack().unstack()
```

This gives the following output:

group	A	B
converted	90.000000	21.000000
viewed	1030.000000	970.000000
conversion_ratio	0.087379	0.021649

Figure 2.44: Reversing rows with columns

Congratulations! You have reshaped the data in the desired manner. You can now bring any data to a format that you like. pandas also provides for a simpler way to reshape that allows making comparisons while analyzing data very easy. Let's have a look at it in the next section.

Pivot Tables

Creating a **pivot table** is a special case of stacking a DataFrame. The **pivot** function, which is used to create a pivot table, takes three arguments and creates a new table, whose row and column indices are the unique values of the respective parameters.

For example, consider the same **data** DataFrame used in the previous exercise:

	converted	group
0	0	B
1	0	B
2	0	A
3	0	B
4	0	A

Figure 2.45: The first few rows of the dataset being considered

We can use the **pivot** function to change the columns to values in group and see if a certain index converted it or not, as follows:

```
data.pivot(columns = 'group', values='converted').head()
```

This gives the following output:

group	A	B
0	NaN	0.0
1	NaN	0.0
2	0.0	NaN
3	NaN	0.0
4	0.0	NaN

Figure 2.46: Data after being passed through the pivot command

In the preceding figure, note that the columns and indices have changed but the observations individually have not. We can see that the data that had either a 0 or 1 value remains as is, but the groups that were not considered have their remaining values filled in as missing.

There is also a function called **pivot_table**, which aggregates fields together using the function specified in the **aggfunc** parameter and creates outputs accordingly. It is considered to be an alternative to aggregations such as **groupby** functions.

For instance, let's apply the **pivot_table** function to the same DataFrame to aggregate data:

```
data.pivot_table(index='group', columns='converted', aggfunc=len)
```

This gives the following output:

converted	0	1
group		
A	940	90
B	949	21

Figure 2.47: Applying pivot_table to data

Note that the use of the **len** argument results in columns 0 and 1 that show how many times each of these values appeared in each group.

Remember that, unlike **pivot**, it is essential to pass the **aggfunc** function when using the **pivot_table** function.

Visualizing Data

An important aspect of exploring data is to be able to represent the data visually. When data is represented visually, the underlying numbers and distribution become very easy to understand and differences become easy to spot.

Plots in Python are very similar to those in any other paradigm of traditional marketing analytics. We can directly make use of our previous understanding of plots and use them in Python. pandas supports inbuilt functions to visualize the data in them through the **plot** function. You can choose which ones are which via the **kind** parameter to the plot function. Some of the most commonly used ones, as used on **sales.csv**, are as follows:

- **kde** or **density** for density plots
- **bar** or **barh** for bar plots
- **box** for boxplot
- **area** for area plots
- **scatter** for scatter plots

- **hexbin** for hexagonal bin plots
- **pie** for pie plots

You can specify which values to pass as the *x* and *y* axes by specifying the column names as **x** and **y** in the DataFrames.

Exercise 9: Visualizing Data With pandas

Using the **sales** DataFrame created from the previous exercise, we will create visualizations to explore the distribution of the **Revenue** KPI. We will look at how different order method types influence the revenue and how it varies compare to the planned revenue, quantity, and gross profit year on year.

1. Import the module that we will be needing, that is, pandas.

   ```
   import pandas as pd
   ```

2. Load the **sales.csv** file into a DataFrame named **sales** and have a look at the first few rows, as follows:

   ```
   sales = pd.read_csv("sales.csv")
   sales.head()
   ```

   You will get the following output:

	Year	Product line	Product type	Product	Order method type	Retailer country	Revenue	Planned revenue	Product cost	Quantity	Unit cost	Unit price	Gross profit	Unit sale price
0	2004	Golf Equipment	Golf Accessories	Course Pro Golf and Tee Set	Sales visit	United States	5819.70	6586.16	1733.2	619.0	2.8	10.64	4086.50	5.105
1	2004	Golf Equipment	Golf Accessories	Course Pro Golf and Tee Set	Sales visit	United Kingdom	NaN	NaN	NaN	NaN	NaN	NaN	NaN	NaN
2	2005	Golf Equipment	Golf Accessories	Course Pro Golf and Tee Set	Sales visit	United States	10904.28	11363.52	2990.4	1068.0	2.8	10.64	7913.88	10.210
3	2005	Golf Equipment	Golf Accessories	Course Pro Golf and Tee Set	Sales visit	United Kingdom	27987.84	28855.68	7593.6	2712.0	2.8	10.64	20394.24	10.320
4	2006	Golf Equipment	Golf Accessories	Course Pro Golf and Tee Set	Sales visit	United States	NaN	NaN	NaN	NaN	NaN	NaN	NaN	NaN

Figure 2.48: Output of sales.head()

3. Now take the **Revenue** field and plot it's distribution with the **kde** parameter as follows:

   ```
   sales['Revenue'].plot(kind = 'kde')
   ```

You will get the following density plot:

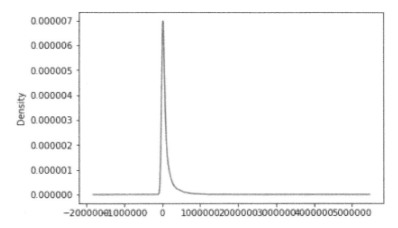

Figure 2.49: Distribution of revenue in sales.csv

4. Next, group the **Revenue** by `Order method type` and make a barplot:

```
sales.groupby('Order method type').sum().plot(kind = 'bar', y = 'Revenue')
```

This gives the following output:

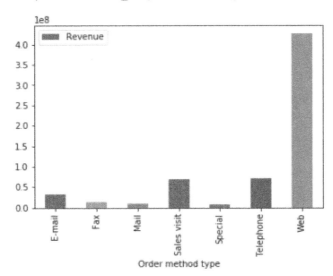

Figure 2.50: Revenue generated through each Order method type in sales.csv

5. Let's now group the columns by year and create boxplots to get an idea on a relative scale:

```
sales.groupby('Year')['Revenue', 'Planned revenue', 'Quantity', 'Gross
profit'].plot(kind= 'box')
```

You should get the following plots:

```
Year
2004      AxesSubplot(0.125,0.125;0.775x0.755)
2005      AxesSubplot(0.125,0.125;0.775x0.755)
2006      AxesSubplot(0.125,0.125;0.775x0.755)
2007      AxesSubplot(0.125,0.125;0.775x0.755)
dtype: object
```

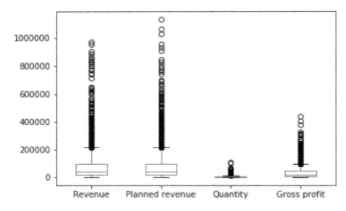

Figure 2.51: Boxplots for Revenue, Planned Revenue, Quantity, and Gross Profit for 2004 to 2007

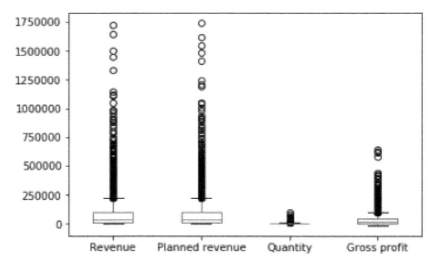

Figure 2.52: Boxplots for Revenue, Planned Revenue, Quantity, and Gross Profit for 2005

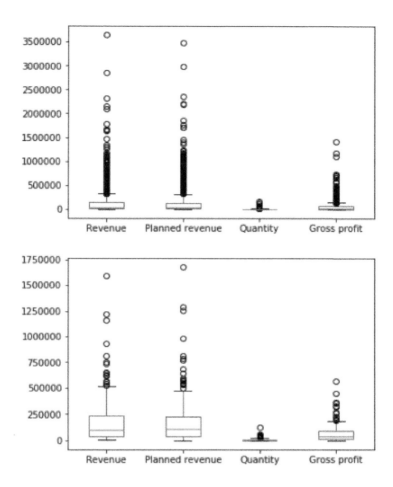

Figure 2.53: Boxplots for Revenue, Planned Revenue, Quantity, and Gross Profit for 2006 and 2007

Now the plots convey the message we want to convey in a suitable way, but we don't have a lot of control over the plots because we are using pandas to figure things out for us. There are other ways to plot the data which allow us to express the data with more freedom. Let's look at them in this section

Visualization through Seaborn

An important kind of plot that we missed before is the histogram. We can still pass the **kind** parameter as **hist** in the plot function, but instead of using default pandas to visualize it, another library, called seaborn, is heavily used in Python. It provides a high-level API to easily generate top-quality plots used in a lot of domains, including statistics.

You can change the environment from regular pandas/Matplotlib to seaborn directly through the **set** function of seaborn. Seaborn also supports a **distplot** function, which plots the actual distribution of the pandas series passed to it, which means no longer worrying about binning and other issues. To generate histograms through seaborn, we can pass the **kde** parameter as **False** and get rid of the distribution line:

```
import seaborn as sns
sns.set()
sns.distplot(sales[Gross profit'].dropna(), kde = False)
```

This gives the following output:

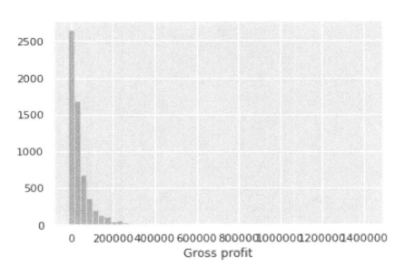

Figure 2.54: Histogram for Gross Profit through Seaborn

However, the actual power of seaborn comes with using it for advanced features such as the PairPlot API.

> **Note**
>
> You can have a look at some of the things you can do directly with seaborn at
> https://elitedatascience.com/python-seaborn-tutorial.

Visualization with Matplotlib

Python's default visualization library is Matplotlib. Originally developed to bring visualization capabilities from the MATLAB academic tool into open source Python, Matplotlib provides low-level additional features that can be added to plots made from any other visualization library, because all of them—the ones used in pandas and seaborn—are built on top of it.

To start using Matplotlib, we first import the `matplotlib.pyplot` object as `plt`. This `plt` object becomes the basis for generating figures in Matplotlib. Every time we want to change the plot we want to look at, we use classes defined on this `plt` object and modify them for more, and better, data analysis.

> **Note**
>
> You can have a look at some of the things you can do directly with Matplotlib at https://matplotlib.org/api/_as_gen/matplotlib.pyplot.html.

The following is an example Matplotlib figure that illustrates the different parts of a plot:

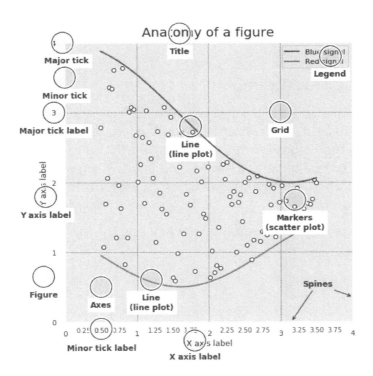

Figure 2.55: Breaking down parts of a Matplotlib plot

Some of the functions we can call on this **plt** object for these options are as follows:

Function	Description
legend(*args, **kwargs)	Place a legend on the axes
grid([b, which, axis])	Configure the grid lines
axes([arg])	Add an axes to the current figure and make it the current axes
xlabel, ylabel	Set the label for the x-axis, y-axis
xticks, yticks	Get or set the current tick locations and labels of the x-axis, y-axis
tick_params	Change the appearance of ticks, tick labels, and gridlines
title(label[, fontdict, loc, pad])	Set a title for the axes

Figure 2.56: Functions that can be used on plt

Note

A tutorial for Matplotlib is available at https://realpython.com/python-matplotlib-guide/.

Activity 2: Analyzing Advertisements

In this activity, we will wrap up our learning from the chapter and practice exploring the data, generating insights, and creating visualizations. Your company has curated its advertisement views through different mediums and the sales made on the same day in **Advertising.csv**. Read the file, have a look at the dataset, explore some of the features, analyze the relationships, and visualize some of the insights in the data to get a clearer understanding of it:

1. Open the Jupyter Notebook and load pandas and the visualization libraries that you will need.

2. Load the data into a pandas DataFrame named **ads** and look at the first few rows. Your DataFrame should look as follows:

Date	TV	newspaper	radio	sales
2018-01-01	230100.0	69200.0	37800.0	22100.0
2018-01-02	44500.0	45100.0	39300.0	10400.0
2018-01-03	17200.0	69300.0	45900.0	9300.0
2018-01-04	151500.0	58500.0	41300.0	18500.0
2018-01-05	180800.0	58400.0	10800.0	12900.0

Figure 2.57: The first few rows of Advertising.csv

3. Understand the distribution of the dataset using the **describe** function and filter out any irrelevant data.

4. Have a closer look at the spread of the features using the **quantile** function and generate relevant insights. You will get the following output:

	TV	newspaper	radio	sales
0.1	24880.0	5990.0	3400.0	7960.0
0.2	59180.0	9380.0	7680.0	9700.0
0.3	86750.0	15970.0	11940.0	10870.0
0.4	119000.0	21320.0	17120.0	11800.0
0.5	149750.0	25750.0	22900.0	12900.0
0.6	186060.0	32700.0	27860.0	14800.0
0.7	210730.0	39110.0	33500.0	16600.0
0.8	228540.0	49640.0	38920.0	18920.0
0.9	261440.0	59070.0	43520.0	21710.0
1.0	296400.0	114000.0	49600.0	27000.0

Figure 2.58: The deciles of ads

5. Look at the histograms of individual features to understand the values better. You should get the following outputs:

```
<matplotlib.axes._subplots.AxesSubplot at 0x7f192a2e4410>
```

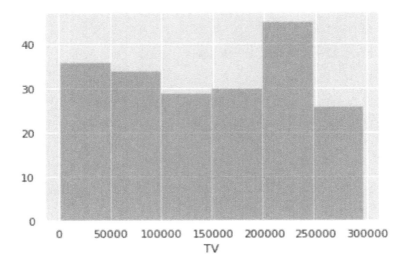

Figure 2.59: Histogram of the TV feature

```
<matplotlib.axes._subplots.AxesSubplot at 0x7f1928221450>
```

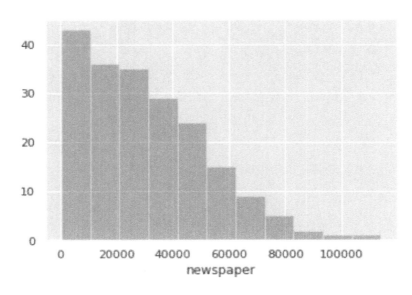

Figure 2.60: Histogram of the newspaper feature

```
<matplotlib.axes._subplots.AxesSubplot at 0x7f1928124290>
```

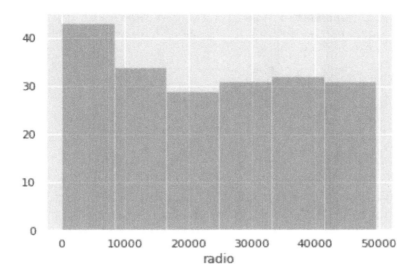

Figure 2.61: Histogram of the radio feature

```
<matplotlib.axes._subplots.AxesSubplot at 0x7f19280d7f90>
```

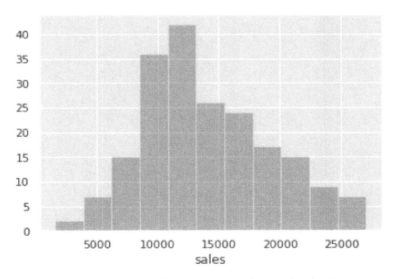

Figure 2.62: Histogram of the sales feature

Now identify the right attributes for analysis and the KPIs.

6. Create focused, more specific, insights pertaining to the KPIs and create visualizations to explain relationships in the data. Understand the scope of the data being used and set expectations for further analysis.

> **Note**
>
> The solution for this activity can be found on page 329.

Summary

In this chapter, we have explored the way data is processed and have figured out intuitive details about it. We can now perform advanced analysis and create visualizations to make processing easy to understand. We can use the knowledge that we have gained to solve further problems, explore hidden relationships, and do further analysis easily. Let's look at some applications of this with problems we can solve in the next chapter.

Unsupervised Learning: Customer Segmentation

Learning Objectives

By the end of this chapter, you will be able to:

- Describe the advantages of using unsupervised learning techniques (clustering) over more traditional segmentation techniques
- Perform the preprocessing steps for preparing data for clustering
- Use k-means clustering to perform customer segmentation
- Determine the properties of groups created using clustering

This chapter covers various customer segmentation methods, deals with the concepts of similarity and data standardization, and explains k-means clustering.

Introduction

In the previous chapter, we saw how to build plots using the built-in function of pandas, and learned how to estimate the mean, median, and other descriptive statistics about specific consumer or product groups.

In this chapter, we will learn about clustering, a form of unsupervised learning technique, and then begin a discussion of how to calculate the similarity between two data points. Next, we will discuss how to standardize data so that multiple data features can be used without one overwhelming the others. We will also go through how similarity can be calculated by computing the distance between data points. Finally, we will discuss k-means clustering, how to perform it, and how to explore the resulting groups.

Customer Segmentation Methods

Customer segmentation is the act of separating (segmenting) your target customers into different groups based on demographic or behavioral data so that marketing strategies can be tailored more specifically to each group. Being able to accurately segment a customer population is becoming increasingly important in today's digital world, where products and advertisements are created to target more and more specific subsets of the population. It is also an important part of allocating marketing resources properly because, by targeting specific customer groups, you can achieve higher return on investment for your marketing initiatives.

Every marketing group does some amount of customer segmentation. However, the methods they use to do this might not always be clear. These may be based on intuitions and hunches about certain demographic groups, or they might be the output of some marketing software, where the methods used are actually obscure. There are advantages and disadvantages of every possible method, and understanding them allows you to make use of the right tool for the job. In the following sections, we will discuss some of the most commonly used approaches for customer segmentation and also discuss their pros and cons.

Traditional Segmentation Methods

There are different methods for performing customer segmentation. Probably the most common general method is for a marketing analyst to sit down with the data they have about customers, whether it's demographic or behavioral, and to try to come up with rough groupings based on intuitions and arbitrary thresholds. An example of this would be deciding to segment customers into different income tiers, based on $10,000 increments.

These kinds of methods have the advantage of being simple and easy to understand. However, this becomes much more complex when you add additional variables. Importantly, as you increase the number of groups in the number of variables, it becomes hard to choose thresholds in a way such that you don't end up with groups with very few customers in them. For example, how many individuals would be there in the group "18- to 25-year-olds making $100,000+"?

This becomes more important when looking at the behavioral data of customers. Creating groups based on intuition can result in underlying patterns in the data being overlooked. For example, there may be segments of the population that respond well to very specific kinds of marketing offers. If the analyst performing the segmentation doesn't happen to know about this specific group and the types of ads they respond to, they may miss out on capturing them as a unique group. For instance, a marketing analyst who separates customers into those who respond to offers for expensive products and those who respond to offers for inexpensive products could miss a group of customers only interested in electronics, regardless of whether they are expensive or inexpensive.

Unsupervised Learning (Clustering) for Customer Segmentation

Another method for performing customer segmentation is using unsupervised learning. Using unsupervised learning is often a very powerful technique as it tends to pick up on patterns in data that might otherwise be missed. It's perfect for customer segmentation because it finds data points that are most like each other and groups them together, which is exactly what good customer segmentation techniques should do.

Clustering is a type of unsupervised machine learning that looks for groups or "clusters" in data without knowing them ahead of time. The following are some of the advantages and disadvantages of using clustering for customer segmentation.

Here are the advantages of clustering:

- Can find customer groups that are unexpected or unknown to the analyst
- Flexible and can be used for a wide range of data
- Reduces the need for deep expertise about connections between the demographics of customers and behaviors
- Quick to perform; scalable to very large datasets

Here are the disadvantages of clustering:

- Customer groups created may not be easily interpretable.

- If data is not based on consumer behavior (such as products or services purchased), it may not be clear how to use the clusters that are found.

As you can see, one downside of clustering is that it may find groups that don't seem to make a lot of sense on the surface. Often this can be fixed by using a better suited clustering algorithm. Determining how to evaluate and fine-tune clustering algorithms will be the topic of our next chapter.

Similarity and Data Standardization

For a clustering algorithm to try to find groups of customers, they need some measure of what it means for a customer to be similar or different. In this section, we will learn how to think about how similar two data points are and how to standardize data to prepare it for clustering.

Determining Similarity

In order to use clustering for customer segmentation (to group customers together with other customers who have similar traits), you first have to decide what "similar" means, or in other words, you need to be very specific about defining what kind of customers are similar. The customer traits you use should be those that are most related to the kind of marketing campaigns you would like to do.

Ideally, each feature you choose should have roughly equal importance in your mind in terms of how well it captures something important about the customer. For example, segmenting customers based on the flavor of toothpaste they tend to buy may not make sense if you want to design marketing strategies for selling cars.

Customer behavior, such as how they have responded to marketing campaigns in the past, is often the most relevant kind of data. However, in the absence of this, it's often useful to segment customers based on other traits, such as their income and age.

Standardizing Data

To be able to group customers based on continuous variables, we first need to rescale these parameters such that the data is on similar scales. Take age and income, for instance. These are on very different scales. It's not uncommon to see incomes that are different by $10,000, but it would be very odd to see two people whose ages differed by 10,000 years. Therefore, we need to be explicit about how big a change in one of these variables is about the same as changing the others in terms of customer similarity. For example, we might say that a difference of 10 years of age between two customers makes those two customers as different for our purposes as if they had an income disparity of $10,000. However, making these kinds of determinations manually for each variable would be difficult. This is the reason why we typically standardize the data, to put them all on a standard scale.

One way to standardize parameters for clustering is to calculate their **z-score**, which is done in two steps:

1. The first step is to subtract the mean of the data from each data point. This centers the data around 0, to make the data easier to look at and interpret, although this is not strictly required for clustering.

2. The second step is to divide the parameters by their **standard deviation**.

The standard deviation is a measure of how spread out our points are. It is calculated by comparing the average of the data to each data point. Data such as income, where the points can be spread out by many thousands, will have much larger standard deviations than data, such as age, where the differences between the data points tend to be much smaller. The following formula is used for calculating the standardized value of a data point:

$$Z_i = \frac{x_i - mean\ (x)}{std(x)}$$

Figure 3.1: The standardization equation

Here, z_i corresponds to the ith standardized value, x represents all values, $mean(x)$ is the mean value of all x values, and $std(x)$ is the standard deviation of the x values.

In this example, by dividing all of our ages by the standard deviation of the ages, we transform the data such that the standard deviation is equal to 1. When we do the same thing with the income, the standard deviation of the income will also be equal to 1. Therefore, a difference of 1 between two customers on either of these measures would indicate a similar level of difference between them.

The downside of performing this kind of transformation is that the data becomes harder to interpret. We all have an intuitive sense of what $10,000 or 10 years means, but it's harder to think of what one standard deviation's worth of income means. However, we do this to help the machine learning algorithm, as it doesn't have the same intuitive understanding of the data that we do.

> **Note**
>
> Because standardization depends on both the mean and standard deviation of your data, the standardization is specific to your population's data. For example, if all of your customers are seniors, one year will account for a larger distance after standardization than if your customers included all age groups, since the standard deviation in age in your population would be much lower.

Exercise 10: Standardizing Age and Income Data of Customers

In this exercise, you will deal with data pertaining to the ages and incomes of customers and learn how to standardize this data using z-scoring:

1. First, you need to import the packages that you will be using, namely NumPy and pandas. NumPy is a widely used package for scientific computing, which we will use to create random data. pandas is a package that allows data to be stored and accessed using DataFrames, which are data structures that have rows and columns that make dealing with data much easier. Use the following code:

    ```
    import numpy as np
    import pandas as pd
    ```

2. Create some data to stand in as your age and income data. Here, we have created each with different scales to better simulate what income and age data might really look like:

    ```
    np.random.seed(100)
    df = pd.DataFrame()
    df['income'] = np.random.normal(50000, scale=10000, size=100)
    df['age'] = np.random.normal(40, scale=10, size=100)
    df = df.astype(int)
    ```

We first set the **random state** of NumPy, so that everyone will generate the same data. Then we create a DataFrame, **df**, to hold the data. We use the **np.random. normal** function to create some data with a normal distribution on different scales. We generate 100 numbers for income and age, and then we store them in our DataFrame. We then convert to **int** so that we end up with whole numbers.

3. Use the **head** function to look at the first five rows of the data, as follows:

```
df.head()
```

The data should look like this:

	income	age
0	32502	22
1	53426	28
2	61530	10
3	47475	40
4	59813	37

Figure 3.2: The printed output of the first five rows of the data

4. We can calculate the standard deviation of both columns simultaneously using the **std** function, which will return the standard deviation for all columns in our DataFrame:

```
df.std()
```

You should see the following output:

```
income     9746.405471
age          10.646624
dtype: float64
```

Figure 3.3: The standard deviation of the two columns

5. Similarly, use the **mean** function to calculate the means of the two columns, as follows:

```
df.mean()
```

You should get the following values for income and age:

```
income      48957.85
age            38.77
dtype: float64
```

Figure 3.4: The mean of the two columns

6. Next, you need to standardize the variables using their standard deviation and mean. Use the following snippet:

```
df['z_income'] = (df['income'] - df['income'].mean())/df['income'].std()
df['z_age'] = (df['age'] - df['age'].mean())/df['age'].std()
```

This will create two new columns, **z_income** and **z_age**, in our DataFrame, which contain the standardized values of income and age.

7. Use the **head** function on the DataFrame again to look at the original data and their standardized values:

```
df.head()
```

Your output should look as follows:

	income	age	z_income	z_age
0	32502	22	-1.688402	-1.575147
1	53426	28	0.458441	-1.011588
2	61530	10	1.289927	-2.702265
3	47475	40	-0.152143	0.115530
4	59813	37	1.113759	-0.166250

Figure 3.5: The first five rows of the DataFrame after the standardized columns have been created

Note

The standardized columns should have a mix of small positive and negative values. They represent the number of standard deviations the original data point was from the mean (with positive being above the mean and negative being below it).

8. Similarly, use the **std** function on the DataFrame to look at the standard deviations:

```
df.std()
```

Note that the standard deviation of the standardized columns should have a value of 1, as you will observe in the screenshot here:

```
income        9746.405471
age             10.646624
z_income         1.000000
z_age            1.000000
dtype: float64
```

Figure 3.6: The standard deviations of each column in the DataFrame

9. Finally, use the **mean** function on the DataFrame to look at the mean of all columns:

```
df.mean()
```

The mean of the standardized values should have values very close to 0 (though not exactly 0 due to floating point precision), as shown here:

```
income        4.895785e+04
age           3.877000e+01
z_income      1.376677e-16
z_age        -3.219647e-16
dtype: float64
```

Figure 3.7: The mean values of each column in the DataFrame

Congratulations! You've successfully standardized age and income data of customers. If you are to use this data for clustering, you would use the **z_income** and **z_age** columns of the DataFrame.

Calculating Distance

Once the data is standardized, we need to calculate the similarity between customers. Typically, this is done by calculating the distance between the customers in the feature space. In a two-dimensional scatterplot, the **Euclidean distance** between two customers is just the distance between their points, as you can see in the following plot:

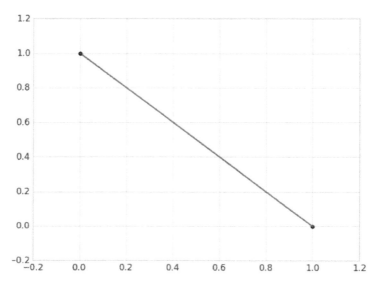

Figure 3.8: A plot showing the Euclidean distance between two points

In the preceding plot, the length of the red line is the Euclidean distance between the two points. The larger this distance, the less similar the customers are. This is easier to think about in two dimensions, but the math for calculating Euclidean distance applies just as well to multiple dimensions.

For two data points, p and q, the distance between them is calculated as follows:

$$d(p, q) = \sqrt{\sum (p_i - q_i)^2}$$

Figure 3.9: Equation for calculating the Euclidean distance between two points

Here, $p = (p1+p2+...pn)$, $q = (q1+q2+...qn)$, and n is the number of features.

We can therefore find the distance between customers regardless of how many features/dimensions we want to use.

> **Note**
>
> This section describes finding the Euclidean distance between two points, which is the most common type of distance metric to use for clustering. Another common distance metric is the Manhattan distance.

Exercise 11: Calculating Distance Between Three Customers

In this exercise, you will calculate the distance between three customers to learn how distance is calculated as well as the importance of standardization. For this, you need to calculate the distance between data points, both before and after standardization. The following is the data regarding the customers:

Customer	Age (in years)	Income (in USD)
1	40	$40,000
2	40	$30,000
3	30	$40,000

Figure 3.10: Table showing incomes and ages of three customers

1. First, import the **math** package, as shown:

   ```
   import math
   ```

2. Next, create a list of incomes and ages, corresponding to the ages and incomes of the three customers. Use the following values:

   ```
   ages = [40, 40, 30]
   incomes = [40000, 30000, 40000]
   ```

3. Calculate the distance between the first and the second customer using the following snippet:

   ```
   math.sqrt((ages[0] - ages[1])**2 + (incomes[0] - incomes[1])**2)
   ```

The result should be 1000.

4. Now calculate the distance between the first and third customer using the following snippet:

```
math.sqrt((ages[0] - ages[2])**2 + (incomes[0] - incomes[2])**2)
```

The result should be 10.

Note that this distance is much smaller in comparison to that obtained in the previous step because the difference between these two customers comes from their ages, where the absolute difference is much smaller than the difference in incomes between the first two customers.

5. Now standardize the ages and incomes using the mean and standard deviation we found from the previous exercise (the mean and standard deviation for age is 40 and 10, and for income it's 50,000 and 10,000, respectively). Use the snippet given here:

```
z_ages = [(age - 40)/10 for age in ages]
z_incomes = [(income - 50000)/10000 for income in incomes]
```

6. Calculate the distance between the standardized scores of the first and second customer:

```
math.sqrt((z_ages[0] - z_ages[1])**2 + (z_incomes[0] - z_incomes[1])**2)
```

The result should be 1.

7. Also, calculate the distance between the standardized scores of the first and third customer.

```
math.sqrt((z_ages[0] - z_ages[2])**2 + (z_incomes[0] - z_incomes[2])**2)
```

The result should again be 1.

As you can see, the distances are now equivalent, because the second customer's income is one standard deviation away from the first customer's while having the same age, and the third customer's age is one standard deviation away from the first customer's while having the same income.

Activity 3: Loading, Standardizing, and Calculating Distance with a Dataset

For this activity, you have been provided with a dataset named **customer_interactions.csv** (https://github.com/TrainingByPackt/Data-Science-for-Marketing-Analytics/blob/master/Lesson03/customer_interactions.csv) that contains data regarding the amount spent by customers on your products and the number of times they have interacted with your business (for instance, by visiting your website). You've been asked to calculate how similar the first two customers in the dataset are to each other based on how frequently they interact with the business and their yearly spend on your business. Execute the following steps to complete this activity:

1. Load the data from the **customer_interactions.csv** file into a pandas DataFrame, and look at the first five rows of data. You should see the following values:

	spend	interactions
0	5818	23
1	6255	15
2	6139	15
3	6070	19
4	4837	24

Figure 3.11: The first few rows of the data in the customer_interactions.csv file

2. Calculate the Euclidean distance between the first two data points in the DataFrame.

   The output should be close to 437.07.

3. Calculate the standardized values of the variables and store them in new columns named **z_spend** and **z_interactions**. Your DataFrame should now look like this:

	spend	interactions	z_spend	z_interactions
0	5818	23	0.923351	0.647282
1	6255	15	1.145958	-0.809740
2	6139	15	1.086868	-0.809740
3	6070	19	1.051719	-0.081229
4	4837	24	0.423632	0.829410

Figure 3.12: The first few rows of the data after new columns are created for the standardized variables

4. Calculate the distance between the first two data points using the standardized values.

You should get a final value that is close to 1.47.

> **Note**
>
> The solution for this activity can be found on page 333.

k-means Clustering

k-means clustering is a very common unsupervised learning technique with a very wide range of applications. It is powerful because it is conceptually relatively simple, scales to very large datasets, and tends to work quite well in practice. In the following section, you will learn the conceptual foundations of k-means clustering, how to apply k-means clustering to data, and how to deal with high-dimensional data (that is, data with many different variables) in the context of clustering.

Understanding k-means Clustering

k-means clustering is an algorithm that tries to find the best way of grouping data points into k different groups, where k is a parameter given to the algorithm. For now, we will choose k arbitrarily. We will revisit how to choose k in practice in the next chapter. The algorithm then works iteratively to try to find the best grouping. There are two steps to this algorithm:

1. The algorithm begins by randomly selecting k points in space to be the centroids of the clusters. Each data point is then assigned to the centroid that it is closest to it.

2. The centroids are updated to be the mean of all of the data points assigned to them. The data points are then reassigned to the centroid closest to them.

Step two is repeated until none of the data points change the centroid they are assigned to after the centroid is updated.

One point to note here is that this algorithm is not deterministic, that is, the outcome of the algorithm depends on the starting locations of the centroids. Therefore, it is not always guaranteed to find the best grouping. However, in practice it tends to find good groupings while still being computationally inexpensive even for large datasets. k-means clustering is fast and easily scalable, and is therefore the most common clustering algorithm used.

> **Note**
>
> In the next chapter, you will learn about how to evaluate how good your grouping is, and explore other alternative algorithms for clustering.

Exercise 12: k-means Clustering on Income/Age Data

In this exercise, you will first standardize the age and income data from the **ageinc.csv** dataset provided within the **Lesson03** folder on the GitHub repository for this book, and perform k-means clustering using the scikit-learn package:

1. Open your Jupyter Notebook and import the pandas package:

    ```
    import pandas as pd
    ```

2. Load the **ageinc.csv** dataset present within the **Lesson03** folder:

    ```
    ageinc_df = pd.read_csv('ageinc.csv')
    ```

3. Create the standardized value columns for the income and age values and store them in the **z_income** and **z_age** variables, using the following snippet:

    ```
    ageinc_df['z_income'] = (ageinc_df['income'] - ageinc_df['income'].
    mean())/ageinc_df['income'].std()
    ageinc_df['z_age'] = (ageinc_df['age'] - ageinc_df['age'].mean())/ageinc_
    df['age'].std()
    ```

4. Use Matplotlib to plot the data to get a sense of what it looks like. For this, you need to first import **pyplot**. To make sure the plot shows up in the Jupyter Notebook, we will tell the notebook to allow Matplotlib to plot inline. Note that this only has to be done once per notebook where we're plotting. Finally, we will use a scatterplot to plot the data:

    ```
    import matplotlib.pyplot as plt
    %matplotlib inline

    plt.scatter(ageinc_df['income'], ageinc_df['age'])
    ```

5. Label the axes as "Income" and "Age" and use the following code to display the figure:

    ```
    plt.xlabel('Income')
    plt.ylabel('Age')
    plt.show()
    ```

    The resulting figure should look like this:

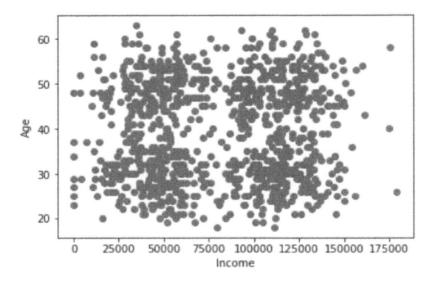

Figure 3.13: A scatterplot of the age and income data

6. Now use the **sklearn** package, a package that has numerous machine learning algorithms, to perform k-means clustering, using the standardized variables. Use the following snippet to perform k-means clustering with four clusters:

    ```
    from sklearn import cluster

    model = cluster.KMeans(n_clusters=4, random_state=10)
    model.fit(ageinc_df[['z_income','z_age']])
    ```

    In the preceding snippet, we first imported the cluster module from the **sklearn** package. Then, we defined the model to be a k-means algorithm with specific parameters (four clusters; the random state just ensures that everyone gets the same answer since the k-means algorithm is not deterministic). The final line fits the model to our data. We specifically only fit it to our **z_income** and **z_age** columns, since we don't want to use the unstandardized variables for clustering.

7. Next, we will create a column called **cluster** that contains the label of the cluster each data point belongs to, and use the **head** function to inspect the first few rows. Consider the following snippet:

```
ageinc_df['cluster'] = model.labels_
ageinc_df.head()
```

Your output will appear as follows:

	income	age	z_income	z_age	cluster
0	101743	58	0.550812	1.693570	2
1	49597	27	-0.777331	-1.130565	3
2	36517	52	-1.110474	1.146963	1
3	33223	49	-1.194372	0.873660	1
4	72994	53	-0.181416	1.238064	1

Figure 3.14: The first few rows of the data with the clusters each data point is assigned to

8. Finally, plot the data points, color, and shape, coded by which cluster they belong to. Use the unstandardized data to do the plotting so the variables are easier to interpret–since we already obtained the clustering from the standardized scores, this is just for visualization purposes, and the absolute value of the variables isn't important. We'll define the markers and colors we want to use for each cluster and then use a loop to plot the data points in each cluster separately with their respective color and shape. We then change the labels of the axes and display the figure:

```
colors = ['r', 'b', 'k', 'g']
markers = ['^', 'o', 'd', 's']

for c in ageinc_df['cluster'].unique():
    d = ageinc_df[ageinc_df['cluster'] == c]
    plt.scatter(d['income'], d['age'], marker=markers[c], color=colors[c])

plt.xlabel('Income')
plt.ylabel('Age')
plt.show()
```

The final plot you obtain should look as follows:

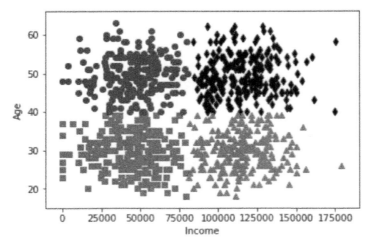

Figure 3.15: A plot of the data with the color/shape indicating which cluster each data point is assigned to

Congratulations! You've successfully performed k-means clustering using the scikit-learn package. In this exercise, we dealt with a dataset that had only two dimensions. In the next section, we'll take a look at how to deal with datasets containing more dimensions.

High-Dimensional Data

It's common to have data that has more than just two dimensions. For example, if in our age and income data we also had yearly spend, we would have three dimensions. If we had some information about how these customers responded to advertised sales, or how many purchases they had made of our products, or how many people lived in their household, we could have many more dimensions.

When we have additional dimensions, it becomes more difficult to visualize our data. In the previous exercise, we only had two variables, and so we could easily visualize data points and the clusters formed. With higher dimensional data, however, different techniques need to be used. Dimensionality reduction techniques are commonly used for this. The idea of **dimensionality reduction** is that data that is multi-dimensional is reduced, usually to two dimensions, for visualization purposes, while trying to preserve the distance between the points.

We will use **principal component analysis** (**PCA**) to perform dimensionality reduction. PCA is a method of transforming the data. It takes the original dimensions and creates new dimensions that capture the most variance in the data. In other words, it creates dimensions that contain the most amount of information about the data, so that when you take the first two principal components (dimensions), you are left with most of the information about the data, but reduced to only two dimensions:

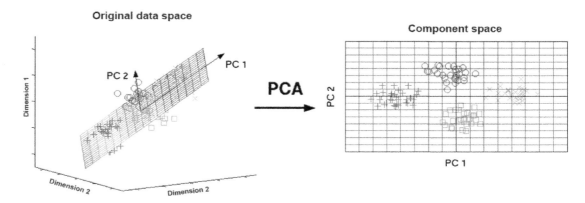

Figure 3.16: How PCA works

> **Note**
>
> There are many other uses of PCA other than dimensionality reduction for visualization. You can read more about PCA here: https://towardsdatascience.com/principal-component-analysis-intro-61f236064b38.

Exercise 13: Dealing with High-Dimensional Data

In this exercise, we will deal with a dataset (**three_col.csv**) that has three columns. We will standardize the data and perform k-means clustering in a way that will scale to data with many columns. To visualize the data, we will perform dimensionality reduction using PCA:

1. Open your Jupyter Notebook and import the pandas package:

   ```
   import pandas as pd
   ```

2. Read in the **three_col.csv** dataset present within the **Lesson03** folder and inspect the columns:

   ```
   df = pd.read_csv('three_col.csv')
   df.head()
   ```

	income	age	days_since_purchase
0	56432	31	492
1	137580	38	551
2	68285	59	304
3	93617	51	507
4	113441	54	509

Figure 3.17: The first few rows of the data in the three_col.csv file

3. Standardize the three columns and save the names of the standardized columns in a list, **zcols**. Use the following loop to standardize all of the columns instead of doing them one at a time:

```
cols = df.columns
zcols = []
for col in cols:
  df['z_' + col] = (df[col] - df[col].mean())/df[col].std()
  zcols.append('z_' + col)
```

4. nspect the new columns using the **head** command, as follows:

```
df.head()
```

	income	age	days_since_purchase	z_income	z_age	z_days_since_purchase
0	56432	31	492	-0.606833	-0.748848	0.818321
1	137580	38	551	1.505879	-0.135469	1.349109
2	68285	59	304	-0.298237	1.704668	-0.873001
3	93617	51	507	0.361289	1.003663	0.953267
4	113441	54	509	0.877413	1.266540	0.971260

Figure 3.18: The first few rows of the data with the standardized columns

5. Perform k-means clustering on the standardized scores. For this, you will first need to import the **cluster** module from the **sklearn** package. Then, define a k-means clustering object (**model**, in the following snippet) with the **random_state** set to 10 and using four clusters. Finally, we will use the **fit_predict** function to fit our k-means model to the standardized columns in our data as well as to label the data:

```
from sklearn import cluster

model = cluster.KMeans(n_clusters=4, random_state=10)
df['cluster'] = model.fit_predict(df[zcols])
```

6. Now we will perform PCA on our data. For this, you need to first import the **decomposition** module from **sklearn**, define a PCA object with **n_components** set to **2**, use this PCA object to transform the standardized data, and store the transformed dimensions in **pc1** and **pc2**:

```
from sklearn import decomposition

pca = decomposition.PCA(n_components=2)
df['pc1'], df['pc2'] = zip(*pca.fit_transform(df[zcols]))
```

7. Plot the clusters in the reduced dimensionality space, using the following loop to plot each cluster with its own shape and color:

```
import matplotlib.pyplot as plt
%matplotlib inline

colors = ['r', 'b', 'k', 'g']
markers = ['^', 'o', 'd', 's']

for c in df['cluster'].unique():
  d = df[df['cluster'] == c]
  plt.scatter(d['pc1'], d['pc2'], marker=markers[c], color=colors[c])

plt.show()
```

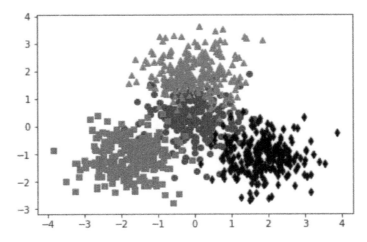

Figure 3.19: A plot of the data reduced to two dimensions denoting the various clusters

Note that the x and y axes here are principal components, and therefore are not easily interpretable. However, by visualizing the clusters, we can get a sense of how good the clusters are based on how much they overlap.

8. To quickly investigate what each cluster seems to be capturing, we can look at the means of each of the variables in each cluster. Use the following snippet:

```
for cluster in df['cluster'].unique():
  print("Cluster: " + str(cluster))
  for col in ['income', 'age', 'days_since_purchase']:
    print(col + ": {:.2f}".format(df.loc[df['cluster'] == cluster, col].
mean()))
```

Here is a tabular representation of the output (notice the difference in the means between the four clusters):

cluster	income	age	days_since_purchase
0	114704.12	29.34	302.92
1	46153.20	29.34	498.19
2	45002.10	49.49	299.66
3	113118.22	49.77	502.58

Figure 3.20: The means of the three columns

> **Note**
>
> This is just one example of how to investigate the different clusters. You can also look at the first few examples of data points in each to get a sense of the differences. In more complex cases, using various visualization techniques to probe more deeply into the different clusters may be useful.

Congratulations! You have successfully used PCA for dimensionality reduction. We can see that each cluster has different characteristics: cluster 0 represents customers with high incomes, low ages, and relatively fewer days since the last purchase; cluster 1 represents low income, low age, and more days since the last purchase; cluster 2 represents low income, high age, and fewer days since last purchase; and cluster 3 has high income, high age, and more days since last purchase.

Activity 4: Using k-means Clustering on Customer Behavior Data

Imagine that you work for the marketing department of a company that sells different types of wine to customers. Your marketing team launched 32 initiatives over the past one year to increase the sales of wine (data for which is present in the **offer_info. csv** file in the **Lesson03** folder). Your team has also acquired data that tells you which customers have responded to which of the 32 marketing initiatives recently (this data is present within the **customer_offers.csv** file). Your marketing team now wants to begin targeting their initiatives more precisely, so they can provide offers customized to groups that tend to respond to similar offers.

> **Note**
>
> Some knowledge of wine might be useful for drawing the inferences at the end of this activity. Feel free to Google the wine types to get an idea of what they are.

Your task is to use k-means clustering to discover a few groups of customers and explore what those groupings are and the types of offers that customers in those groups tend to respond to. Execute the following steps to complete this activity:

1. Read in the data in the **customer_offers.csv** file and set the **customer_name** column to the index.

2. Perform k-means clustering with three clusters and save the cluster that each data point is assigned to.

> **Note**
>
> We won't standardize the data this time, because all variables are binary. We will talk more about other variable types in the next chapter.

3. Use PCA to visualize the clusters. Your plot will look as follows:

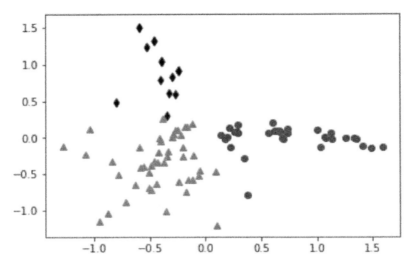

Figure 3.21: A plot of the data reduced to two dimensions denoting three clusters

4. Investigate how each cluster differs from the average in each of our features. In other words, find the difference between the proportion of customers in each cluster that responded to an offer and the proportion of customers overall that responded to an offer, for each of the offers. Plot these differences on a bar chart. The outputs should appear as follows:

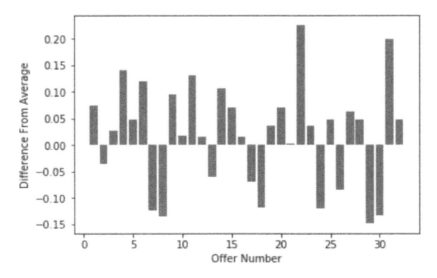

Figure 3.22: Plot for cluster 0

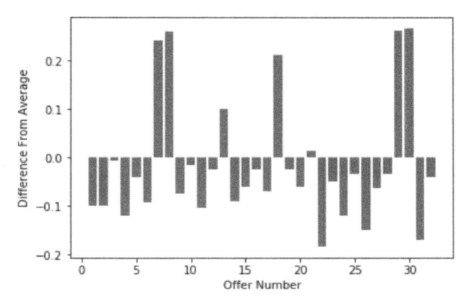

Figure 3.23: Plot for cluster 1

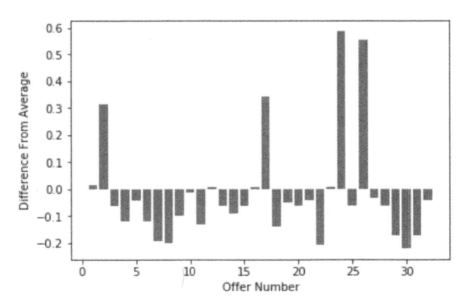

Figure 3.24: Plot for cluster 2

5. Load the information about what the offers were from **offer_info.csv**. For each cluster, find the five offers where the data points in that cluster differ most from the mean, and print out the varietal of those offers. You should get the following values:

```
3        Champagne
5         Prosecco
10       Champagne
21       Champagne
30       Champagne
Name: varietal, dtype: object
6             Prosecco
7            Espumante
17           Espumante
28       Pinot Grigio
29              Malbec
Name: varietal, dtype: object
0              Malbec
1          Pinot Noir
16         Pinot Noir
23         Pinot Noir
25         Pinot Noir
Name: varietal, dtype: object
```

Figure 3.25: The five offers where the cluster differs most from the mean

> **Note**
>
> The solution for this activity can be found on page 334.

Summary

In this chapter, we explored the idea of using unsupervised machine learning to perform customer segmentation. We established how to think about similarity in the customer data feature space and also learned the importance of standardizing data if they are on very different scales. Finally, we learned about k-means clustering, a commonly used, fast, and easily scalable clustering algorithm.

In this chapter, we used predefined values for the number of groups we asked the k-means algorithms to look for. In the next chapter, we will learn about how to choose the number of groups, how to evaluate your groupings, and additional methods for using machine learning to perform customer segmentation.

Choosing the Best Segmentation Approach

Learning Objectives

By the end of this chapter, you will be able to:

- Tune hyperparameters (such as the number of clusters) of clustering algorithms using various methods
- Use the mean-shift, k-mode, and k-prototype clustering techniques
- Evaluate and fine-tune clustering

This chapter covers various clustering algorithms (apart from k-means) and explains how they can be evaluated.

Introduction

In the previous chapter, we introduced the concept of clustering, and practiced it using k-means clustering. However, several issues remained unresolved, such as how to choose the number of clusters and how to evaluate a clustering technique once the clusters are created. This chapter aims to expand on the content of the previous one and fill in some of those gaps.

There are a number of different methods for approaching the problem of choosing the number of clusters when using k-means clustering, some relying on judgment and some using more technical quantitative measures. You can even use clustering techniques that don't require you to explicitly state the number of clusters; however, these methods have their own tradeoffs and hyperparameters that need to be tuned. We'll study these in this chapter.

We also have only dealt with data that is fairly easy for k-means to deal with: continuous variables or binary variables. In this chapter, we'll explain how to deal with data containing categorical variables with many different possible values, using the k-mode and k-prototype clustering methods.

Finally, we'll learn how to tell whether one method of clustering is better than another. For this purpose, we want to be able to tweak the hyperparameters of a modeling algorithm and be able to tell whether that led to a better or worse clustering, as well as compare the completely different types of algorithms to each other. Here, we will learn how to evaluate clustering.

Choosing the Number of Clusters

In the previous chapter, we just used a predefined number of clusters, but in the real world, we don't always know what number of clusters to expect. There are different ways of trying to come up with the correct number of clusters. In this chapter, we will start with two. First, we will learn about **simple visual inspection**, which has the advantages of being easy and intuitive but relies heavily on individual judgement and subjectivity. We will then learn about the **elbow method with sum of squared errors**, which is partially quantitative but still relies on individual judgement and is more abstract than choosing based on visual inspection. Later in this chapter, we will also learn about using the **silhouette score**, which removes subjectivity from the judgment but is also quite abstract.

As we learn about these different methods, there is one overriding principle you should keep in mind: the quantitative measures only tell you how well that number of clusters fits the data. It does not tell you how useful those clusters are. A general principle is that you shouldn't use a clustering method if the resulting clusters are incomprehensible. Using fewer clusters and fewer variables can often lead to easier-to-interpret clusters. In general, real-world data is quite messy and there are a lot of judgment calls to be made. Learning about these methods is important to be able to tell how good your clusters are and to make sure your methods are well founded, but keep in mind that they are only one factor. Often, the differences between using a different number of clusters will be rather small in terms of the quantitative differences, and at that point you should be prepared to use your judgment on what's best.

Simple Visual Inspection

One method of choosing the number of clusters is to simply perform clustering with a few different numbers and visually inspect the results. You can usually tell by looking at data how well separated the different clusters are. When dealing with more than two dimensions, we learned in the previous chapter how to visualize the data.

Clusters are better when they are well separated, without too much overlap, and when they capture the most densely populated parts of the data space. Too few clusters will often lead to plots that look like a single cluster is spanning more than one densely packed space. On the other hand, too many clusters will often look like two are competing for a single densely packed space. In higher dimensions, this can become complicated, because two-dimensional representations of the high dimensional space are not perfect, so the more dimensions there are, the poorer the visualization is of how the data is actually clustered.

Choosing the number of clusters on the basis of visual inspection is often appealing because it is a decision based on looking at what's happening with the data most directly. People are usually pretty good at looking at how much different clusters overlap and deciding whether a given number of clusters leads to too much overlap. This is not a quantitative method, however, leaving a lot to subjectivity and individual judgment, but for many simple problems, it's a great way to decide how many clusters to use.

Exercise 14: Choosing the Number of Clusters Based on Visual Inspection

In this exercise, you will apply k-means clustering to age and income data using different numbers of clusters (ranging from two to six), and use visual inspection to evaluate the results:

1. Import pandas and load the age and income data from the **ageinc.csv** dataset into a DataFrame named **ageinc_df**:

    ```
    import pandas as pd
    ageinc_df = pd.read_csv('ageinc.csv')
    ```

2. Now import the **matplotlib** library and plot a scatterplot of the **age** and **income** fields using the following code:

    ```
    import matplotlib.pyplot as plt
    %matplotlib inline

    plt.scatter(ageinc_df['income'], ageinc_df['age'])
    plt.xlabel('Income')
    plt.ylabel('Age')
    plt.show()
    ```

    Look carefully at the plot you obtain, which should look like the one shown here:

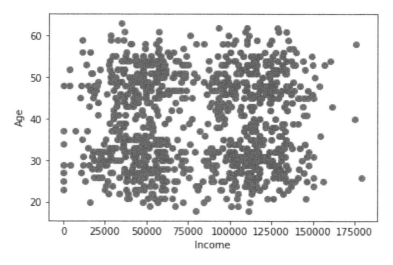

Figure 4.1: Scatterplot of age versus income

You may already notice that the data looks clustered into four groups. This should become more explicit once you've performed and visualized the k-means clustering.

3. Standardize the data, as performed in previous exercises, and store the standardized values in **z_income** and **z_age** columns, as follows:

```
ageinc_df['z_income'] = (ageinc_df['income'] - ageinc_df['income'].
mean())/ageinc_df['income'].std()
ageinc_df['z_age'] = (ageinc_df['age'] - ageinc_df['age'].mean())/ageinc_
df['age'].std()
```

4. Now you can perform k-means clustering using the standardized data. First, import the **cluster** module from the **sklearn** package and define the colors and shapes that you'll use for each cluster (since you'll be visualizing six clusters in all, define at least six different colors and shapes), as follows:

```
from sklearn import cluster

colors = ['r', 'b', 'k', 'g', 'm', 'y']
markers = ['^', 'o', 'd', 's', 'P', 'X']
```

5. Then, using a **for** loop, cluster the data using a different number of clusters, ranging from two to six, and visualize the resulting plots obtained in a subplot. Use a separate **for** loop to plot each cluster in each subplot, so we can use different shapes for each cluster. Use the following snippet:

```
plt.figure(figsize=(12,16))

for n in range(2,7):
    model = cluster.KMeans(n_clusters=n, random_state=10)
    ageinc_df['cluster'] = model.fit_predict(ageinc_df[['z_income','z_age']])

    plt.subplot(3, 2, n-1)
    for c in ageinc_df['cluster'].unique():
        d = ageinc_df[ageinc_df['cluster'] == c]
        plt.scatter(d['income'], d['age'], marker=markers[c], color=colors[c])

plt.show()
```

You should see the following plots when this is done:

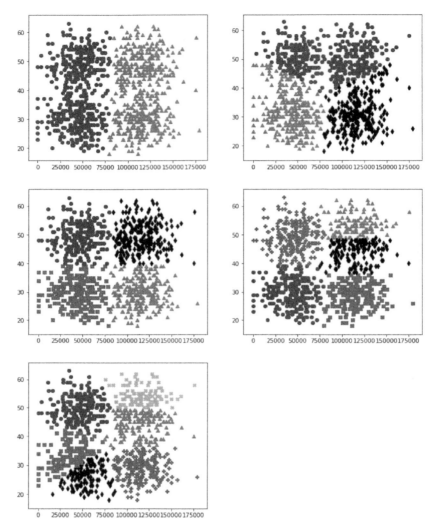

Figure 4.2: (Clockwise from top left) Scatterplots of income and age data with cluster numbers progressing from two to six

By observing the resulting plots, we can see that with too few clusters, we end up with clusters spanning pretty sparse regions in between more densely packed regions. However, with too many, we end up with clusters that border each other but don't seem separated by a region of sparseness. Therefore, four clusters seem to capture things very well.

The Elbow Method with Sum of Squared Errors

Often, it's difficult to tell by visualization alone how many clusters should be used for a particular problem. Different people may disagree about the number of clusters to use, and there may not be a clear answer. Furthermore, dimensionality-reduction techniques are not perfect—they attempt to take all the information in multiple dimensions and reduce it to only two. In some cases, this can work well, but as the number of dimensions increases, the data becomes more complex, and these visual methods quickly reach their limitations. When this happens, it's not easy to determine through visual inspection what the right number of clusters to use is. In these harder cases, it's often better to reach for a more quantitative measure. One such classic measure is to look for an elbow in a plot of the sum of squared errors.

The sum of squared errors is the sum of the "errors" (difference between a data point and the centroid of its assigned cluster) for all data points, squared. It can be calculated with the following equation:

$$SS = \sum_k \sum_{x_i \in k} (x_i - \mu_k)^2$$

Figure 4.3: Equation for calculating the sum of squared errors of data points in a dataset

Here, μk is the location of the centroid of cluster k, and each xi is a data point assigned to cluster k. As we increase k, we should expect the sum of squared errors to decrease since there are more centroids. When plotted together, however, there will often be an "elbow" in the plot, where the "gain" in terms of reduced errors seems to slow for each new cluster. Hence, the plot of the sum of squared errors versus number of clusters (k) will look as follows:

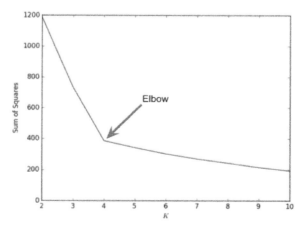

Figure 4.4: A plot of the sum of squared errors for different values of k, showing an "elbow" (inflection point) at k=4

Exercise 15: Determining the Number of Clusters Using the Elbow Method

In this exercise, you need to determine the number of clusters (between 2 and 10) that is best to use for the age and income data using the elbow method with the sum of squared errors:

1. Import pandas and load the age and income data from the **ageinc.csv** dataset into a DataFrame named **ageinc_df**:

   ```
   import pandas as pd
   ageinc_df = pd.read_csv('ageinc.csv')
   ```

2. Standardize the data, as performed in previous exercises, and store the standardized values in **z_income** and **z_age** columns, as follows:

   ```
   ageinc_df['z_income'] = (ageinc_df['income'] - ageinc_df['income'].
   mean())/ageinc_df['income'].std()
   ageinc_df['z_age'] = (ageinc_df['age'] - ageinc_df['age'].mean())/ageinc_
   df['age'].std()
   ```

3. You need to calculate the sum of squared errors for clusterings using 2 to 10 clusters, but we will start by going through the process for a clustering with **k=2**. Import the **cluster** module from the **sklearn** package. Cluster the data using **k=2** and save the resulting labels in a variable called **cluster_assignments** and cluster centers in a variable called **centers**, as shown here:

   ```
   from sklearn import cluster

   model = cluster.KMeans(n_clusters=2, random_state=10)
   X = ageinc_df[['z_income','z_age']].as_matrix()
   model.fit_predict(X)
   cluster_assignments = model.labels_
   centers = model.cluster_centers_
   ```

4. To perform the calculation for the sum of squared errors, import **numpy**. Calculate the difference between each data point and the center of its assigned cluster, square it, and use the built-in NumPy **sum** method to sum all of these squared errors together using the following code:

   ```
   import numpy as np

   print(np.sum((X - centers[cluster_assignments]) ** 2))
   ```

   The result should be 1189.7476232504307.

5. Now import **matplotlib.pyplot** for plotting. Loop through **k=2** to **k=10**, calculate the squared error for each, and store the result as a list in a variable called **ss**:

```
import matplotlib.pyplot as plt
%matplotlib inline


ss = []
krange = list(range(2,11))
X = ageinc_df[['z_income','z_age']].values
for n in krange:
    model = cluster.KMeans(n_clusters=n, random_state=10)
    model.fit_predict(X)
    cluster_assignments = model.labels_
    centers = model.cluster_centers_
    ss.append(np.sum((X - centers[cluster_assignments]) ** 2))
```

Finally, create a plot with k on the *x*-axis and the squared error on the *y*-axis, as shown here:

```
plt.plot(krange, ss)
plt.xlabel("$K$")
plt.ylabel("Sum of Squares")
plt.show()
```

The resulting plot should look as follows:

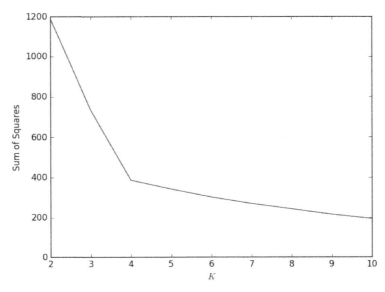

Figure 4.5: A plot of the sum of squared errors for different values of k, showing an "elbow" (inflection point) at k=4

By observing the preceding plot, you will notice that there's a clear elbow in the plot at **k=4**, so we take that as our best number for k. Prior to that, an additional cluster gives us big gains in reducing the sum of squared errors. Beyond that, we seem to be getting diminishing returns.

Activity 5: Determining Clusters for High-End Clothing Customer Data Using the Elbow Method with the Sum of Squared Errors

You are working at a company that sells high-end clothing. The company has collected data on customer age, income, their annual spend at the business, and the number of days since their last purchase. The company wants to start targeted marketing campaigns, but doesn't know how many different types of customers they have. Therefore, it wants the customer population segmented based on the data gathered and wants to know how many customer clusters there are and what group each customer falls into. You need to achieve this objective with both visualization and the elbow method with the sum of squared errors. Execute the following steps to complete the activity:

1. Read in the data from **four_cols.csv**.

2. Inspect the data using the **head** function. The first five rows are shown here:

	income	age	days_since_purchase	annual_spend
0	37453	48	504	4441
1	50775	50	566	4239
2	71047	41	326	5834
3	52239	52	259	5456
4	112343	27	279	1749

Figure 4.6: The first five rows of the four_cols data set

3. Standardize all columns.

4. Plot the data, using dimensionality reduction (principal component analysis). The plot should look as follows:

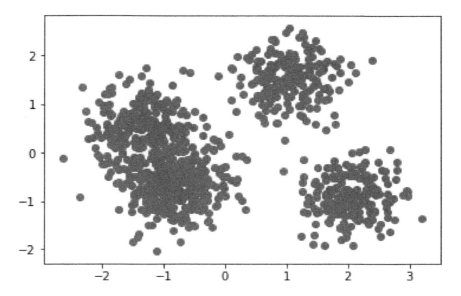

Figure 4.7: Data visualized after being reduced to two dimensions

5. Visualize clustering with two and seven clusters. You should get plots similar to the ones shown here:

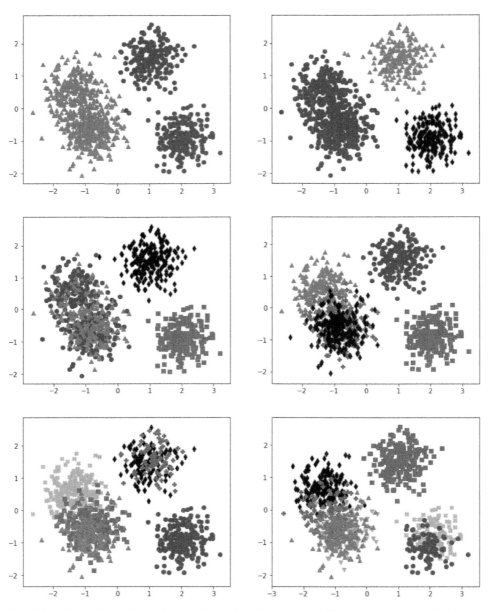

Figure 4.8: The dimensionality-reduced data visualized with different numbers of clusters. Each different color/shape indicates a different cluster

6. Create a plot of the sum of squared errors and look for an elbow. The plot should appear similar to this:

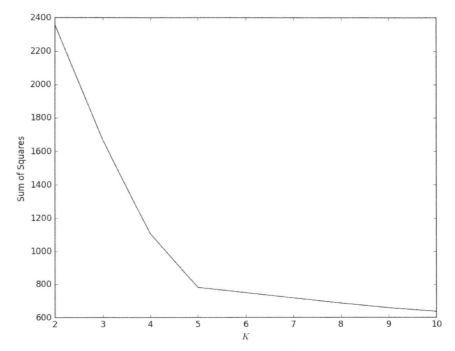

Figure 4.9: A plot showing the sum of squared errors for different numbers of clusters. Notice the "elbow" at k=5

> **Note**
>
> The solution for this activity can be found on page 336.

Different Methods of Clustering

k-means is a useful clustering algorithm because it is simple, widely applicable, and scales very well to large datasets. However, it is not the only clustering algorithm available. Each clustering algorithm has its own strengths and weaknesses, so it's often worth having more than one in your toolkit. We'll look at some of the other popular clustering algorithms in this section.

Mean-Shift Clustering

Mean-shift clustering is an interesting algorithm in contrast to the k-means algorithm because unlike k-means, it does not require you to specify the number of clusters. Mean-shift clustering works by starting at each data point and shifting the data points toward the area of greatest density. When all of the data points have found their local density peak, the algorithm is complete. This tends to be computationally expensive, so this method does not scale well to large datasets (k-means clustering, on the other hand, scales very well). The following diagram illustrates this:

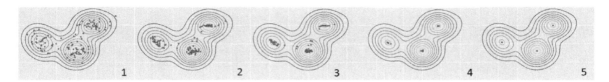

Figure 4.10: Illustration of the workings of the mean-shift algorithm

While not needing to choose the number of clusters sounds great, there is the difficult issue of choosing the bandwidth that the algorithm will use, or in other words, how far each data point will look when searching for a higher density area. A common method (which we will use shortly) for determining the best bandwidth is to estimate it based on the distances between nearby points, but this method requires one to choose a quantile that determines the proportion of points to look at. In practice, this ends up being a very similar problem to the problem of choosing a number of clusters where at some point you, the user, have to make a choice of what hyperparameter to use. Why, then, bother with mean-shift clustering? Because despite also needing an input hyperparameter, the mean-shift algorithm is different than k-means and therefore will simply fit certain datasets better than k-means. Later in this chapter, we will learn how to compare these methods.

> **Note**
>
> There are many clustering algorithms. To read about the ones implemented in sklearn, see here: https://scikit-learn.org/stable/modules/clustering.html#overview-of-clustering-methods.

Exercise 16: Performing Mean-Shift Clustering to Cluster Data

In this exercise, we will use mean-shift clustering to cluster the age and income data of customers from the **ageinc.csv** dataset:

1. Import **pandas** and load the age and income data from the **ageinc.csv** dataset into a DataFrame named **ageinc_df**:

   ```
   import pandas as pd
   ageinc_df = pd.read_csv('ageinc.csv')
   ```

2. Standardize the data and store the standardized values in the **z_income** and **z_age** columns, as follows:

   ```
   ageinc_df['z_income'] = (ageinc_df['income'] - ageinc_df['income'].
   mean())/ageinc_df['income'].std()
   ageinc_df['z_age'] = (ageinc_df['age'] - ageinc_df['age'].mean())/ageinc_
   df['age'].std()
   ```

3. Now you need to perform mean-shift clustering on the standardized columns of the data. First, import the **cluster** module from the **sklearn** package, and also save the standardized columns to **X**. Now use the **estimate_bandwidth** function to estimate the best bandwidth to use, with a quantile parameter set to 0.1. Train the model with the estimated bandwidth, and set **bin_seeding** to **True** (this speeds up the algorithm). Finally, fit the model to the data, as follows:

   ```
   from sklearn import cluster

   X = ageinc_df[['z_income','z_age']]
   bandwidth = cluster.estimate_bandwidth(X, quantile=0.1)
   ms = cluster.MeanShift(bandwidth=bandwidth, bin_seeding=True)

   ms.fit(X)
   ```

4. Print the resulting number of clusters by finding the number of unique labels that mean-shift clustering has created, as follows:

   ```
   ageinc_df['cluster'] = ms.labels_
   print("Number of clusters: %d" % len(ageinc_df['cluster'].unique()))
   ```

5. Plot the resulting clustering by importing **matplotlib**, defining the shapes and colors we will use for the plot and looping through to scatter plot each cluster (like we did for the previous exercise):

```
import matplotlib.pyplot as plt
%matplotlib inline

colors = ['r', 'b', 'k', 'g']
markers = ['^', 'o', 'd', 's']

for c in ageinc_df['cluster'].unique():
  d = ageinc_df[ageinc_df['cluster'] == c]
  plt.scatter(d['income'], d['age'], marker=markers[c], color=colors[c])

plt.show()
```

The resulting plot should look as follows:

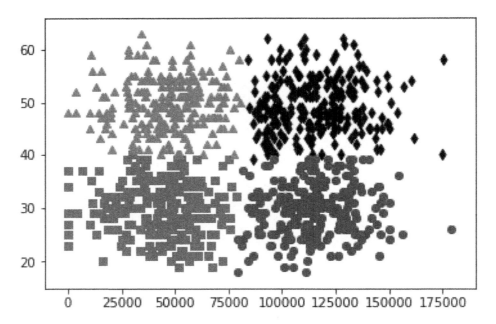

Figure 4.11: The data clustered using mean-shift clustering. Each different color/shape indicates a different cluster

Congratulations! You've successfully used mean-shift clustering to cluster age and income data. In the next section, we'll learn about other clustering algorithms.

k-modes and k-prototypes Clustering

k-means clustering is great when you have numerical data. However, when you have categorical data (that is, data that can't be converted into a numerical order, such as race, language, and country) with more than two categories, it becomes more complicated. In statistics, one common strategy for dealing with categorical data is to use dummy variables—the practice of creating a new variable for each category—so that each of these dummy variables is a binary. When clustering, this can lead to complications, because if you have many different categories, you are adding many different dimensions for each categorical variable and the result will often not properly reflect the kinds of groupings you're looking for.

Luckily, it turns out there are two related methods that make dealing with categorical data more natural. **k-modes** is a clustering algorithm that uses the **mode** of a cluster rather than the **mean**, but otherwise performs just like the k-means algorithm. Since the mode is defined as the most common value in a set, this makes it a poor choice for continuous variables, which typically only have one data point associated with a specific number, but it's a great choice for categorical data (and in fact, works only with categorical data), where many data points will fall into the same categories.

k-prototypes clustering allows you to deal with cases where there is a mix of categorical and continuous variables. Instead of defining a centroid for each cluster like k-means or k-modes, k-prototypes clustering chooses a data point to be the "prototype," and uses that as if it is the centroid of the cluster, updating to a new data point closer to the center of all data points assigned to that cluster using the same process as k-means or k-modes.

Exercise 17: Clustering Data Using the k-prototypes Method

For this exercise, you have been provided with the **age_education.csv** dataset containing demographic data on the age and educational attainment of 1,000 customers. You need to create customer segmentations with this data by applying k-prototype clustering to data that has a mix of categorical (**education**) and continuous (**age**) variables:

1. Import pandas and read in the data in **age_education.csv**:

```
import pandas as pd

df = pd.read_csv('age_education.csv')
```

2. Inspect the data using the **head** function:

```
df.head()
```

The first five rows of the data will look as follows:

	age	education
0	27.007219	college
1	47.615409	highschool
2	51.382815	highschool
3	54.906622	highschool
4	27.719939	less_than_highschool

Figure 4.12: The first five columns of the age and education data

3. Standardize the **age** variable, since it is our only numeric variable, and store the values in the **z_age** column:

```
df['z_age'] = (df['age'] - df['age'].mean())/df['age'].std()
```

4. Import **Kprototypes** from the **kmodes** module. The **kmodes** module expects NumPy matrices rather than pandas DataFrames, so convert the standardized age and education columns as a matrix in the **X** variable by using the **values** function. Perform k-prototypes clustering using three clusters, specifying the **education** column (in column index 1) as **categorical**, and save the result of the clustering as a new column called **cluster**:

```
from kmodes.kprototypes import KPrototypes

X = df[['z_age', 'education']].values
kp = KPrototypes(n_clusters=3)
df['cluster'] = kp.fit_predict(X, categorical=[1])
```

> **Note**
>
> If all variables were categorical, we would use k-modes instead of k-prototypes clustering. The code would be the same, except all references to **kprototypes** would be changed to **kmodes**. We will use **kmodes** in the next activity.

5. Create dummy variables for our categorical variable using the pandas **get_dummies** function, and concatenate them onto our DataFrame so we can analyze the results:

```
df = pd.concat([df,pd.get_dummies(df['education'])],axis=1)
```

6. Plot the proportions of each educational level in each cluster in a bar plot by looping through each cluster, filtering to the data points in the current cluster and storing the result in **cluster_df**, calculating the proportions using the pandas **mean** function, and finally plotting them using the matplotlib **barh** function:

```python
import matplotlib.pyplot as plt
%matplotlib inline

plt.figure(figsize=(8,12))

for i in range(3):
    cluster_df = df[df['cluster'] == i]
    means = cluster_df[['college','highschool','less_than_highschool']].
mean()

    ax = plt.subplot(3, 1, i+1)
    plt.barh([1,2,3],means)
    ax.set_yticks([1,2,3])
    ax.set_yticklabels(['college','highschool','less_than_highschool'])
    ax.set_title('Cluster ' + str(i))
plt.show()
```

Your resulting plot should look as follows:

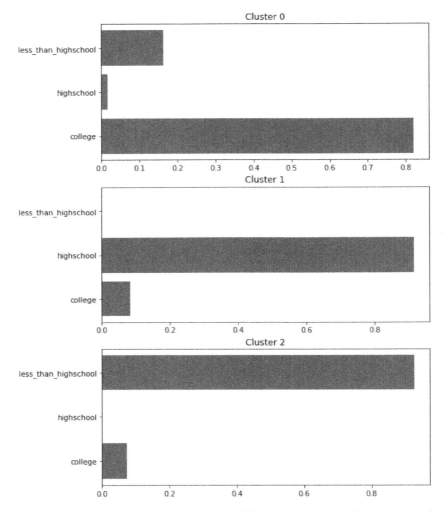

Figure 4.13: The proportions of customers of different educational levels in each cluster

> **Note**
>
> We use this method of visualizing the education data instead of the usual scatterplots because the categorical data increases the dimensionality. If we used dimensionality reduction to visualize the data, we would not be able to visualize how the clusters capture the different education levels.

Congratulations! You have successfully used k-prototypes clustering to segment people based on their age and educational attainment levels. You can see in the preceding plots that cluster 0 captures college-educated customers, cluster 1 captures those with a high-school education, and cluster 2 captures those with less than a high-school education.

Activity 6: Using Different Clustering Techniques on Customer Behavior Data

In this activity, you've been given data about a number of different marketing promotions that have been offered to customers. You also have data on which offers each customer responded to. Based on this information, you're asked to cluster the customers. Using the customer offer data (in `customer_offers.csv`), try using different clustering techniques, and visualize the results using principal component analysis:

1. Read in the data from `customer_offers.csv`.

2. Use mean-shift clustering (with quantile = 0.1) to cluster the data.

3. Use k-modes clustering (with k = 4) to cluster the data.

4. Use k-means clustering (with k=4 and random_state=100) to cluster the data.

5. Using dimensionality reduction (principal component analysis), visualize the resulting clustering of each method. The resulting plots should look as follows:

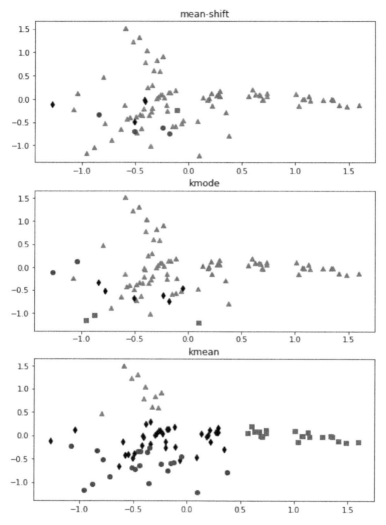

Figure 4.14: Clustering as a result of mean-shift, k-mode, and k-means clustering

Note

The solution for this activity can be found on page 338.

Evaluating Clustering

Being able to perform clustering in different ways is only useful if you know how to evaluate different clustering methods and compare them in an objective way. Subjective methods, such as visual inspection, can always be used, but the silhouette score is a powerful objective method that can be used with data that is more difficult to visualize. We'll learn more about this in the next section.

Silhouette Score

The silhouette score is a formal measure of how well a clustering fits the data. The higher the score, the better. Typically, the score is calculated for each data point separately, and the average is taken as a measure of how well the model fits the whole dataset altogether.

There are two main components to the score. The first component measures how well the data point fits into the cluster that it is assigned to. This is defined as the average distance between it and all other members of that same cluster. The second component measures how well the data point fits into the next nearest cluster. It is calculated in the same way by measuring the average distance between the data point and all of the data points assigned to the next nearest cluster. The difference between these two numbers can be taken as a measure of how well the data point fits into the cluster it is assigned to as opposed to a different cluster. Therefore, when calculated for all data points, it's a measure of how good each data point fits into the particular cluster it's been assigned to.

More formally, given data point xi, where axi is the average distance between that data point and all other data points in the same cluster and bxi is the average distance between data point xi and the data points in the next nearest cluster, the silhouette score is defined as follows:

$$s(x_i) = \frac{b_{x_i} - a_{x_i}}{\max\left(a_{x_i}, b_{x_i}\right)}$$

Figure 4.15: Equation for calculating the silhouette score for a data point

Note that since we divide by the maximum of axi and bxi, we end up with a number between –1 and 1. A negative score means that this data point is actually on average closer to the other cluster, whereas a high positive score means it's a much better fit to the cluster it is assigned to. When we take the average score across all data points, we will therefore still get a number between –1 and 1, where the closer we are to one the better the fit.

Note that the silhouette score is a general measure of how well a clustering fits the data, so it can be used to not only compare two different models of different types, but also choose hyperparameters, such as the number of clusters or choice of quantile for calculating bandwidth for mean-shift clustering.

Exercise 18: Calculating Silhouette Score to Pick the Best k for k-means and Comparing to the Mean-Shift Algorithm

In this exercise, we will perform k-means clustering using different numbers of clusters and use the silhouette score to determine the best number of clusters to use. We will also compare the scores obtained using the k-means and mean-shift algorithms:

1. Import pandas and read the data in **four_cols.csv**:

    ```
    import pandas as pd
    df = pd.read_csv('four_cols.csv')
    ```

2. Standardize the data in each column by looping through each column, and store the results in new columns named with a **z_** prefix. Use the following code:

    ```
    cols = df.columns
    zcols = []
    for col in cols:
        df['z_' + col] = (df[col] - df[col].mean())/df[col].std()
        zcols.append('z_' + col)
    ```

3. To begin the clustering, import **cluster** and **metrics** from **sklearn**, and import **matplotlib**:

    ```
    from sklearn import cluster
    from sklearn import metrics
    import matplotlib.pyplot as plt
    %matplotlib inline
    ```

4. Start with k-means clustering. Create a list of the numbers we'll use for k, 2 to 10, and store it in a variable called **krange**. Create an empty list called **avg_silhouettes**, which we will use to store the silhouette scores. Loop through the values in **krange**, perform k-means clustering for each value of k, and use the **silhouette_score** function from **metrics** to calculate the silhouette score. Append the silhouette score to **avg_silhouettes**:

    ```
    krange = list(range(2,11))
    avg_silhouettes = []
    for n in krange:
        model = cluster.KMeans(n_clusters=n, random_state=10)
        cluster_assignments = model.fit_predict(df[zcols])
    ```

```
    silhouette_avg = metrics.silhouette_score(df[zcols], cluster_
  assignments)
    avg_silhouettes.append(silhouette_avg)
```

5. Finally, plot the result by plotting **krange** against **avg_silhouettes**:

```
plt.plot(krange, avg_silhouettes)
plt.xlabel("$K$")
plt.ylabel("Average Silhouette Score")
plt.show()
```

Your plot will look as follows:

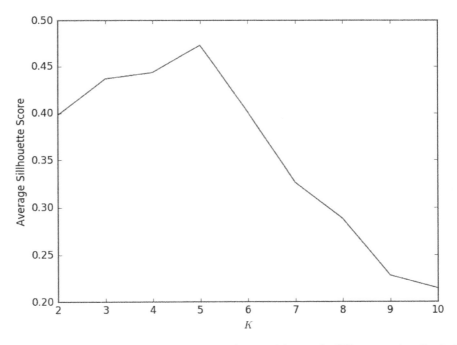

Figure 4.16: A plot of the average silhouette score obtained for each different value for k. k=5 has the best value

From the preceding plot, you can infer that k=5 has the best silhouette score.

6. Perform k-means clustering with the best k found from the preceding plot and print its silhouette score using the following code:

```
model = cluster.KMeans(n_clusters=5, random_state=10)
model.fit_predict(X)

km_silhouette = metrics.silhouette_score(df[zcols], model.labels_)

print('k-means silhouette score: ' + str(km_silhouette))
```

The k-means silhouette score should be 0.47313271918107647.

7. Now perform mean-shift clustering with a quantile of 0.1 and print the silhouette score of the resulting clustering, as follows:

```
bandwidth = cluster.estimate_bandwidth(df[zcols], quantile=0.1)
ms = cluster.MeanShift(bandwidth=bandwidth, bin_seeding=True)

ms.fit(X)
ms_silhouette = metrics.silhouette_score(df[zcols], ms.labels_)

print('mean-shift silhouette score: ' + str(ms_silhouette))
```

The mean-shift silhouette score should be 0.47287372381945053.

Note that the mean-shift silhouette score is very close to the k-means score using the best value of k. This means both provide an equally good fit for this dataset.

Train and Test Split

A very common concern in machine learning is the problem of overfitting. **Overfitting** is when a machine learning model fits so well to the data that was used to create it, that it doesn't generalize to new data. This problem is usually a larger concern with supervised learning, where there is a label with the correct result expected from the algorithm. However, it can also be a concern with clustering when you are trying to choose the best clustering technique or hyperparameters that fit the data. One issue is that you could try out so many different kinds of parameters and algorithms that the one that comes out on top is the best fit just because of some small peculiarity in training data that isn't true of the data more generally.

It's therefore considered best practice to always evaluate your models using a held out portion of the data called the **test set**. Prior to doing any kind of clustering, the data is divided into the **training set** and the **test set**. The model is then fit using the training set, meaning that the centroids are defined based on running the k-means algorithm on that portion of the data. Then, the test data is assigned to clusters based on those centroids, and the model is evaluated based on how well that test data is fit. Since the model has not been trained using the test set, this is just like the model encountering new data, and you can see how well your model generalizes to this new data, which is what we really care about.

Exercise 19: Using a Train-Test Split to Evaluate Clustering Performance

In this exercise, we will separate the data from **four_cols.csv** into a training and test set. We will use the training set to fit our clustering algorithms, and then evaluate them on the test set:

1. Import pandas and read in the data from **four_cols.csv**:

    ```
    import pandas as pd
    df = pd.read_csv('four_cols.csv')
    ```

2. Standardize the data in each column and save the results in new columns named with a **z_** prefix:

    ```
    cols = df.columns
    zcols = []
    for col in cols:
        df['z_' + col] = (df[col] - df[col].mean())/df[col].std()
        zcols.append('z_' + col)
    ```

3. Import **model_selection** from **sklearn** to use the **train_test_split** function to split the data into training and testing sets. Store the resulting DataFrames in **X_train** and **X_test**:

    ```
    from sklearn import model_selection

    X_train, X_test = model_selection.train_test_split(df[zcols], random_state = 100)
    ```

4. Inspect the training and test sets using the **head** function:

    ```
    X_train.head()
    ```

The first five instances of the training data will appear as follows:

	z_income	z_age	z_days_since_purchase	z_annual_spend
114	1.296394	-1.147250	-0.914520	-0.200457
309	-0.116798	0.973360	0.788546	0.727396
406	-1.697256	0.327957	1.305708	1.151438
611	-0.983877	0.235756	-1.262266	0.715401
934	1.629281	0.512358	0.949045	0.699207

Figure 4.17: The first five rows of the training data

Use the following code to inspect the test set:

```
X_test.head()
```

The first five instances of the test data will appear as follows:

	z_income	z_age	z_days_since_purchase	z_annual_spend
445	-0.591641	0.604558	-0.441941	0.678214
157	0.882064	-0.962849	-1.779428	-1.534958
656	0.513568	-0.778448	-1.422765	-2.131135
310	-1.094577	1.342161	-0.629189	0.795171
297	1.192704	-1.239450	-1.431681	-0.877004

Figure 4.18: The first five rows of the test data

5. Check the lengths of the two sets to see how the **train_test_split** function works:

```
print('Length of training set: ' + str(len(X_train)))
print('Length of test set: ' + str(len(X_test)))
```

You will observe that the length of training set is 750, and that of the test set is 250.

> **Note**
>
> By default, the **train_test_split** function produces splits where the test data is 25% of the data and the training is 75%. This can be altered with the **test_size** parameter.

6. Now to perform mean-shift clustering on the data, import **cluster** and **metrics** from **sklearn**. Use a quantile of 0.1 to estimate the bandwidth on the training data, create a mean-shift model, **ms**, with the resulting bandwidth, and use the **fit** function of the mean-shift model to fit on the training data:

```
from sklearn import cluster
from sklearn import metrics

bandwidth = cluster.estimate_bandwidth(X_train, quantile=0.1)
ms = cluster.MeanShift(bandwidth=bandwidth, bin_seeding=True)

ms.fit(X_train)
```

> **Note**
>
> Notice that we have been using **fit_predict** previously, but here we are just using **fit**. We can call the **fit** and **predict** methods separately to fit using one set of data and then predict (in this case, get cluster labels) with different data.

7. Use the **predict** method of the mean-shift model to produce cluster labels for the test data and store the labels in an **ms_labels** variable. Calculate the silhouette score for the test set using the **silhouette_score** function on these labels, store the values in an **ms_silhouette** variable, and print them out:

```
ms_labels = ms.predict(X_test)

ms_silhouette = metrics.silhouette_score(X_test, ms_labels)
print('mean-shift silhouette score: ' + str(ms_silhouette))
```

You should get the mean-shift silhouette score as 0.4702247778303609.

8. Now perform k-means clustering with five clusters, again using the training set to fit and the testing set to calculate the silhouette score. Print the score for the clustering as follows:

```
model = cluster.KMeans(n_clusters=5, random_state=10)
model.fit(X_train)

km_labels = model.predict(X_test)
km_silhouette = metrics.silhouette_score(X_test, km_labels)

print('k-means silhouette score: ' + str(km_silhouette))
```

You should get the k-means silhouette score as 0.4710211103342539.

> **Note**
>
> The silhouette scores of the two methods should be very close. This just means they're performing pretty similarly, so there is no reason based on performance to strongly prefer one or the other.

9. Perform mean-shift clustering again, this time with quantile set to 0.01. Again, fit on the training data and calculate the silhouette score on the test data:

```
bandwidth = cluster.estimate_bandwidth(X_train, quantile=0.01)
ms = cluster.MeanShift(bandwidth=bandwidth, bin_seeding=True)

ms.fit(X_train)

ms_labels = ms.predict(X_test)

ms_silhouette = metrics.silhouette_score(X_test, ms_labels)
print('mean-shift (low quantile) silhouette score: ' + str(ms_silhouette))
```

You should get the mean-shift (low quantile) silhouette score as 0.030474668518421098. This much lower silhouette score shows that the algorithm performs much better with a higher value for the quantile.

Activity 7: Evaluating Clustering on Customer Behavior Data

In this activity, we will build on *Activity 2*, where we clustered the **customer_offers** dataset. In the previous activity, we performed clustering using different methods, but this time we'll use what we've learned about evaluating and comparing clustering methods to choose the best clustering method and hyperparameters for this data. Execute the following steps to complete this activity:

1. Import the data from **customer_offers.csv**.

2. Perform a train-test split using **random_state = 100**.

3. Plot the silhouette scores for k-means clustering using k ranging from 2 to 10. Your plot should look as follows:

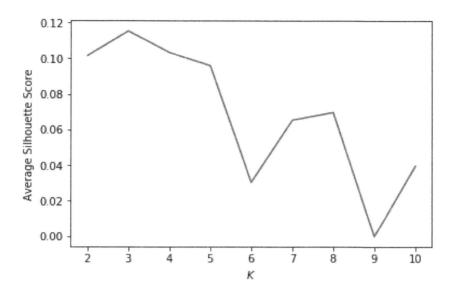

Figure 4.19: Average silhouette score for different values of k

Use the plot to determine a value of k to use for k-means clustering.

4. Now use the value of k with the highest silhouette score found in the previous step to perform k-means clustering on the test set with **random_state=100**, and print out the silhouette score.

    The expected output for k-means silhouette score is 0.115298516478898.

5. Perform mean-shift clustering and print out its silhouette score on the test set.

    The expected output for mean-shift silhouette score is 0.07308587709358311.

6. Perform k-modes clustering and print out its silhouette score on the test set.

    The expected output for k-mode silhouette score is 0.11750917239635501.

> **Note**
>
> The solution for this activity can be found on page 339.

Summary

It's important to not only be able to perform clustering, but also use several different types of clustering algorithms and evaluate the performance of each using multiple methods, so that the correct tool can be used for the job. In this chapter, we learned various methods for choosing the number of clusters, including judgment-based methods such as visual inspection of cluster overlap and elbow determination using the sum of squared errors, and objective methods such as evaluating the silhouette score. Each of these methods has strengths and weaknesses—the more abstract and quantified the measure is, the further removed we are from understanding why a particular clustering seems to be failing or succeeding. However, as we have seen, making judgments is often difficult, especially with complex data, and this is where quantifiable methods, in particular the silhouette score, tend to shine. In practice, sometimes one measure will not give a clear answer while another does; this is all the more reason to have multiple tools in your toolkit.

In addition to learning new methods for evaluating clustering, we also learned new methods for clustering, such as the mean-shift algorithm, and k-modes and k-prototypes algorithms. Finally, we learned one of the basic concepts of evaluating a model, which will be important as we move forward: using a test set. By separating data into training and testing sets, we are treating the test set as if it's new data that we didn't have at the time that we developed the model. This allows us to see how well our model does with this new data. As we move into examples of supervised learning, this concept becomes all the more important.

In the next chapter, we will learn about using regression, a type of supervised learning, for making predictions about continuous outcomes such as revenue.

5

Predicting Customer Revenue Using Linear Regression

Learning Objectives

By the end of this chapter, you will be able to:

- Describe use cases for regression modeling

- Prepare transaction data for regression

- Engineer features for regression analysis

- Perform regression modeling and interpret the results

This chapter covers regression and explains how to transform data to use for regression analysis and interpret the results.

Introduction

In the previous lesson, you learned about applying and assessing various unsupervised clustering techniques to segment data into groups. In this chapter, you will learn about regression, a supervised learning technique used to predict continuous outcomes. We will begin with an explanation of regression. Then, we will discuss feature engineering and data cleaning for regression. Finally, we will learn how to perform regression and interpret the results.

Understanding Regression

Machine learning deals with supervised and unsupervised problems. In unsupervised learning problems, there is no historical data that tells you the correct grouping for data. Therefore, these problems are dealt with by looking at hidden structures in the data and grouping that data based on those hidden structures. This is in contrast with supervised learning problems, wherein historical data that has the correct grouping is available.

Regression is a type of supervised learning. The objective of a regression model is to predict a continuous outcome based on data. This is as opposed to predicting which group a data point belongs to (called **classification**, which will be covered in *Chapter 7, Predicting Customer Churn*). Because regression is a supervised learning technique, the model built thus requires past data where the outcome is known, so that it can learn the patterns in the historical data and make predictions about the new data. The following figure illustrates three regression problems:

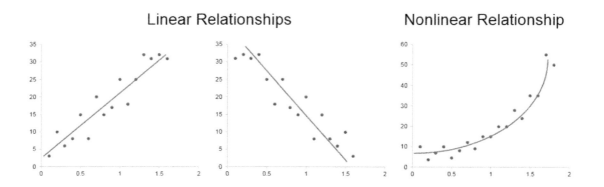

Figure 5.1: Regression problems

The first two plots in the preceding figure show linear regression, where the outcome (on the vertical axis) is related to the predictor (on the horizontal axis) in a simple linear way. The third plot shows a more complex, non-linear relationship, where a curved line is required to capture the relationship. In this chapter, we will look at linear regression.

We will look at non-linear relationships in the next chapter.

Regression has many different use cases, since many problems in marketing are related to predicting a continuous outcome, such as predicting how much a customer will spend in the next year to assess customer value, or predicting the number of sales of a store. However, before we can perform regression, we need to transform the data and create features that will be useful for predicting our outcome. We will learn how to do this in the next section.

Feature Engineering for Regression

Feature engineering is the process of taking data and transforming it for use in predictions. The idea is to create features that capture aspects of what's important to the outcome of interest. This process requires both data expertise and domain knowledge—you need to know what can be done with the data that you have, as well as knowledge of what might be predictive of the outcome you're interested in.

Once the features are created, they need to be assessed. This can be done by simply looking for relationships between the features and the outcome of interest. Alternatively, you can test how much a feature impacts the performance of a model, to decide whether to include it or not. We will first look at how to transform data to create features, and then how to clean the data of the resulting features to ensure models are trained on high-quality data.

Feature Creation

In order to perform a regression, we first need data to be in a format that allows it. In many cases, data is in the form of customer transactions. This needs to be transformed into features that can be used to perform a prediction. These features then become our predictors.

Features are transformed versions of the data that capture what we think is possibly predictive of our outcome of interest. If we are trying to predict the future value of a customer (that is, how much we expect a customer to spend on a company's product in the future), examples of useful features might include the number of purchases a customer has made previously, the amount they have spent, or the length of time since their last order.

We'll also need to be able to link these categories to our outcome of interest. For example, if we are trying to build a model that will allow us to predict a customer's spend for the next year using data for the current year, we will need two historical periods to build our model: one period where we already know the customer's spend, and another earlier period that we will use to calculate features. We can then build a model that uses the features from the earlier period to predict the outcome in the later period. This model will then be able to use features created using data we have at present to predict an outcome about a future period. The following figure illustrates the role of feature engineering in a machine learning workflow:

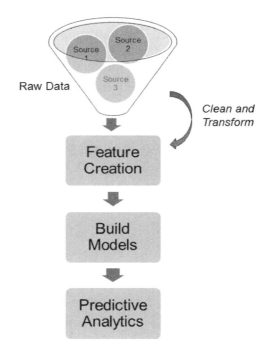

Figure 5.2: Role of feature engineering in a machine learning workflow

Data Cleaning

Generally, feature creation and data cleaning go hand in hand. As you create your features, you might notice problems with the data that need to be dealt with. The following are common problems you'll notice with data:

- **Data could be missing**. The easiest way to deal with missing data is to just remove those data points that are missing some data if it makes sense to do so. Otherwise, you can attempt to insert a value for a missing variable based on the average or median of the other data points.

- **Outliers could be present**. Outliers are data points that lie far outside of the normal range of a variable, or in other words, far from the norm. A standard definition is that an outlier is any data point more than three standard deviations above the median. They are dangerous because they might not reflect normal behavior but can have a disproportionate effect on our model. Again, the easiest method of dealing with outliers is to simply remove them. The following figure illustrates an outlier:

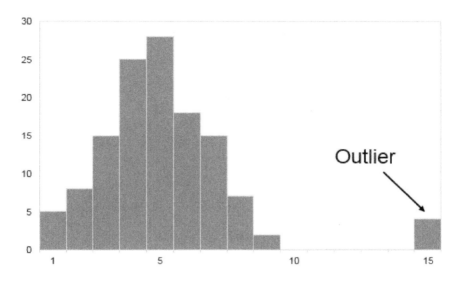

Figure 5.3: A histogram showing an outlier value

Exercise 20: Creating Features for Transaction Data

In this exercise, we have some historical transaction data from 2010 and 2011. For each transaction, we have a customer identifier (**CustomerID**), the number of units purchased (**Quantity**), the date of the purchase (**InvoiceDate**), and the unit cost (**UnitPrice**), as well as some other information about the item purchased. We want to prepare this data for a regression of customer transaction data from 2010 against the spend for 2011. We will therefore create features from the data for the year 2010 and compute the target (the amount of money spent) for 2011. When we create this model, it should generalize to future years for which we don't have the result yet. So, we could use 2020 data to predict 2021 spending behavior in advance, unless the market or business has changed significantly since the time period the data used to fit the model relates to:

1. Import **pandas** and read the data from **retail_transactions.csv** to a DataFrame **df**:

```
import pandas as pd

df = pd.read_csv('retail_transactions.csv')
```

2. Use the **head** function to view the data:

    ```
    df.head()
    ```

    The first five instances of your dataset should appear as follows:

	InvoiceNo	StockCode	Description	Quantity	InvoiceDate	UnitPrice	CustomerID	Country
0	546729	22775	PURPLE DRAWERKNOB ACRYLIC EDWARDIAN	12	2011-03-16 11:36:00	1.25	18231.0	United Kingdom
1	559898	21868	POTTING SHED TEA MUG	6	2011-07-13 12:18:00	1.25	16225.0	United Kingdom
2	548648	71459	HANGING JAM JAR T-LIGHT HOLDER	24	2011-04-01 13:20:00	0.85	12949.0	United Kingdom
3	540543	22173	METAL 4 HOOK HANGER FRENCH CHATEAU	4	2011-01-09 15:23:00	2.95	14395.0	United Kingdom
4	561390	20726	LUNCH BAG WOODLAND	10	2011-07-27 09:52:00	1.65	17068.0	United Kingdom

Figure 5.4: The first five rows of the retail transactions data

3. Convert the **InvoiceDate** column to date format using the following code:

    ```
    df['InvoiceDate'] = pd.to_datetime(df['InvoiceDate'])
    ```

4. Calculate the revenue for each row, by multiplying **Quantity** with **UnitPrice**:

    ```
    df['revenue'] = df['UnitPrice']*df['Quantity']
    ```

5. You will observe that each invoice is spread over multiple rows, one for each type of product purchased. These can be combined such that data for each transaction is on a single row. To do so, we can perform a **groupby** operation on **InvoiceNo**. However, before that, we need to specify how to combine those rows that are grouped together. Use the following code:

    ```
    operations = {'revenue':'sum',
                  'InvoiceDate':'first',
                  'CustomerID':'first'
                 }
    df = df.groupby('InvoiceNo').agg(operations)
    ```

In the preceding code snippet, we first specified the aggregation functions that we will use for each column, and then performed **groupby** and applied those functions. **InvoiceDate** and **CustomerID** will be the same for all rows for the same invoice, so we can just take the first entry for them. For **revenue**, we sum the revenue across all items for the same invoice to get the total revenue for that invoice.

6. Finally, use the **head** function to display the result:

```
df.head()
```

Your DataFrame should now appear as follows:

InvoiceNo	revenue	InvoiceDate	CustomerID
536365	139.12	2010-12-01 08:26:00	17850.0
536366	22.20	2010-12-01 08:28:00	17850.0
536367	278.73	2010-12-01 08:34:00	13047.0
536368	70.05	2010-12-01 08:34:00	13047.0
536369	17.85	2010-12-01 08:35:00	13047.0

Figure 5.5: The first five rows of the data after aggregating by invoice number

7. Since we will be using the year to decide which rows are being used for prediction and which we are predicting, create a separate column named **year** for the year, as follows:

```
df['year'] = df['InvoiceDate'].apply(lambda x: x.year)
```

8. The dates of the transactions may also be an important source of features. The days since a customer's last transaction as of the end of the year, or how early in the year a customer had their first transaction, can tell us a bit about the customer's purchasing history, which could be important. Therefore, for each transaction, we'll calculate how many days difference there is between the last day of 2010 and the invoice date:

```
df['days_since'] = (pd.datetime(year=2010, month=12, day=31) -
                    df['InvoiceDate']).apply(lambda x: x.days)
```

9. Currently, we have the data grouped by invoice, but we really want it grouped by customer. We'll start by calculating all of our predictors. We will again define a set of aggregation functions for each of our variables and apply them using **groupby**. We'll calculate the sum of revenue. For **days_since**, we will calculate the maximum and minimum number of days (giving us features telling us how long this customer has been active in 2010, and how recently), as well as the number of unique values (giving us how many separate days this customer made a purchase on). Since these are for our predictors, we will only apply these functions to our data from 2010, and we'll store it in a variable, **X**, and use the **head** function to see the results:

```
operations = {'revenue':'sum',
              'days_since':['max','min','nunique'],
             }

X = df[df['year'] == 2010].groupby('CustomerID').agg(operations)

X.head()
```

You should see the following:

	revenue	days_since		
	sum	max	min	nunique
CustomerID				
12347.0	711.79	23	23	1
12348.0	892.80	14	14	1
12370.0	1868.02	16	13	2
12377.0	1001.52	10	10	1
12383.0	600.72	8	8	1

Figure 5.6: The first five rows of data after aggregating by customer ID

10. As you can see from the preceding figure, because we performed multiple types of aggregations on the **days_since** column, we ended up with multi-level column labels. To simplify this, we can reset the names of the columns to make them easier to reference later. Use the following code and print the results:

```
X.columns = [' '.join(col).strip() for col in X.columns.values]

X.head()
```

Your columns should now appear as follows:

CustomerID	revenue sum	days_since max	days_since min	days_since nunique
12347.0	711.79	23	23	1
12348.0	892.80	14	14	1
12370.0	1868.02	16	13	2
12377.0	1001.52	10	10	1
12383.0	600.72	8	8	1

Figure 5.7: The first five rows of data

11. We'll calculate one more feature: the average spend per order. We can calculate this by dividing **revenue sum** by **days_since nunique** (this is really the average spend per day, not per order, but we're assuming that if two orders were put in on the same day, we can treat them as part of the same order for our purposes):

```
X['avg_order_cost'] = X['revenue sum']/X['days_since nunique']
```

12. Now that we have our predictors, we need the outcome that we'll be predicting, which is just the sum of revenue for 2011. We can calculate this with a simple **groupby** and store the values in the **y** variable, as follows:

```
y = df[df['year'] == 2011].groupby('CustomerID')['revenue'].sum()
```

13. Now we can put our predictors and outcomes into a single DataFrame, **wrangled_df**, and rename the columns to have more intuitive names. Finally, look at the resulting DataFrame, using the **head** function:

```
wrangled_df = pd.concat([X,y], axis=1)
wrangled_df.columns = ['2010 revenue',
                       'days_since_first_purchase',
                       'days_since_last_purchase',
                       'number_of_purchases',
                       'avg_order_cost',
                       '2011 revenue']

wrangled_df.head()
```

Your DataFrame will appear as follows:

CustomerID	2010 revenue	days_since_first_purchase	days_since_last_purchase	number_of_purchases	avg_order_cost	2011 revenue
12346.0	NaN	NaN	NaN	NaN	NaN	77183.60
12347.0	711.79	23.0	23.0	1.0	711.79	3598.21
12348.0	892.80	14.0	14.0	1.0	892.80	904.44
12349.0	NaN	NaN	NaN	NaN	NaN	1757.55
12350.0	NaN	NaN	NaN	NaN	NaN	334.40

Figure 5.8: The first five rows of the data after feature creation

14. Note that many of the values in our DataFrame are NaN. This is caused by customers who were active either only in 2010 or only in 2011, so there is no data for the other year. In a future chapter, we will work on predicting which of our customers will churn, but for now, we'll just drop all customers not active in both years. Note that this means that our model will predict the spend of customers in the next year assuming that they remain active customers. To drop the customers without values, drop rows where either of the revenue columns are null, as follows:

```
wrangled_df = wrangled_df[~wrangled_df['2010 revenue'].isnull()]
wrangled_df = wrangled_df[~wrangled_df['2011 revenue'].isnull()]
```

15. As a final data-cleaning step, it's often a good idea to get rid of outliers. A standard definition is that an outlier is any data point more than three standard deviations above the median, so we will use this to drop customers that are outliers in terms of 2010 or 2011 revenue:

```
wrangled_df = wrangled_df[wrangled_df['2011 revenue'] < ((wrangled_
df['2011 revenue'].median()) + wrangled_df['2011 revenue'].std()*3)]
wrangled_df = wrangled_df[wrangled_df['2010 revenue'] < ((wrangled_
df['2010 revenue'].median()) + wrangled_df['2010 revenue'].std()*3)]
```

16. It's often a good idea, after you've done your data cleaning and feature engineering, to save the new data as a new file, so that, as you're developing your model, you don't need to run the data through the whole feature engineering and cleaning pipeline each time you want to rerun your code. We can do this using the **to_csv** function. We can also take a look at our final DataFrame using the **head** function:

```
wrangled_df.to_csv('wrangled_transactions.csv')

wrangled_df.head()
```

Your DataFrame will now look as follows:

CustomerID	2010 revenue	days_since_first_purchase	days_since_last_purchase	number_of_purchases	avg_order_cost	2011 revenue
12347.0	711.79	23.0	23.0	1.0	711.79	3598.21
12348.0	892.80	14.0	14.0	1.0	892.80	904.44
12370.0	1868.02	16.0	13.0	2.0	934.01	1677.67
12377.0	1001.52	10.0	10.0	1.0	1001.52	626.60
12383.0	600.72	8.0	8.0	1.0	600.72	1249.84

Figure 5.9: The final cleaned data

Assessing Features Using Visualizations and Correlations

Once we have our features of interest created, the next step is to assess those features, which can be done in the following sequence:

1. First, we should do a sanity check of our features to make sure their values are what we would expect. We can plot a histogram of each feature to make sure the distribution of the feature is also what we would expect. This can often reveal unexpected problems with our data.

2. The next step is to examine the relationships between our features and the outcome of interest. This can be done in the following two ways:

   Creating scatterplots: Often, the most effective means of assessing a relationship is to create a scatterplot that plots a feature against the outcome of interest and see whether there is any obvious relationship.

Assessing correlations: Another quick and effective method for assessing a relationship is to see whether there is a correlation between the variables. Correlations are linear relationships between two variables. They can be positive (as one variable increases, the other increases) or negative (as one increases, the other decreases). Correlation can be calculated easily using statistical packages, resulting in a single number that can often reveal whether there is a strong relationship between two variables. The following figure illustrates the different correlations, from perfect positive to perfect negative correlation:

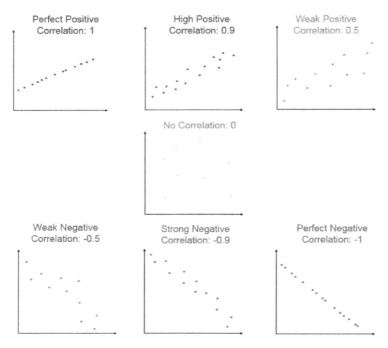

Figure 5.10: A visualization of the different correlations

Exercise 21: Examining Relationships between Predictors and Outcome

In this exercise, we will use the features we calculated in the previous exercise and see whether these variables have any relationships with our outcome of interest (sales revenue from customers in 2011):

1. Use pandas to import the data you saved at the end of the last exercise, using **CustomerID** as the index:

    ```
    import pandas as pd

    df = pd.read_csv('wrangled_transactions.csv', index_col='CustomerID')
    ```

2. The seaborn library has a number of nice plotting features. Its **pairplot** function will plot the histograms and pair-wise scatterplots of all of our variables in one line, allowing us to examine both the distributions of our data and the relationships between the data points easily. Use the following code:

```
import seaborn as sns
%matplotlib inline

sns.pairplot(df)
```

You will get the following plot:

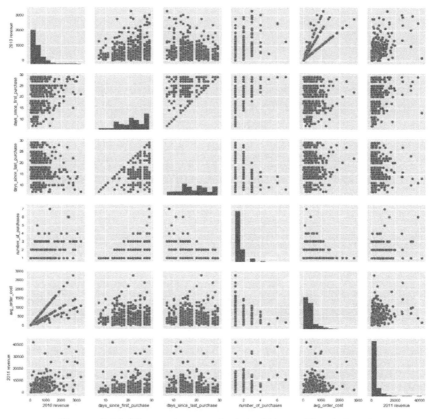

Figure 5.11: The seaborn pairplot of the entire dataset

In the preceding plot, the diagonal shows a histogram for each variable, whereas each row shows the scatterplot between one variable and each other variable. The bottom row of figures shows the scatterplots of the 2011 revenue (our outcome of interest) against each of our other variables. Because the datapoints are overlapping and there is a fair amount of variance, the relationships don't look very clear-cut in the visualizations.

3. Therefore, we can use correlations to help us interpret relationships. The **corr** pandas function will generate correlations between all of the variables in a DataFrame:

```
df.corr()
```

Your output should appear as follows:

	2010 revenue	days_since_first_purchase	days_since_last_purchase	number_of_purchases	avg_order_cost	2011 revenue
2010 revenue	1.000000	0.109692	-0.254964	0.504438	0.779401	0.548234
days_since_first_purchase	0.109692	1.000000	0.641574	0.327502	-0.074321	0.061743
days_since_last_purchase	-0.254964	0.641574	1.000000	-0.398268	-0.054051	-0.171294
number_of_purchases	0.504438	0.327502	-0.398268	1.000000	-0.012466	0.355751
avg_order_cost	0.779401	-0.074321	-0.054051	-0.012466	1.000000	0.357384
2011 revenue	0.548234	0.061743	-0.171294	0.355751	0.357384	1.000000

Figure 5.12: The correlations between each variable and each other variable in the dataset.

Again, we can look at the last row to see the relationships between our predictors and outcome of interest (2011 revenue). Positive numbers indicate a positive relationship—for instance, the higher the 2010 revenue from a customer, the greater the expected revenue from them in 2011 should be. Negative numbers mean the reverse—for example, the more days there have been since a customer's last purchase, the lower we would expect the 2011 revenue from them to be. Also, the higher the absolute number, the stronger the relationship.

Activity 8: Examining Relationships Between Storefront Locations and Features about Their Area

For this activity, you've been provided with data on a number of storefront locations of a company, and information about the surrounding area. This information includes the revenue of the storefront at each location, the age of the location in years, and information about the surrounding area (in a 20-mile radius), such as the number of competitors, the median income of the area, the number of members enrolled on the company's loyalty rewards program living in the area, and the population density of the area. You've been asked to explore this data and look for how these features are related to the revenue of the storefront in that location. Use correlations and visualizations to explore the data. Follow these steps to complete the activity:

1. Load the data from **location_rev.csv** and take a look at the data. Your data should appear as follows:

	revenue	num_competitors	median_income	num_loyalty_members	population_density	location_age
0	42247.80	3.0	30527.57	1407.0	3302.0	12.0
1	38628.37	3.0	30185.49	1025.0	4422.0	11.0
2	39715.16	1.0	32182.24	1498.0	3260.0	12.0
3	35593.30	5.0	29728.65	2340.0	4325.0	10.0
4	35128.18	4.0	30691.17	847.0	3774.0	11.0

Figure 5.13: The first five rows of the location revenue data

2. Use seaborn's **pairplot** function to visualize the data and its relationships. The plots should appear as shown here:

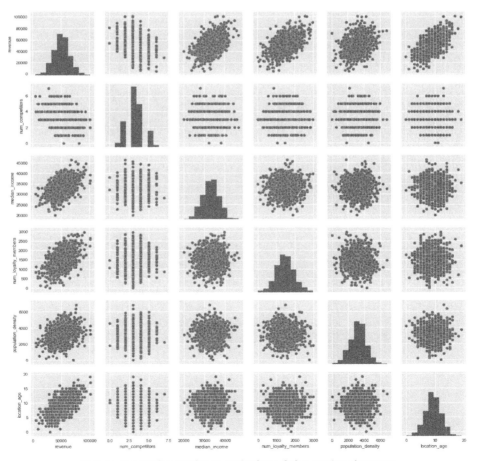

Figure 5.14: The seaborn pairplot of the entire dataset

3. Finally, use correlations to investigate the relationship between the different variables and location revenue. Your DataFrame should appear as follows:

	revenue	num_competitors	median_income	num_loyalty_members	population_density	location_age
revenue	1.000000	-0.261470	0.474922	0.510666	0.285655	0.607897
num_competitors	-0.261470	1.000000	-0.000547	0.010845	-0.037712	-0.008686
median_income	0.474922	-0.000547	1.000000	0.009734	0.058734	-0.013919
num_loyalty_members	0.510666	0.010845	0.009734	1.000000	-0.029442	0.010732
population_density	0.285655	-0.037712	0.058734	-0.029442	1.000000	-0.001524
location_age	0.607897	-0.008686	-0.013919	0.010732	-0.001524	1.000000

Figure 5.15: The correlations between each variable and each other variable in the dataset

> Note
>
> The solution for this activity can be found on page 341.

Performing and Interpreting Linear Regression

Linear regression is a type of regression model that uses linear relationships between predictors and the outcome to predict the outcome. Linear regression models can be thought of as a line running through the feature space that minimizes the distance between the line and the data points. This is best visualized when there is a single predictor (see *Figure 5.14*), where it is equivalent to drawing a line of best fit on a scatterplot between the two variables but can be generalized to many predictors:

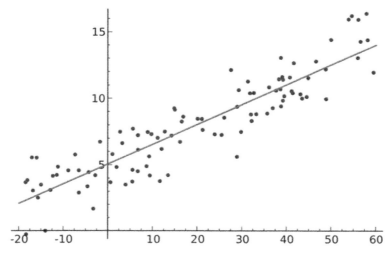

Figure 5.16: A visualization of a linear regression line (red) fit to data (blue data points)

The line is generated by trying to find the line that best minimizes the error (difference) between the line and the data points. We'll learn more about types of errors in the next chapter, where we'll learn to use them to evaluate models, but it's important to note that they are also used in the process of fitting the model.

One of the big benefits of linear regression is that it is a very simple model. The model can be described in a simple equation, as follows:

$$Y = a + b_1X_1 + b_2X_2 \dots b_iX_i$$

Here, Y is the predicted value of the outcome variable, *a* is the intercept (where the line crosses the x-axis), each X is the value of a variable, and each *b* is the respective weight assigned to that variable.

Advantages: A big advantage of this simplicity is that it makes the model easy to interpret. By looking at the coefficients, we can easily see how much we would predict Y to change for each unit change in the predictor. For example, if we had a model predicting sales revenue from each customer for the next year and the coefficient for the number of purchases in the previous year predictor was 10, we can say that for each purchase in the previous year, we could expect the revenue from a customer to be $10 higher.

Disadvantages: Linear regression models also have significant weaknesses that stem from their simplicity. *They can only capture linear relationships*, while relationships in the real world are often more complex. Linear models assume that, no matter how high the value of a predictor is, adding more to it will have the same effect as if the predictor was lower. In reality, this is often not the case. If a product appeals to customers in a middle-income range, we would expect that a boost in income for a customer with low income would increase sales to that customer, while a boost in income for a customer with high income could very well decrease sales to that customer. This would be a non-linear relationship:

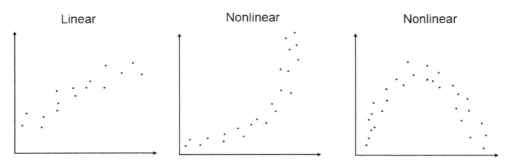

Figure 5.17: Some examples of linear and non-linear relationships

In addition to non-linear relationships, *linear models are unable to capture interactions between variables easily.* In statistics, an interaction is a situation in which, when two variables are combined, their effect is larger than (or less than) the sum of their effect alone. For example, it could be the case that while television advertisements and radio advertisements both have a positive effect on sales in an area, when both are done at once, the sum of their effect is less than the effect each would have alone due to saturating the market with ads. Linear models don't have a built-in way of dealing with these kinds of effects, since they assume a simple linear relationship between the predictors and the outcome.

This does not mean that linear models are completely unable to account for non-linear relationships or interactions. By performing transformations on predictors, a non-linear relationship can be turned into a linear one, and interaction terms can be created by multiplying two predictors together; they can then be added to the model. However, this can be difficult and time-consuming to do, and increases the complexity of the model, which makes it harder to interpret, thereby eliminating many of the benefits of using linear models to begin with.

Exercise 22: Building a Linear Model Predicting Customer Spend

In this exercise, we will build a linear model on customer spend using the features created in *Exercise 20, Creating Features for Transaction Data*:

1. Import **pandas** and read in the data from **wrangled_transactions.csv** with **CustomerID** as the index:

   ```
   import pandas as pd
   df = pd.read_csv('wrangled_transactions.csv', index_col='CustomerID')
   ```

2. Look at the correlations between the variables again using the **corr** function:

   ```
   df.corr()
   ```

   Your DataFrame will look as follows:

	2010 revenue	days_since_first_purchase	days_since_last_purchase	number_of_purchases	avg_order_cost	2011 revenue
2010 revenue	1.000000	0.109692	-0.254964	0.504438	0.779401	0.548234
days_since_first_purchase	0.109692	1.000000	0.641574	0.327502	-0.074321	0.061743
days_since_last_purchase	-0.254964	0.641574	1.000000	-0.398268	-0.054051	-0.171294
number_of_purchases	0.504438	0.327502	-0.398268	1.000000	-0.012466	0.355751
avg_order_cost	0.779401	-0.074321	-0.054051	-0.012466	1.000000	0.357384
2011 revenue	0.548234	0.061743	-0.171294	0.355751	0.357384	1.000000

Figure 5.18: The correlations between each pair of variables

Recall that there is only a weak relationship between **days_since_first_purchase** and 2011 revenue—we will therefore not include that predictor in our model.

3. Store the predictor columns and outcome columns in the **X** and **y** variables, respectively:

```
X = df[['2010 revenue',
        'days_since_last_purchase',
        'number_of_purchases',
        'avg_order_cost'
        ]]
y = df['2011 revenue']
```

4. Use **sklearn** to perform a train-test split on the data, so that we can assess the model on a dataset it was not trained on, as shown here:

```
from sklearn.model_selection import train_test_split

X_train, X_test, y_train, y_test = train_test_split(X, y, random_state = 100)
```

5. Import **LinearRegression** from **sklearn**, create a **LinearRegression** model, and fit it on the training data:

```
from sklearn.linear_model import LinearRegression

model = LinearRegression()
model.fit(X_train,y_train)
```

6. Examine the model coefficients by checking the **coef_** property. Note that these are in the same order as our X columns: **2010 revenue**, **days_since_last_purchase**, **number_of_purchases**, and **avg_order_cost**:

```
model.coef_
```

This should result in an array with the values 4.14, -1.66, 394.96, and -0.49.

7. Check the intercept term of the model by checking the **intercept_** property:

```
model.intercept_
```

This should give a value of 538.74. From steps 6 and 7, we can arrive at the model's full equation:

2011 revenue = 538.74 + 4.14*(**2010 revenue**) − 1.66*(**days_since_last_purchase**) + 394.96*(**number_of_purchases**) − 0.49*(**avg_order_cost**)

8. We can now use the fitted model to make predictions about a customer outside of our dataset. Make a DataFrame that holds data for one customer, where 2010 revenue is 1,000, the number of days since the last purchase is 20, the number of purchases is 2, and the average order cost is 500. Have the model make a prediction on this one customer's data:

```
single_customer = pd.DataFrame({
    '2010 revenue': [1000],
    'days_since_last_purchase': [20],
    'number_of_purchases': [2],
    'avg_order_cost': [500]
})

model.predict(single_customer)
```

The result should be an array with a single value of 5197.79217043, indicating the predicted 2011 revenue for a customer with this data.

9. We can plot the model's predictions on the test set against the true value. First, import **matplotlib**, and make a scatterplot of the model predictions on **X_test** against **y_test**. Limit the x and y axes to a maximum value of 10,000 so that we get a better view of where most of the data points lie. Finally, add a line with slope 1, which will serve as our reference—if all of the points lie on this line, it means we have a perfect relationship between our predictions and the true answer:

```
import matplotlib.pyplot as plt
%matplotlib inline

plt.scatter(model.predict(X_test),y_test)
plt.xlim(0,10000)
plt.ylim(0,10000)
plt.plot([0, 10000], [0, 10000], 'k-', color = 'r')
plt.xlabel('Model Predictions')
plt.ylabel('True Value')
plt.show()
```

Your plot will look as follows:

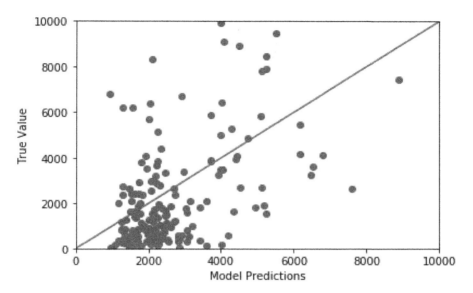

Figure 5.19: The model predictions plotted against the true values

In the preceding plot, the red line indicates where points would lie if the prediction was the same as the true value. Since many of our points are quite far from the red line, this indicates that the model is not completely accurate. However, there does seem to be some relationship, with higher model predictions having higher true values.

10. To further examine the relationship, we can use correlation. From **scipy**, we can import the **pearsonr** function, which calculates the correlation between two arrays, just like pandas did for the whole of our DataFrame. We can use it to calculate the correlation between our model predictions and the true value as follows:

```
from scipy.stats.stats import pearsonr

pearsonr(model.predict(X_test),y_test)
```

You should get two numbers returned: (0.69841798296908, 2.17897009995024370e-28). The first number is the correlation, which is close to 0.7, indicating a strong relationship. The second number is the p-value, which indicates the probability that you would see a relationship this strong if the two sets of numbers were unrelated—the very low number here means that this relationship is unlikely to be due to chance.

> **Note**
>
> Note that R-squared is another common metric that is used to judge the fit of a model and is calculated by simply squaring the correlation between the model's prediction and the actual result. We will learn more about it in *Chapter 6, Other Regression Techniques and Tools for Evaluating Regression Models*.

Activity 9: Building a Regression Model to Predict Storefront Location Revenue

You have data on the revenue and area of a bunch of storefronts at various locations. You're asked to build a model that can (1) describe the relationship between revenue and factors related to the storefront's location, and (2) can predict the revenue of a store based on its location and age. Build a linear regression model to predict storefront location revenue based on information about the area the storefront is located in and explore the model coefficients:

1. Import the data from **location_rev.csv** and view the first few rows, which should look as follows:

	revenue	num_competitors	median_income	num_loyalty_members	population_density	location_age
0	42247.80	3.0	30527.57	1407.0	3302.0	12.0
1	38628.37	3.0	30185.49	1025.0	4422.0	11.0
2	39715.16	1.0	32182.24	1498.0	3260.0	12.0
3	35593.30	5.0	29728.65	2340.0	4325.0	10.0
4	35128.18	4.0	30691.17	847.0	3774.0	11.0

Figure 5.20: The first five rows of the location revenue data

2. Create a variable, **X**, with the predictors in it, and store the outcome (revenue) in a separate variable, **y**.

3. Split the data into a training and test set. Use `random_state = 100`.

4. Create a linear regression model and fit it on the training data.

5. Print out the model coefficients.

6. Print out the model intercept.

7. Produce a prediction for a location that has 3 competitors; a median income of 30,000; 1,200 loyalty members; a population density of 2,000; and a location age of 10. The result should be an array with a single value of 27573.21782447, indicating the predicted revenue for a customer with this data.

8. Plot the model's predictions versus the true values on the test data. Your plot should look as follows:

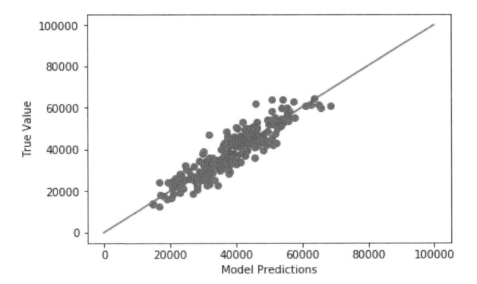

Figure 5.21: The model predictions plotted against the true value

9. Calculate the correlation between the model predictions and the true values of the test data.

The result should be (0.9061597827907563, 1.1552714895198058e-94).

Summary

In this chapter, we learned about regression, a supervised learning technique used to predict continuous outcomes. We discussed what regression is, and how to approach feature engineering and data cleaning for regression. We also discussed how to perform linear regression, and how to interpret the results.

In the next chapter, we will explore how to evaluate regression models in more depth, and will also explore types of regression other than linear regression.

Other Regression Techniques and Tools for Evaluation

Learning Objectives

By the end of this chapter, you will be able to:

- Calculate mean absolute error and root mean squared error, which are common measures of the accuracy of a regression model

- Use evaluation metrics or lasso regression to perform feature selection for linear models

- Use tree-based regression models (regression trees and random forest regression)

- Compare the accuracy of different regression models

This chapter covers other regression techniques such as lasso regression, and explains how to evaluate various regression models using common measures of accuracy.

Introduction

In the previous chapter, we learned how to prepare data for regression modeling. We also learned how to apply linear regression to data and interpret the results.

In this chapter, we will build on this knowledge by learning how to evaluate a model. This will be used to choose which features to use for a model, as well as to compare different models. Then, we will learn about using lasso regression for feature selection. Finally, we will learn about tree-based regression methods, and why they sometimes outperform linear regression techniques.

Evaluating the Accuracy of a Regression Model

In order to evaluate regression models, we first need to define some metrics. The common metrics used to evaluate regression models rely on the concepts of residuals and errors, which are quantifications of how much a model mispredicts a particular data point. In the following sections, we will first learn about residuals and errors. We will then learn about two evaluation metrics, **mean absolute error** (**MAE**) and **root mean squared error** (**RMSE**), and how they are used to evaluate regression models.

Residuals and Errors

An important concept in understanding how to evaluate regression models is the **residual**. The residual refers to the difference between the value predicted by the model and the true value for a data point. It can be thought of as by how much your model missed a particular value. The following diagram illustrates this:

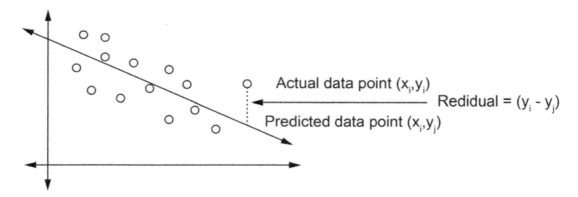

Figure 6.1: Estimating the residual

The residual is taken to be an estimate of the error of a model, where the error is the difference between the true process underlying the data generation and the model. We can't directly observe the error because we don't know the true process, and therefore, we use the residual values as our best guess at the error. For this reason, error and residual are closely related and are often used interchangeably.

Mean Absolute Error

There are multiple ways to use residuals to evaluate a model. One way is to simply take the absolute value of all residuals and calculate the average. This is called the **mean absolute error** (**MAE**), and can intuitively be thought of as the average difference you should expect between your model's predictions and the true value:

$$\text{MAE} = \frac{1}{n} \sum_{j=1}^{n} \left| y_j - \hat{y}_j \right|$$

Figure 6.2: Equation for calculating the MAE of a model

In the preceding equation, y_j is the true value of the outcome variable for data point j, and ŷj is the prediction of the model for that data point. By subtracting these terms and taking the absolute value, we get the residual. n is the number of data points, and thus by summing over all data points and dividing by n, we get the mean of the absolute error.

Therefore, a value of zero would mean that your model predicts everything perfectly, and larger values mean a less accurate model. If we have multiple models, we can look at the MAE and prefer the model with the lower value.

Root Mean Squared Error

One issue with the MAE is that it accounts for all errors equally. For many real-world applications, small errors are okay and expected, whereas large errors could lead to larger issues. However, with MAE, two medium-sized errors could add up and outweigh one large error. This means that the MAE may prefer a model that is fairly accurate for most predictions but is occasionally extremely inaccurate over a model with more consistent errors over all predictions. For this reason, instead of using the absolute error, a common technique is to use the **squared error**.

By squaring the error term, large errors are weighted more heavily than small ones that add up to the same total amount of error. If we then try to optimize the mean squared error rather than the mean absolute error, we will end up with a preference for models with more consistent predictions, since those large errors are going to be penalized so heavily. The following figure illustrates how the squared error grows more quickly than the absolute error, as the size of the residual increases:

Residual	Absolute Error	Squared Error
+1 or -1	1	1
+2 or -2	2	4
+3 or -3	3	9
+4 or -4	4	16

Figure 6.3: Squared error versus absolute error

One downside of this, however, is that the error term becomes harder to interpret. The MAE gives us an idea of how much we should expect the prediction to differ from the true value on average, while the mean squared error is more difficult to interpret. Therefore, it is common to take the route of the mean squared error, resulting in the **root mean squared error** (**RMSE**), as shown by the following equation:

$$\text{RMSE} = \sqrt{\frac{1}{n}\sum_{j=1}^{n}\left(y_j - \hat{y}_j\right)^2}$$

Figure 6.4: Equation for calculating the RMSE of a model

Exercise 23: Evaluating Regression Models of Location Revenue Using MAE and RMSE

In this exercise, you will calculate both MAE and RMSE for models built using the storefront location revenue data used in *Chapter 5*. We will compare models built using all of the predictors to a model built excluding one of the predictors:

1. Import **pandas** and use it to create a DataFrame from the data in **location_rev.csv**. Call this DataFrame **df**, and view the first five rows using the **head** function:

    ```
    import pandas as pd

    df = pd.read_csv('location_rev.csv')
    df.head()
    ```

    You should see the following output:

	revenue	num_competitors	median_income	num_loyalty_members	population_density	location_age
0	42247.80	3.0	30527.57	1407.0	3302.0	12.0
1	38628.37	3.0	30185.49	1025.0	4422.0	11.0
2	39715.16	1.0	32182.24	1498.0	3260.0	12.0
3	35593.30	5.0	29728.65	2340.0	4325.0	10.0
4	35128.18	4.0	30691.17	847.0	3774.0	11.0

Figure 6.5: The first five rows of the data in location_rev.csv

2. Import **train_test_split** from **sklearn**. Define the **y** variable as **revenue**, and **X** as **num_competitors**, **median_income**, **num_loyalty_members**, **population_density**, and **location_age**. Perform a train-test split on the data, using **random_state=15**, and save the results in **X_train**, **X_test**, **y_train**, and **y_test**, as shown:

    ```
    from sklearn.model_selection import train_test_split

    X = df[['num_competitors',
            'median_income',
            'num_loyalty_members',
            'population_density',
            'location_age'
            ]]

    y = df['revenue']

    X_train, X_test, y_train, y_test = train_test_split(X, y, random_state = 15)
    ```

3. Import **LinearRegression** from **sklearn**, and use it to fit a linear regression model to the training data:

```
from sklearn.linear_model import LinearRegression

model = LinearRegression()
model.fit(X_train,y_train)
```

4. Get the model's predictions for the **X_test** data, and store the result in a variable called **predictions**:

```
predictions = model.predict(X_test)
```

5. Calculate the error by calculating the difference between **predictions** and **y_test**:

```
error = predictions - y_test
```

6. Use the error to calculate both the RMSE and the MAE, and print these values out. Use the following code:

```
rmse = (error**2).mean()**.5
mae = abs(error).mean()

print('RMSE: '+ str(rmse))
print('MAE: '+ str(mae))
```

You'll receive the following output:

RMSE: 5133.736391468814

MAE: 4161.387875602789

7. Instead of calculating the RMSE and the MAE ourselves, we can import functions from **sklearn** to do it for us. Note that **sklearn** only contains a function to calculate the mean squared error, so we need to take the root of this value to get the RMSE. Use the following code:

```
from sklearn.metrics import mean_squared_error, mean_absolute_error
print('RMSE: ' + str(mean_squared_error(predictions, y_test)**0.5))
print('MAE: ' + str(mean_absolute_error(predictions, y_test)))
```

This should result in the same output as when we calculated these values ourselves (see step 6).

8. Now, we'll rebuild the model after dropping **n_competitors** from the predictors and evaluate the new model. Create **X_train2** and **X_test2** variables by dropping **num_competitors** from **X_train** and **X_test**. Train a model using **X_train2** and generate new predictions from this model using **X_test2**:

```
X_train2 = X_train.drop('num_competitors', axis=1)
X_test2 = X_test.drop('num_competitors', axis=1)

model.fit(X_train2, y_train)
predictions2 = model.predict(X_test2)
```

9. Calculate the RMSE and MAE for the new model's predictions and print them out, as follows:

```
print('RMSE: ' + str(mean_squared_error(predictions2, y_test)**0.5))
print('MAE: ' + str(mean_absolute_error(predictions2, y_test)))
```

This should result in the following output:

RMSE: 5702.030002037039

MAE: 4544.416946418695

Note that both of these values are higher than the values we calculated for the previous model. This means that dropping **num_competitors** from our model increased the error in our model on the test set. In other words, our model was more accurate when it contained **num_competitors**. Thus, we can see how the MAE or the RMSE can be used to determine which features it is important to have in a model and those that have little impact on performance and can therefore be left out.

Activity 10: Testing Which Variables are Important for Predicting Responses to a Marketing Offer

You've been given some data about a company's marketing campaign, which offered discounts for various products. You are interested in building a model to predict the number of responses to the offer, and have information about how much discount the offer included (**offer_discount**), how many customers the offer reached (**offer_reach**), and a value for the offer quality that the marketing team assigned to that offer (**offer_quality**). You want to build a model that is accurate but does not contain unnecessary variables. Use the RMSE to evaluate how the model performs when all variables are included, and compare this to what happens when each variable is dropped from the model. Follow the steps given here:

1. Import **pandas**, read in the data from **offer_responses.csv**, and use the **head** function to view the first five rows of the data. Your output should appear as follows:

	responses	offer_discount	offer_quality	offer_reach
0	4151.0	26.0	10.257680	31344.0
1	3397.0	35.0	15.194380	24016.0
2	3274.0	21.0	13.971468	28832.0
3	3426.0	27.0	6.054338	26747.0
4	5745.0	42.0	16.801365	46968.0

Figure 6.6: The first five rows of the offer_responses data

2. Import **train_test_split** from **sklearn** and use it to split the data into a training and test set, using responses as the **y** variable and all others as the predictor (**X**) variables. Use **random_state=10** for the train-test split.

3. Import **LinearRegression** and **mean_squared_error** from **sklearn**. Fit a model to the training data (using all of the predictors), get predictions from the model on the test data, and print out the calculated RMSE on the test data. The RMSE with all variables should be approximately 966.2461828577945.

4. Create **X_train2** and **X_test2** by dropping **offer_quality** from **X_train** and **X_test**. Train and evaluate the RMSE of a model using **X_train2** and **X_test2**. The RMSE without **offer_quality** should be 965.5346123758474.

5. Perform the same sequence of steps from step 4, but this time dropping **offer_discount** instead of **offer_quality**. The RMSE without **offer_discount** should be 1231.6766556327284.

6. Perform the same sequence of steps but this time dropping **offer_reach**. The RMSE without **offer_reach** should be 1185.8456831644114.

> **Note**
>
> The solution for this activity can be found on page 344.

Using Regularization for Feature Selection

In the previous section, we saw how an evaluation metric such as the RMSE can be used to decide whether a variable should be included in a model or not. However, this method can be cumbersome when there are many variables involved.

When a model contains extraneous variables (variables that are not related to the outcome of interest), it can become more difficult to interpret the model. It can also lead to **overfitting**, where the model may change drastically if you use a different subset of the data to train the model. Therefore, it is important to select only those features that are related to the outcome for training the model.

One common way to select which features will be used by a model is to use **regularization**. The idea of regularization is that the model will be asked not only to try to predict the training points as accurately as possible, but will have the additional constraint of trying to minimize the weight that it puts on each of the variables. With some forms of regularization, this leads to some variables being dropped entirely. Specifically, a type of model called **lasso regression** uses a form of regularization that encourages the model to drop variables that are not useful for production. Other than using regularization to find the coefficients for the model, it is just like ordinary linear regression, resulting in a model that can be written down as a simple equation. Therefore, this type of model is useful for feature selection for linear regression models.

Exercise 24: Using Lasso Regression for Feature Selection

For this exercise, you've been given data on the revenue of stores at different locations, and a series of 20 scores based on internal metrics. You aren't told what the scores mean, but are asked to build a predictive model that uses as few of these as possible without sacrificing the ability to predict the location revenue:

1. Import **pandas**, read the data from **20scores.csv** into a DataFrame called **df**, and display the first five rows of data using the **head** function:

```
import pandas as pd

df = pd.read_csv('20scores.csv')
df.head()
```

You should see the following output:

	revenue	score0	score1	score2	score3	score4	score5	score6	score7	score8	...	score10	score11	score12	score13
0	30698.74	0.067763	1.762772	0.211119	0.619655	-1.586284	0.051320	-0.529940	-0.177908	-0.387431	...	-1.246132	-1.817742	-0.189583	-1.636507
1	46813.75	0.943657	-0.696100	3.503075	1.323145	-0.579567	-1.379598	0.013465	1.061996	-0.952645	...	1.115770	0.455824	0.109667	-0.790210
2	39493.35	-0.070838	-1.817580	-0.156724	-0.159741	-1.564338	-0.817489	0.125174	-1.053015	0.181246	...	-0.006912	-0.009129	-0.324959	1.040768
3	48130.55	-0.133306	0.815997	2.261204	0.794839	-0.947440	0.049189	-0.042403	1.657086	-2.870217	...	2.183177	0.364106	0.686530	0.112862
4	35129.09	0.452780	1.529394	0.085364	-0.787245	1.351148	-0.340774	0.354099	-0.319731	-0.776033	...	2.000792	1.035293	-0.719229	-3.073072

Figure 6.7: The first five rows of the 20scores.csv data

2. Import **train_test_split** and perform a train-test split on the data with **random_state=10**, storing revenue in the **y** variable and all other features in the **X** variable, as shown:

```
from sklearn.model_selection import train_test_split

x_cols = df.columns[1:]
X = df[x_cols]

y = df['revenue']

X_train, X_test, y_train, y_test = train_test_split(X, y, random_state = 10)
```

3. Import **LinearRegression** from **sklearn** and fit a linear regression model on the training data:

```
from sklearn.linear_model import LinearRegression

model = LinearRegression()
model.fit(X_train,y_train)
```

4. Look at the model's coefficients, as follows:

```
model.coef_
```

You should get the following result:

```
array([ 3.10465458e+01,  1.35929333e+00, -1.71996170e+01, -4.26396854e+00,
       -4.56514104e+00,  2.71178012e+01,  1.12523398e+01, -9.62768549e+00,
        1.28097189e+01, -3.82102937e+01, -3.92691076e+00, -4.49267755e+00,
        9.12581579e+03,  2.81237962e+01,  1.26722148e+01,  1.99096955e+01,
       -1.73401880e+01,  3.77047162e+03, -7.57356369e+00,
    4.99844116e+03])
```

Note that all of these values are non-zero, so the model is using all variables.

5. Now import **Lasso** from **sklearn** and fit a lasso regression to the training data (using **random_state=10**). Also make sure to normalize the data; this ensures that the data the model is fitting to is on the same scale, so the regularization treats all variables equally. This is not required with normal linear regression because there is no regularization involved:

```
from sklearn.linear_model import Lasso

lasso_model = Lasso(normalize=True, random_state=10)
lasso_model.fit(X_train,y_train)
```

6. Examine the coefficients of the lasso model using the following code:

```
lasso_model.coef_
```

This should produce the following output:

```
array([ 4.26184401e+00,  0.00000000e+00, -0.00000000e+00, -0.00000000e+00,
       -0.00000000e+00,  0.00000000e+00,  0.00000000e+00, -0.00000000e+00,
        0.00000000e+00, -1.28279999e+01, -0.00000000e+00, -0.00000000e+00,
        9.10035968e+03,  0.00000000e+00,  0.00000000e+00,  0.00000000e+00,
       -0.00000000e+00,  3.74239596e+03, -0.00000000e+00,
    4.97252311e+03])
```

Note that many of these coefficients are now 0. The model has decided not to use these variables. If we knew what the variables were, we could examine which variables the model has chosen to use.

7. Import **mean_squared_error** from **sklearn** and use it to calculate the RMSE of the linear regression model on the test data:

```
from sklearn.metrics import mean_squared_error

predictions = model.predict(X_test)
print(mean_squared_error(predictions, y_test)**0.5)
```

The output should be 491.78833768572633.

8. Similarly, calculate the RMSE of the lasso model on the test data:

```
lasso_predictions = lasso_model.predict(X_test)
print(mean_squared_error(lasso_predictions, y_test)**0.5)
```

The output should be 488.60931274387747.

You can observe that, although the lasso regression is not using most of the variables, its RMSE is very similar to the linear model that uses all of them. This shows that it has not lost any predictive power, even though it has greatly simplified the model by removing variables.

Activity 11: Using Lasso Regression to Choose Features for Predicting Customer Spend

You've been given a number of data elements about customers: how much they spent in the previous year (**prev_year_spend**), the number of days since their last purchase (**days_since_last_purchase**), the number of days since their first purchase (**days_since_first_purchase**), the total number of transactions (**total_transactions**), the customer's age (**age**), the customer's income (**income**), and a customer engagement score (**engagement_score**), which is a score created based on customers' engagement with previous marketing offers. You are asked to investigate which of these is related to the customer spend in the current year (**cur_year_spend**), and create a simple linear model to describe these relationships. Follow the steps given here:

1. Import **pandas**, use it to read the data in **customer_spend.csv**, and use the **head** function to view the first five rows of data. The output should appear as follows:

	cur_year_spend	prev_year_spend	days_since_last_purchase	days_since_first_purchase	total_transactions	age	income	engagement_score
0	5536.46	1681.26	7	61	34	61	97914.93	-0.652392
1	871.41	1366.74	12	34	33	68	30904.69	0.007327
2	2046.74	1419.38	10	81	22	54	48194.59	0.221666
3	4662.70	1561.21	12	32	34	49	93551.98	1.149641
4	3539.46	1397.60	17	72	34	66	66267.57	0.835834

Figure 6.8: The first five rows of customer_spend.csv

2. Use **train_test_split** from **sklearn** to split the data into training and test sets, with **random_state=100** and **cur_year_spend** as the **y** variable:

3. Import **Lasso** from **sklearn** and fit a lasso model (with **normalize=True** and **random_state=10**) to the training data.

4. Get the coefficients from the lasso model, and store the names of the features that have non-zero coefficients along with their coefficient values in the **selected_features** and **selected_coefs** variables, respectively.

5. Print out the names of the features with non-zero coefficients and their associated coefficient values using the following code. The following is the expected output:

Feature	Value of coefficient
prev_year_spend	0.7986123149372604
days_since_first_purchase coefficient	14.244498219709854
total_transactions coefficient	46.31232726625005
income coefficient	0.05781233517110743

Figure 6.9: Expected coefficients of the features

Note

The solution for this activity can be found on page 346.

Tree-Based Regression Models

Linear models are not the only type of regression models. Another powerful technique is to use **regression trees**. Regression trees are based on the idea of a **decision tree**. A decision tree is a bit like a flowchart, where at each step you ask whether a variable is greater than or less than some value. After flowing through several of these steps, you reach the end of the tree and receive an answer for what value the prediction should be. The following figure illustrates the workings of regression trees:

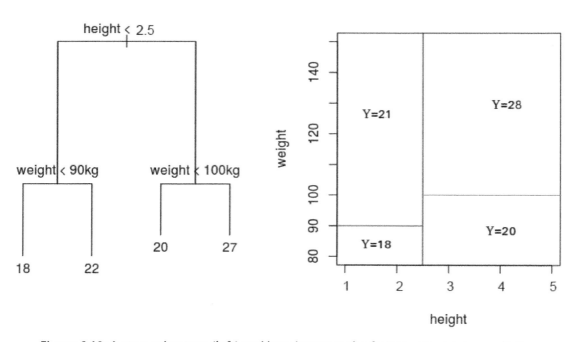

Figure 6.10: A regression tree (left) and how it parses the feature space into predictions

Decision trees are interesting because they can pick up on trends in data that linear regression might miss or capture poorly. Whereas linear models assume a simple linear relationship between predictors and an outcome, regression trees result in step functions, which can fit certain kinds of relationships more accurately.

One important hyperparameter for regression trees is the *maximum depth of the tree*. The more depth that a tree is allowed, the more complex a relationship it can model. While this may sound like a good thing, choosing too high a maximum depth can lead to a model that is highly overfitted to the data. In fact, the tendency to overfit is one of the biggest drawbacks of regression trees.

Random Forests

To overcome the issue of overfitting, instead of training a single tree to find patterns in data, many trees are trained over random subsets of the data. The predictions of these trees are then averaged to produce a prediction. Combining trees together in this way is called a **<u>random forest</u>**. This technique has been found to overcome many of the weaknesses of regression trees. The following figure illustrates an ensemble of tree models, each of whose predictions are averaged to produce the ensemble's predictions:

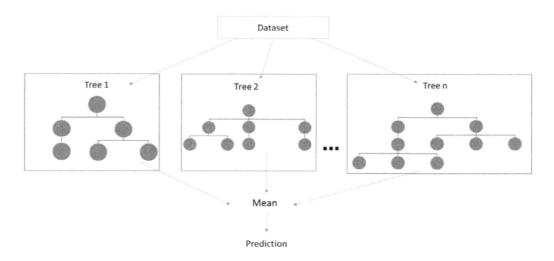

Figure 6.11: An ensemble of tree models

Random forests are based on the idea of creating an **ensemble**, which is where multiple models are combined together to produce a single prediction. This is a powerful technique that can often lead to very good outcomes. In the case of random forests, creating an ensemble of regression trees together in this way has been shown to not only decrease overfitting, but also produce very good predictions in a wide variety of scenarios.

Because tree-based methods and linear regression are so drastically different in the way they fit to data, they often work well in different circumstances. When the relationships in data are linear (or close to it), linear models will tend to produce more accurate predictions, with the bonus of being easy to interpret. When relationships are more complex, tree-based methods may perform better. Testing each and choosing the best model for the job requires evaluating the models based on their predictive accuracy with a metric such as the RMSE.

Exercise 25: Using Tree-Based Regression Models to Capture Non-Linear Trends

In this exercise, we'll look at a very simple dataset where we have data on customers' spend and their age. We want to figure out how spending habits change with age in our customers, and how well different models can capture this relationship:

1. Import **pandas** and use it to read in the data in **age_spend.csv**. Use the **head** function to view the first five rows of the data:

    ```
    import pandas as pd

    df = pd.read_csv('age_spend.csv')
    df.head()
    ```

    Your output will appear as follows:

	spend	age
0	2725.0	20.0
1	3010.0	38.0
2	2782.0	25.0
3	2809.0	31.0
4	2774.0	54.0

    Figure 6.12: The first five rows of the age_spend data

2. Import **train_test_split** from **sklearn** and use it to perform a train-test split of the data, with **random_state=10** and **y** being spend and **X** being age:

    ```
    from sklearn.model_selection import train_test_split

    X = df[['age']]

    y = df['spend']

    X_train, X_test, y_train, y_test = train_test_split(X, y, random_state = 10)
    ```

3. Import **DecisionTreeRegressor** from **sklearn** and fit two decision trees to the training data, one with **max_depth=2** and one with **max_depth=5**:

```
from sklearn.tree import DecisionTreeRegressor

max2_tree_model = DecisionTreeRegressor(max_depth=2)
max2_tree_model.fit(X_train,y_train)

max5_tree_model = DecisionTreeRegressor(max_depth=5)
max5_tree_model.fit(X_train,y_train)
```

4. Import **LinearRegression** from **sklearn** and fit a linear regression model to the training data, as shown:

```
from sklearn.linear_model import LinearRegression

model = LinearRegression()
model.fit(X_train,y_train)
```

5. Import **mean_squared_error** from **sklearn**. For the linear model and the two regression tree models, get predictions from the model for the test set and use these to calculate the RMSE. Use the following code:

```
from sklearn.metrics import mean_squared_error

linear_predictions = model.predict(X_test)
print('Linear model RMSE: ' + str(mean_squared_error(linear_predictions,
y_test)**0.5))

max2_tree_predictions = max2_tree_model.predict(X_test)
print('Tree with max depth of 2 RMSE: ' + str(mean_squared_error(max2_
tree_predictions, y_test)**0.5))

max5_tree_predictions = max5_tree_model.predict(X_test)
print('tree with max depth of 5 RMSE: ' + str(mean_squared_error(max5_
tree_predictions, y_test)**0.5))
```

You should get the following RMSE values for the linear and decision tree models with max depths of 2 and 5, respectively: 159.07639273785358, 125.1920405443602, and 109.73376798374653.

Notice that the linear model has the largest error, the decision tree with a max depth of 2 does better, and the decision tree with a max depth of 5 has the lowest error of the 3.

6. Import **matplotlib**. Create a variable called **ages** to store a DataFrame with a single column containing ages from 18 to 70, so that we can have our models give us their predictions for all of these ages:

```
import matplotlib.pyplot as plt
%matplotlib inline

ages = pd.DataFrame({'age':range(18,70)})
```

7. Create a scatter plot with the test data and plot on top of it the predictions from the linear regression model for the range of ages. Plot with **color='r'** and **linewidth=5** to make it easier to see:

```
plt.scatter(X_test.age.tolist(),y_test.tolist())
plt.plot(ages,model.predict(ages), color='r', linewidth=5)
plt.show()
```

The following plot shows the predictions of the linear regression model across the age range plotted on top of the actual data points:

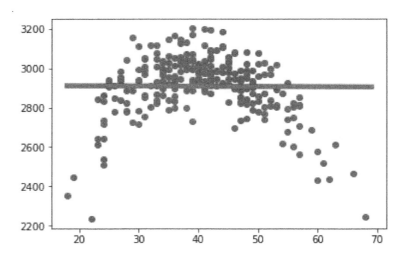

Figure 6.13: The predictions of the linear regression model

We can see that the linear regression model just shows a flat line across ages; it is unable to capture the fact that people aged around 40 spend more, and people younger and older than 40 spend less.

8. Create another scatter plot with the test data, this time plotting the predictions of the **max2_tree** model on top with **color='g'** and **linewidth=5**:

```
plt.scatter(X_test.age.tolist(),y_test.tolist())
plt.plot(ages,max2_tree_model.predict(ages), color='g',linewidth=5)
plt.show()
```

The following plot shows the predictions of the regression tree model with **max_depth** of 2 across the age range plotted on top of the actual data points:

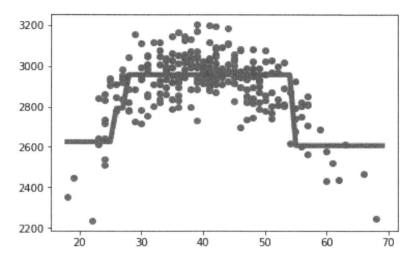

Figure 6.14: The predictions of the regression tree model with max_depth of 2

This model does a better job of capturing the relationship, though it does not capture the sharp decline in the oldest or youngest population.

9. Create another scatter plot with the test data, this time plotting the predictions of the **max5_tree** model on top with **color='k'** and **linewidth=5**:

```
plt.scatter(X_test.age.tolist(),y_test.tolist())
plt.plot(ages,max5_tree_model.predict(ages), color='k',linewidth=5)
plt.show()
```

The following plot shows the predictions of the regression tree model with **max_depth** of 5 across the age range plotted on top of the actual data points:

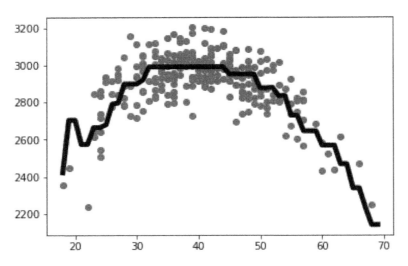

Figure 6.15: The predictions of the regression tree model with max_depth of 5

This model does an even better job of capturing the relationship, properly capturing a sharp decline in the oldest or youngest population.

10. Let's now perform random forest regression on the same data. Import **RandomForestRegressor** from **sklearn**. Fit two random forest models with **random_state=10**, one with **max_depth=2** and the other with **max_depth=5**, and save these as **max2_forest** and **max5_forest**, respectively:

```
from sklearn.ensemble import RandomForestRegressor

max2_forest_model = RandomForestRegressor(max_depth=2, random_state=10)
max2_forest_model.fit(X_train,y_train)

max5_forest_model = RandomForestRegressor(max_depth=5, random_state=10)
max5_forest_model.fit(X_train,y_train)
```

11. Calculate and print the RMSE for the two random forest models using the following code:

```
max2_forest_predictions = max2_forest_model.predict(X_test)
print('Max depth of 2 RMSE: ' + str(mean_squared_error(max2_forest_
predictions, y_test)**0.5))

max5_forest_predictions = max5_forest_model.predict(X_test)
print('Max depth of 5 RMSE: ' + str(mean_squared_error(maxt_forest_
predictions, y_test)**0.5))
```

The following RMSE values should be obtained for the random forest models with max depths of 2 and 5, respectively: 115.51279667457273 and 109.61188562057568.

Note that the random forest model with a max depth of 2 does better than the regression tree with a max depth of 2, and the model with a max depth of 5 does about as well as the regression tree with a depth of 5. Both do better than the linear regression model.

12. Create another scatter plot with the test data, this time plotting the predictions of the **max2_forest** model on top with **color='c'** and **linewidth=5**:

```
plt.scatter(X_test.age.tolist(),y_test.tolist())
plt.plot(ages,max2_forest_model.predict(ages), color='c',linewidth=5)
plt.show()
```

The following plot shows the predictions of the random forest model with **max_depth** of 2 across the age range plotted on top of the actual data points:

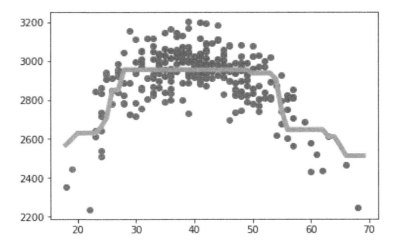

Figure 6.16: The predictions of the random forest model with max_depth of 2

We can see that this model captures the data trend better than the decision tree, but still doesn't quite capture the trend at the very high or low ends of our range.

13. Create another scatter plot with the test data, this time plotting the predictions of the **max2_forest** model on top with **color='m'** and **linewidth=5**:

```
plt.scatter(X_test.age.tolist(),y_test.tolist())
plt.plot(ages,max5_forest_model.predict(ages), color='m',linewidth=5)
plt.show()
```

The following plot shows the predictions of the random forest model with **max_depth** of 5 across the age range plotted on top of the actual data points:

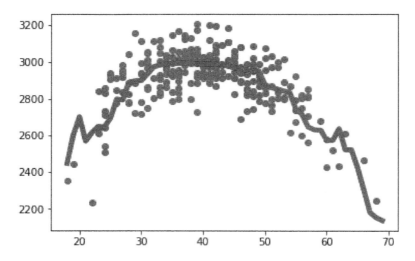

Figure 6.17: The predictions of the random forest model with max_depth of 5

Again, the model the greater max depth does an even better job of capturing the relationship, properly capturing the sharp decline in the oldest or youngest population.

Activity 12: Building the Best Regression Model for Customer Spend Based on Demographic Data

You are given data on customers' spend at your business and some basic demographic data about each customer (age, income, and years of education). You are asked to build the best predictive model possible that can predict, based on these demographic factors, how much a customer would spend at your business. Follow the steps given here:

1. Import **pandas**, read the data in **spend_age_income_ed.csv** into a DataFrame, and use the **head** function to view the first five rows of the data. The output should be as follows:

	spend	age	income	years_of_education
0	3304.0	36.0	45125.0	12
1	3709.0	43.0	41695.0	10
2	3305.0	47.0	39253.0	17
3	2170.0	33.0	32384.0	13
4	2113.0	30.0	33182.0	10

Figure 6.18: The first five rows of the spend_age_income_ed data

2. Perform a train-test split with **random_state=10**.

3. Fit a linear regression model to the training data.

4. Fit two regression tree models to the data, one with **max_depth=2** and one with **max_depth=5**.

5. Fit two random forest models to the data, one with `max_depth=2`, one with `max_depth=5`, and `random_state=10` for both.

6. Calculate and print out the RMSE on the test data for all five models.

   The following table summarizes the expected output for all of the models:

Model	RMSE
Linear model	348.19771532747865
Decision tree with max depth of 2	268.51069264082935
Decision tree with max depth of 5	125.53257106419696
Random forest with max depth of 2	267.88627970886233
Random forest with max depth of 5	115.88545042221628

Figure 6.19: Expected outputs for all 5 models

Note

The solution for this activity can be found on page 347.

Summary

In this chapter, we explored how to evaluate regression models. We learned about using residuals to calculate MAE and RMSE, and how to use these metrics to compare models. We also learned about lasso regression and how it can be used for feature selection. Finally, we learned about tree-based regression models, and looked at how they are able to fit to some of the non-linear relationships that linear regression is unable to handle.

In the next chapter, we will learn about classification models, the other primary type of supervised learning models.

Supervised Learning: Predicting Customer Churn

Learning Objectives

By the end of this chapter, you will be able to:

- Perform classification tasks using logistic regression

- Implement the most widely used data science pipeline (OSEMN)

- Perform data exploration to understand the relationship between the target and explanatory variables.

- Select the important features for building your churn model.

- Perform logistic regression as a baseline model to predict customer churn.

This chapter covers classification algorithms such as logistic regression and explains how to implement the OSEMN pipeline.

Introduction

Churn prediction is one of the most common use cases of machine learning. Churn can be anything—employee churn from a company, customer churn from a mobile subscription, and so on. Predicting customer churn is important for an organization because acquiring new customers is easy, but retaining them is more difficult. Similarly, high employee churn can also affect a company, since it spends a huge sum of money on grooming talent. Also, organizations that have high retention rates benefit from consistent growth, which can also lead to high referrals from existing customers.

Most of the use cases for churn prediction involve supervised classification tasks. We saw what supervised learning is in the previous chapters, and covered regression in detail. In this chapter, we will first begin by learning about classification problems, then we will implement logistic regression and understand the intuition behind the algorithm. Next, we will see how to organize data to build a churn model, followed by an exploration of the data to find some insights from it, and we'll cover some of the statistical inferences that can be drawn from the data. We will find out what the important features are for building our churn model, and finally, we'll apply logistic regression to predict customer churn.

Classification Problems

Classification problems are the most common type of machine learning problem. Classification tasks are different from regression tasks, in the sense that, in classification tasks, we predict a discrete class label, whereas in the case of regression, we predict continuous values. Another notable difference between classification problems and regression problems lies in the choice of performance metrics. With classification problems, accuracy is commonly chosen as a performance metric, while root mean square is quite common in the case of regression.

There are many important business use cases for classification problems where the dependent variable is not continuous, such as churn and fraud detection. In these cases, the response variable has only two values, that is, churn or not churn, and fraud or not fraud. For example, suppose we are studying whether a customer churns ($y = 1$) or doesn't churn ($y = 0$) after signing up for a mobile service contract. Then, the probability that a customer churns is indicated as $p = P(Churn)$, and the possible explanatory variable x includes account age, current billing amount, and average days delinquent (that is, the average number of days a person misses making his or her payment).

The following figure illustrates how a supervised classification task works:

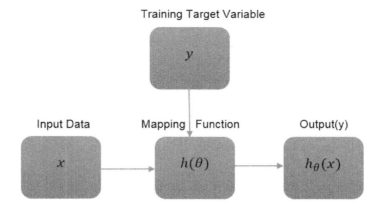

Figure 7.1: Workflow of a supervised classification task

As a supervisor, we provide the model with the variables (x,y), which lets the model calculate the parameter theta (θ). This parameter is learned from the training data and is also termed as a **coefficient**. x includes the explanatory variables and y is the target label that we provide to the model so that the model learns the parameters. Using this, the model produces a function $h(\theta)$, which maps input x to a prediction $h_\theta(x)$.

Classification problems can generally be divided into two types:

- **Binary classification**: The target variable can have only two categorical values or classes. For example, given an image, classify whether it's a cat or not a cat.

- **Multiclass classification**: The target variable can have multiple classes. For example, given an image, classify whether it's a cat, dog, rabbit, or bird.

Understanding Logistic Regression

Logistic regression is one of the most widely used classification methods, and it works well when data is linearly separable. The objective of logistic regression is to squash the output of linear regression to classes 0 and 1.

Revisiting Linear Regression

In the case of linear regression, our function would be as follows:

$$h_\theta(x) = \theta_0 + \theta_1 * x$$

Figure 7.2: Equation of linear regression

Here, x refers to the input data, y is the target variable, and θ_0 and θ_1 are parameters that are learned from the training data.

Also, the cost function in case of linear regression, which is to be minimized is as follows:

$$J(\theta_0, \theta_1) = \frac{1}{2 * No\ of\ rows} \sum_{i=0}^{i=No\ of\ rows} (h_\theta(x^i) - x^i)^2$$

Figure 7.3: Linear regression cost function

This works well for continuous data, but the problem arises when we have a target variable that is categorical, such as, 0 or 1. When we try to use linear regression to predict the target variable, we can get a value anywhere between $-\infty$ to $+\infty$, which is not what we need.

Logistic Regression

If a response variable has binary values, the assumptions of linear regression are not valid for the following reasons:

- The relationship between the independent variable and the predictor variable is not linear.

- The error terms are heteroscedastic.

- The error terms are not normally distributed.

If we proceed, considering these violations, the results would be as follows:

- The predicted probabilities could be greater than 1 or less than 0.

- The magnitude of the effects of independent variables may be underestimated.

With logistic regression, we are interested in modeling the mean of the response variable, p, in terms of an explanatory variable, x, as a probabilistic model in terms of **odd ratio**. A simple logistic regression model formula is as follows:

$$logit(p) = log\left(\frac{p}{1-p}\right) = \theta_0 + \theta_1 * x_1 + \theta_2 * x_2 + \theta_3 * x_3 \ldots$$

Where, p is the probability that an event y occurs, $p(y = 1)$

$\frac{p}{1-p}$ is the odd ratio

$log\left(\frac{p}{1-p}\right)$ is the log odds, or logit

Figure 7.4: Simple logistic regression model formula

With logistic regression, we still use the linear regression formula. However, we will be squashing the output of the linear function to a range of 0 and 1 using a sigmoid function. The sigmoid function is the inverse of the logit function:

$$p = g(z) = \frac{1}{1 + e^{-z}}$$

Figure 7.5: Sigmoid function

Squash the output of the linear equation as follows:

$$linear\ function: h_\theta(x) = \theta_0 + \theta_1 * x_1 + \theta_2 * x_2 + \theta_3 * x_3 \ldots$$

$$taking\ (\theta_0 + \theta_1 * x_1 + \theta_2 * x_2 + \theta_3 * x_3 \ldots)\ as\ \theta^T x$$

$$g(\theta^T x) = \frac{1}{1 + e^{-\theta^T x}}$$

Figure 7.6: Squashing output of linear equation using sigmoid

Here, we take the output of $h_\theta(x)$ and give it to the $g(z)$ function, which returns the squashed function to the range of 0 to 1.

Exercise 26: Plotting the Sigmoid Function

In this exercise, we will plot a sigmoid function using values generated from –10 to +10. This exercise will tell us how a sigmoid function behaves and what it looks like. It gives the idea that, even though logistic regression uses a linear regression equation, which can give values between –10 to +10, a sigmoid function squashes the output to 0 and 1.

1. Import Matplotlib and NumPy libraries:

```
import matplotlib.pyplot as plt
import numpy as np
```

2. Define a function **sigmoid(x)** that constructs a sigmoid function as follows:

```
def sigmoid(x):
    return 1/(1+np.exp(-x))
```

3. Generate values ranging from –10 to +10 using the following code:

```
z=np.arange(-10,10,0.1)
z
```

You will get an output showing you the list of data points generated.

4. Now call the sigmoid function and plot it. Use the following code:

```
sig=sigmoid(z)
plt.plot(z,sig)
plt.yticks([0.0,0.5,1.0])
plt.grid(True)
```

Your plot will look as follows:

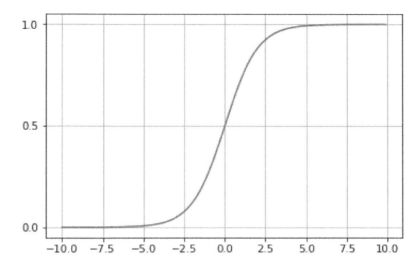

Figure 7.7: Plot of sigmoid function

5. Let's also plot the values of **z** using a linear function 0+0.5*z, as follows:

```
plt.plot(z,0+0.5*z)
plt.grid(True)
```

This will give us the following plot:

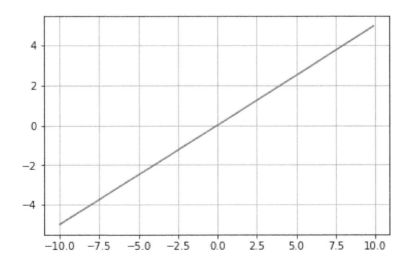

Figure 7.8: Plot using a linear function

From the preceding graph, it is evident that the sigmoid function squashes the values −10 to +10 to between 0 and 1, whereas the linear function is unable to do so.

Cost Function for Logistic Regression

The sigmoid function that we described previously contains a non-linear term. We must convert it into a linear term, else we would have a non-convex function that would be difficult to optimize. The cost function of logistic regression can be defined as follows, which is obtained using Maximum Likelihood Estimation:

$$cost(g(\theta^T x), y) = \begin{cases} -log\left(g(\theta^T x)\right) & y = 1 \\ -log\left(1 - g(\theta^T x)\right) & y = 0 \end{cases}$$

Figure 7.9: Logistic regression cost function

It is easy for the algorithm to optimize the cost function when we have a linear term (see the left plot in the following figure), whereas it becomes difficult for the algorithm to optimize if our cost function is non-linear (see the right plot of the following figure).

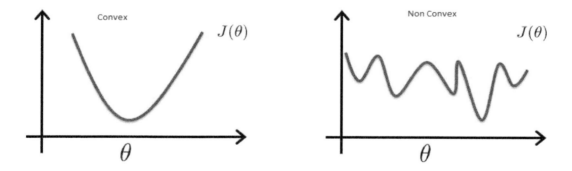

Figure 7.10: Difference between plots with linear and non-linear terms

After converting our cost function for logistic regression to a linear term, we finally get the following equation:

$$J(\theta) = -\frac{1}{no\ of\ rows} \sum_{i=0}^{i=no\ of\ rows} y^i * log\left(g(\theta^T x)\right) + (1 - y^i) * log\left(1 - g(\theta^T x)\right)$$

Figure 7.11: Optimized logistic regression cost function

Here, θ is the parameter the model learns from the training data.

> **Note**
>
> The derivation of the cost function is out of the scope of this book, and we recommend students go through the derivation separately.

Assumptions of Logistic Regression

The following are the assumptions of the logistic regression algorithm:

- Logistic regression does not assume a linear relationship between dependent and independent variables.

- The dependent variable must be binary (that is, have two categories).

- The independent variable need not have intervals, be normally distributed, linearly related, or have equal variance within each group.

- The categories must be mutually exclusive and exhaustive.

Exercise 27: Loading, Splitting, and Applying Linear and Logistic Regression to Data

For this exercise, you will be using the **exam_score.csv** dataset placed in the **Lesson07** folder on GitHub. The dataset comprises scores obtained by students in two subjects. It has also a column that has 0 and 1 values. 1 indicates that the student has passed the exam, whereas 0 indicates that student has not passed the exam. Your teacher has asked you to develop a machine learning model that can predict whether a student will pass (1) or fail (0). Apply linear and logistic regression to predict the output. You will also see why it's not a good idea to use linear regression for this kind of classification problem:

1. Import pandas, NumPy, sklearn, and Matplotlib:

```
import pandas as pd
import numpy as np
from sklearn.model_selection import train_test_split
from sklearn import linear_model
import matplotlib.pyplot as plt
```

2. Read the data to a pandas DataFrame named **data** and look at the first few rows:

```
data= pd.read_csv(r'exam_score.csv',header=None)
data.head(5)
```

You will get the following output:

	0	1	2
0	34.623660	78.024693	0
1	30.286711	43.894998	0
2	35.847409	72.902198	0
3	60.182599	86.308552	1
4	79.032736	75.344376	1

Figure 7.12: The first few rows of the data

3. Split the data into training and testing sets as follows:

```
X_train,X_test,y_train,y_test=train_test_split(data[[0,1]],data[[2]].
astype(int),test_size=0.3,random_state=1,stratify=data[[2]].astype(int))
```

4. Fit the model using linear regression:

```
linear = linear_model.LinearRegression()
linear.fit(X_train, y_train)
```

5. Predict on the test data:

```
linear.predict(X_test)
```

Your output will be as follows:

```
array([[ 1.22083091],
       [ 1.17230948],
       [ 0.94507443],
       [ 0.35609403],
       [ 1.02375539],
       [ 0.8016655 ],
       [ 1.09434499],
       [ 1.05191921],
       [ 0.27273707],
       [ 0.40180325],
       [ 0.84618988],
       [ 1.06105956],
       [ 1.06873208],
       [ 0.35054279],
       [ 1.19900775],
       [ 0.51962942],
       [ 0.16641549],
       [ 1.01137892],
       [ 0.30865603],
       [ 0.30361639],
       [ 0.67983531],
       [-0.20582051],
       [ 0.34259952],
       [ 0.45063479],
       [ 0.74903637],
       [ 0.29760594],
       [ 0.43242695],
       [ 0.97129797],
       [ 0.50748505],
       [ 0.98267487]])
```

Figure 7.13: Output of the prediction on test data

6. Now check the actual target values using **y_test[2]**:

```
y_test[2].values.astype(int)
```

Your output will be as follows:

```
array([1, 1, 1, 1, 1, 1, 0, 0, 1, 0, 0, 0, 1, 1, 0, 1, 1, 1, 0, 0])
```

Figure 7.14: Output of actual target values

7. Plot the linear regression curve:

```
color = ['red', 'green']
y_color = [color[i] for i in y_train[2].values.astype(int)]
marker=['o','v']
y_marker = [marker[i] for i in y_train[2].values.astype(int)]

plt.figure(figsize=(6, 6))
for _m, c, _x, _y in zip(y_marker, y_color, X_train[0].values, X_train[1].
values):
    plt.scatter(_x,_y, c=c,marker=_m)

plt.plot((- linear.coef_[0][1] * np.array((min(X_train[1].values), max(X_
train[1].values))) - linear.intercept_[0]) /
        linear.coef_[0][0], np.array((min(X_train[1].values), max(X_
train[1].values))))
plt.show()
```

Your plot should look as follows:

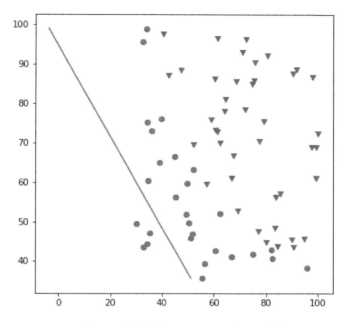

Figure 7.15: Linear regression plot

From the plot you can observe that linear regression was unable to predict the values as 1 and 0. Therefore, the model is not able to distinguish the classes correctly.

8. Let's now try using logistic regression. Fit the model using logistic regression as follows:

```
logit = linear_model.LogisticRegression()
logit.fit(X_train, y_train[2].values.astype(int))
```

9. Predict on the test data:

```
logit.predict(X_test)
```

You should get the following output:

```
array([1, 1, 1, 1, 1, 1, 1, 1, 1, 1, 1, 1, 1, 1, 1, 1, 0, 1, 0, 0, 1, 0,
       1, 1, 1, 1, 1, 1, 1, 1])
```

Figure 7.16: Prediction of output of test data using logistic regression

10. Check the actual target values with y_test[2]:

```
y_test[2].values.astype(int)
```

You should get the following output:

```
array([1, 1, 1, 0, 1, 1, 1, 1, 0, 0, 1, 1, 1, 0, 1, 1, 0, 1, 0, 0, 0, 0,
       0, 1, 1, 0, 0, 1, 1, 1])
```

Figure 7.17: Original value of test data

11. Plot the logistic regression line:

```
color = ['red', 'green']
y_color = [color[i] for i in y_train[2].values.astype(int)]
marker=['o','v']
y_marker = [marker[i] for i in y_train[2].values.astype(int)]

plt.figure(figsize=(6, 6))
for _m, c, _x, _y in zip(y_marker, y_color, X_train[0].values, X_train[1].
values):
    plt.scatter(_x,_y, c=c,marker=_m)
```

```
plt.plot((- logit.coef_[0][1] * np.array((min(X_train[1].values), max(X_
train[1].values))) - logit.intercept_[0]) /
        logit.coef_[0][0], np.array((min(X_train[1].values), max(X_
train[1].values))))
plt.show()
```

Your plot should look as follows:

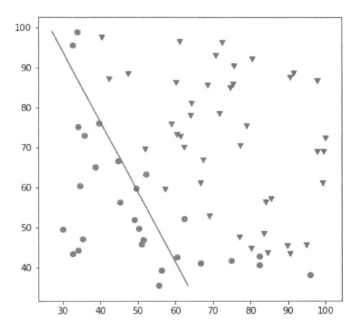

Figure 7.18: Logistic regression plot

From the plot you will observe that logistic regression was able to predict the values as 1 and 0. The graph shows that the model was able to classify most of the data points correctly, but some were misclassified. **logit.predict_proba()** can be used to predict probabilities instead of classes.

Creating a Data Science Pipeline

OSEMN is one of the most common data science pipelines used for approaching any kind of data science problem. It's pronounced *awesome*.

OSEMN stands for the following:

1. **O**btaining the data, which can be from any source, structured, unstructured, or semi-structured.

2. **S**crubbing the data, which is getting your hands dirty and cleaning the data, which can involve renaming columns and imputing missing values.

3. **E**xploring the data to find out the relationships between each of the variables. Searching for any correlation among the variables. Finding the relationship between the explanatory variables and the response variable.

4. **M**odeling the data, which can include prediction, forecasting, and clustering.

5. I**N**terpreting the data, which is combining all the analyses and results to draw a conclusion.

Obtaining the Data

This step refers to collecting data. Data can be obtained from a single source or from multiple sources. In the real world, collecting data is not always easy since the data is often siloed. Data collection in a large organization is done by gathering data from both internal and external sources (such as social media).

Exercise 28: Obtaining the Data

You work at a multinational bank that is aiming to increase it's market share in Europe. Recently, it has been noticed that the number of customers using the banking services has declined, and the bank is worried that existing customers have stopped using them as their main bank. As a data scientist, you are tasked with finding out the reasons behind customer churn and to predict customer churn. The marketing team, in particular, is interested in your findings and want to better understand existing customer behavior and possibly predict customer churn. Your results will help the marketing team to use their budget wisely to target potential churners. To achieve this objective, in this exercise, you will import the banking data (`Churn_Modelling.csv`) provided by the bank and do some initial checks, such as seeing how many rows and columns are present.

> **Note**
>
> We will be using the same Jupyter Notebook for Exercises 28 to 34.

1. Import pandas, NumPy, Matplotlib, and seaborn libraries:

```
import pandas as pd
import numpy as np
import matplotlib.pyplot as plt
import seaborn as sns
```

2. Read the data into a pandas DataFrame named **data**:

```
data= pd.read_csv('Churn_Modelling.csv')
data.head(5)
```

You should get the following output:

	CustomerId	CredRate	Geography	Gender	Age	Tenure	Balance	Prod Number	HasCrCard	ActMem	Estimated Salary	Exited
0	15634602	619	France	Female	42.0	2	0.00	1	1	1	101348.88	1
1	15647311	608	Spain	Female	41.0	1	83807.86	1	0	1	112542.58	0
2	15619304	502	France	Female	42.0	8	159660.80	3	1	0	113931.57	1
3	15701354	699	France	Female	39.0	1	0.00	2	0	0	93826.63	0
4	15737888	850	Spain	Female	43.0	2	125510.82	1	1	1	79084.10	0

Figure 7.19: First few rows of the churn modelling data

3. Check the number of rows and columns in the dataset:

```
data.shape
```

The dataset has around 10,000 rows and 12 columns.

This completes the first step of our OSEMN pipeline. Let's now move on to the next step.

Scrubbing the Data

Scrubbing the data typically involves missing value imputation, data type conversion, standardization, and renaming columns. We will perform these steps in the next exercise.

Exercise 29: Imputing Missing Values

After reading the banking data, our task in this exercise is to find any missing values and perform imputation on the missing values. Ensure that you continue using the same Notebook as that used in the preceding exercise:

1. Check for any missing values first using the following code:

    ```
    data.isnull().values.any()
    ```

2. This will give you an output of **True**. So, let's explore the columns that have these missing values. Use the following code:

    ```
    data.isnull().any()
    ```

    You should get the following output:

```
CustomerId          False
CredRate            False
Geography           False
Gender               True
Age                  True
Tenure              False
Balance             False
Prod Number         False
HasCrCard           False
ActMem              False
EstimatedSalary      True
Exited              False
dtype: bool
```

Figure 7.20: Checking for missing values

3. It seems that the columns **Gender**, **Age**, and **EstimatedSalary** have missing values. Use **describe** to explore the data in the **Age** and **EstimatedSalary** columns and then for the entire DataFrame as well.

```
data[["EstimatedSalary","Age"]].describe()
```

	Estimated Salary	Age
count	9996.000000	9994.000000
mean	100074.744083	38.925255
std	57515.774555	10.489248
min	11.580000	18.000000
25%	50974.077500	32.000000
50%	100168.240000	37.000000
75%	149388.247500	44.000000
max	199992.480000	92.000000

Figure 7.21: Description statistics for column EstimatedSalary and Age

```
data.describe()
```

	CustomerId	CredRate	Age	Tenure	Balance	Prod Number	HasCrCard	ActMem	Estimated Salary	Exited
count	1.000000e+04	10000.000000	9994.000000	10000.000000	10000.000000	10000.000000	10000.00000	10000.000000	9996.000000	10000.000000
mean	1.569094e+07	650.528800	38.925255	5.012800	76485.889288	1.530200	0.70550	0.515100	100074.744083	0.203700
std	7.193619e+04	96.653299	10.489248	2.892174	62397.405202	0.581654	0.45584	0.499797	57515.774555	0.402769
min	1.556570e+07	350.000000	18.000000	0.000000	0.000000	1.000000	0.00000	0.000000	11.580000	0.000000
25%	1.562853e+07	584.000000	32.000000	3.000000	0.000000	1.000000	0.00000	0.000000	50974.077500	0.000000
50%	1.569074e+07	652.000000	37.000000	5.000000	97198.540000	1.000000	1.00000	1.000000	100168.240000	0.000000
75%	1.575323e+07	718.000000	44.000000	7.000000	127644.240000	2.000000	1.00000	1.000000	149388.247500	0.000000
max	1.581569e+07	850.000000	92.000000	10.000000	250898.090000	4.000000	1.00000	1.000000	199992.480000	1.000000

Figure 7.22: Description statistics

Note

Since **Gender** is a categorical variable with only two values, we have used only **Age** and **EstimatedSalary** for our **describe** function.

4. From the descriptive statistics we can observe that the column **HaCrCard** column has a min value of 0 and a maximum value of 1. It seems that this variable is a categorical variable. We will learn how to change this kind of variable to categorical, but first, let's check the count of 0s and 1s using the following syntax:

```
data['HasCrCard'].value_counts()
```

You should get an output that shows the number of 1s as 7055 and the number of 0s as 2945. This shows that approximately 70% of the customers have a credit card and 29% of them do not have a credit card.

5. Use the following syntax to find out the total number of missing values:

```
data.isnull().sum()
```

Your output should indicate that the **Gender**, **Age**, and **EstimatedSalary** columns have 4, 6, and 4 missing values, respectively.

6. Find out the percentage of missing values using the following code:

```
round(data.isnull().sum()/len(data)*100,2)
```

Your output should indicate that the missing values constitute 4, 6, and 4 percent of the total values in the **Gender**, **Age**, and **EstimatedSalary** columns, respetively.

7. Check the datatypes of the missing columns:

```
data[["Gender","Age","EstimatedSalary"]].dtypes
```

Your output will be as follows:

```
Gender                object
Age                   float64
EstimatedSalary       float64
dtype: object
```

Figure 7.23: Data type of columns which have missing values

8. Now we need to impute the missing values. We can do that by dropping the rows that have missing values, filling in the missing values with a test statistic (such as mean, mode, or median), or predicting the missing values using a machine learning algorithm. For **EstimatedSalary**, we will fill in the missing values with the mean of the data in that column using the following code:

```
mean_value=data['EstimatedSalary'].mean()
data['EstimatedSalary']=data['EstimatedSalary'].fillna(mean_value)
```

Note

For estimated salary, since the column is a continuous column, we can use the mean of the values for the estimated salary to replace the missing values.

9. For **Gender**, use **value_count()** to see how many instances of each gender are present:

```
data['Gender'].value_counts()
```

Since there are more Males (5453) than Females (4543), we will use the following code to replace the missing values with the gender that occurs most frequently, that is, Male.

```
data['Gender']=data['Gender'].fillna(data['Gender'].value_counts().
idxmax())
```

10. For **Age**, use **mode()**, to get the mode of the data, which is 37, and then replaces the missing values with the mode of the values in the column using the following code.

```
data['Age'].mode()
mode_value=data['Age'].mode()
data['Age']=data['Age'].fillna(mode_value[0])
```

11. Check whether the missing values have been imputed:

```
data.isnull().any()
```

You should get the following output:

```
CustomerId          False
CredRate            False
Geography           False
Gender              False
Age                 False
Tenure              False
Balance             False
Prod Number         False
HasCrCard           False
ActMem              False
EstimatedSalary     False
Exited              False
dtype: bool
```

Figure 7.24: Check for missing values

In this exercise, we first used the **describe()** function to find out the descriptive stats of the data. Then, we learned how to find missing values, and performed missing value imputation for the **EstimatedSalary**, **Gender**, and **Age** columns.

Exercise 30: Renaming Columns and Changing the Data Type

Scrubbing data also involves renaming columns in the right format and can include removing any special characters and spaces in the column names, shifting the target variable either to the extreme left or right for better visibility, and checking whether the data types of the columns are correct. Our goal is to convert the columns into a more human-readable format.

Therefore, in this exercise, we will rename some of the columns, change the data types, and shift the customer ID column to a suitable position:

1. Rename the following columns and check that they have been appropriately renamed as follows:

```
data = data.rename(columns={
                    'CredRate': 'CreditScore',
                    'ActMem' : 'IsActiveMember',
                    'Prod Number': 'NumOfProducts',
                    'Exited':'Churn'
                    })
data.columns
```

You should get the following output:

```
Index(['CreditScore', 'Geography', 'Gender', 'Age', 'Tenure', 'Balance',
       'NumOfProducts', 'HasCrCard', 'IsActiveMember', 'EstimatedSalary',
       'Churn'],
      dtype='object')
```

Figure 7.25: Renamed columns

2. Move the churn column to the right and drop the **CustomerId** column using the following code:

```
data.drop(labels=['CustomerId'], axis=1,inplace = True) data.
drop(labels=['churn'], axis=1,inplace = True)
column_churn = data['Churn']
data.drop(labels=['Churn'], axis=1,inplace = True)
data.insert(len(data.columns), 'Churn', column_churn.values)
```

3. Change the datatype of the **Geography**, **Gender**, **HasCrCard**, **Churn**, and **IsActiveMember** columns to **category** as shown:

```
data["Geography"] = data["Geography"].astype('category')
data["Gender"] = data["Gender"].astype('category')
data["HasCrCard"] = data["HasCrCard"].astype('category')
data["Churn"] = data["Churn"].astype('category')
data["IsActiveMember"] = data["IsActiveMember"].astype('category')
```

4. Now check whether the datatypes have been converted or not:

```
data.dtypes
```

You should get the following output:

```
CreditScore              int64
Geography             category
Gender                category
Age                    float64
Tenure                   int64
Balance                float64
NumOfProducts            int64
HasCrCard             category
IsActiveMember        category
EstimatedSalary        float64
Churn                 category
dtype: object
```

Figure 7.26: Data type of the columns

In this exercise, we successfully renamed a few columns; converted the **Geography**, **Gender**, **HasCrCard**, **Churn**, and **IsActiveMember** columns to the category type; and shifted the customer ID column to the extreme right.

Exploring the Data

Data exploration is one of the most important steps before building a machine learning model. It's important to know the data well before applying any kind of machine learning algorithm. Typically, the data exploration step consists of the following steps: **Statistical overview**, **Correlation**, and **Visualization**. We will discuss these in the following sections.

Statistical Overview

This step typically involves inspecting the data using general descriptive statistics. In a statistical overview, we summarize the data using the central tendency and distribution of the data, and inspect the target variable using mean, count, and other functions studied in previous chapters.

Correlation

The correlation coefficient measures the linear relationship between two variables. It's usually represented by r and varies from +1 to –1. We can interpret the correlation value as given in the following table:

Correlation Value	Interpretation
–1	Perfect negative linear relationship between the two variables
–0.80	Strong negative linear relationship
–0.50	Moderate negative relationship
–0.30	Weak negative relationship
0	No linear relationship
+0.30	Weak positive relationship
+0.50	Moderate positive relationship
+0.70	Strong positive linear relationship
+1	Perfect positive linear relationship between the two variables

Figure 7.27: Correlation coefficient

Note

When finding out the correlation coefficient, one of our assumption is linear relationship. However in reality, there may or may not be any linear relationship between two variables. Hence it is wise to plot your data and visually verify it.

Exercise 31: Obtaining the Statistical Overview and Correlation Plot

In this exercise, we will find out the number of customers that churned using basic exploration techniques. The churn column has two attributes: 0 means that the customer did not churn and 1 implies that the customer churned. We will also plot the correlation matrix, which will give us a basic understanding of the relationship between the target variable and rest of the variables. Ensure that you continue from the previous Notebook:

1. Inspect the target variable to see how many of the customers have churned. Use the following code

   ```
   data['churn'].value_counts(0)
   ```

   The output will tell you that 7963 customers did not churn, whereas 2037 customers churned.

2. Inspect the percentage of customers who left the bank using the following code:

   ```
   data['churn'].value_counts(1)*100
   ```

   This will again give us an output of 79.63 and 20.37 percent corresponding to the customers that did not churn and those that churned, respectively. Hence, you can infer that the proportion of customers that churned is 20.37% (2,037), and the proportion of those that did not churn is 79.63% (7,963).

3. Inspect the percentage of customers that have a credit card using the following code:

   ```
   data['IsActiveMember'].value_counts(1)*100
   ```

   You should get an output of 51.51 for the number of 1s and 48.49 for the number of 0s, respectively, implying that 51% of the customers hold a credit card, whereas 48% do not hold a credit card.

4. Get a statistical overview of the data:

```
data.describe()
```

You should get the following output:

	CreditScore	Age	Tenure	Balance	NumOfProducts	Estimated Salary
count	10000.000000	10000.000000	10000.000000	10000.000000	10000.000000	10000.000000
mean	650.528800	38.924100	5.012800	76485.889288	1.530200	100074.744083
std	96.653299	10.486207	2.892174	62397.405202	0.581654	57504.269099
min	350.000000	18.000000	0.000000	0.000000	1.000000	11.580000
25%	584.000000	32.000000	3.000000	0.000000	1.000000	51002.110000
50%	652.000000	37.000000	5.000000	97198.540000	1.000000	100134.325000
75%	718.000000	44.000000	7.000000	127644.240000	2.000000	149382.097500
max	850.000000	92.000000	10.000000	250898.090000	4.000000	199992.480000

Figure 7.28: Statistical overview of the data

Inspect some of the statistics, such as mean and max in the above figure. These statistics help us answer questions such as the average age, salary, and number of products held by our customers, or the maximum and minimum number of products held by our customer base. These statistics would be useful for the marketing team and senior management.

5. Inspect the mean attributes of customers who churned compared to those who did not churn:

```
summary_churn = data.groupby('Churn')
summary_churn.mean()
```

You should get the following output:

Churn	CreditScore	Age	Tenure	Balance	NumOfProducts	Estimated Salary
0	651.853196	37.411277	5.033279	72745.296779	1.544267	99718.932023
1	645.351497	44.837997	4.932744	91108.539337	1.475209	101465.677531

Figure 7.29: Mean attributes of the customer with respect to churn

From the preceding figure, you can infer that the average credit score of customers that churned is 645.35, and the average age of the customers that churned is 44.83 years. The average balance and the estimated salary of the customers that churned are 911,108.53 USD and 101,465.67 USD, respectively, which is greater than the values for customers that didn't churn.

6. Also, find the median attributes of the customers:

```
summary_churn.median()
```

You should get the following output:

Churn	CreditScore	Age	Tenure	Balance	NumOfProducts	Estimated Salary
0	653	36.0	5	92072.68	2	99645.04
1	646	45.0	5	109349.29	1	102460.84

Figure 7.30: Median attributes of the customer with respect to churn

Note that the median number of products bought by customers that churned is 1.

7. Now use the **seaborn** library to plot the correlation plot using the following code:

```
corr = data.corr()
plt.figure(figsize=(15,8))
sns.heatmap(corr,
            xticklabels=corr.columns.values,
            yticklabels=corr.columns.values,annot=True)
corr
```

The correlation statistics and plot provides us the correlation between our continuous features. It tell us how each of these variables are related to one another.

	Credit Score	Age	Tenure	Balance	NumOfProducts	Estimated Salary
Credit Score	1.000000	-0.004179	0.000842	0.006268	0.012238	-0.001352
Age	-0.004179	1.000000	-0.009996	0.028141	-0.030590	-0.007215
Tenure	0.000842	-0.009996	1.000000	-0.012254	0.013444	0.007407
Balance	0.006268	0.028141	-0.012254	1.000000	-0.304180	0.013129
NumOfProducts	0.012238	-0.030590	0.013444	-0.304180	1.000000	0.014132
Estimated Salary	-0.001352	-0.007215	0.007407	0.013129	0.014132	1.000000

Figure 7.31: Correlation statistics of features

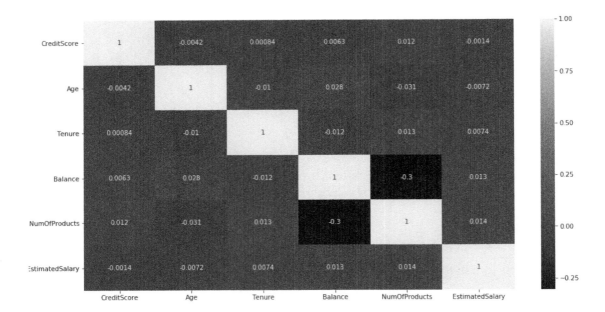

Figure 7.32: Correlation plot of different features

From the correlation plot, it appears that there is a negative (-0.3%) relationship between the number of products purchased and the balance.

> **Note**
>
> A word of warning for interpreting the results of correlation. Correlation does not imply causation. Even if the matrix shows a relationship, do not assume that one variable caused the other. Both may be influenced by a third variable.
>
> Many other interesting observations can be obtained from this analysis. Students are encouraged to find out some more useful insights from the statistical overview. It is always good practice to perform an initial statistical review.

Visualizing the Data

The best way to perform data exploration is to visualize the data to find out how each of the variables are interacting with each other. As pointed out by **Cleveland**, "Data analysis without data visualization is no data analysis." In statistics, the use of graphical methods to reveal the distribution or/and statistics of a selected variable is popularly known as **Exploratory Data Analysis** (**EDA**).

EDA was promoted by **John Tukey** to encourage statisticians to explore data, and possibly formulate hypotheses that could lead to new data collection and experiments. The following table tells us the different kinds of visualization that can be used for Univariate and Bivariate Data.

EDA for Univariate Data	EDA for Bivariate Data

1. Distribution Analysis
    a. Bar Chart
    b. Histogram
2. Deviation Analysis
    a. Boxplot
3. Part Whole Analysis
    a. Pie Chart
    b. Pareto Chart
4. Trend Patterns
    a. Line Graph
	1. Two Categorical Variables Analysis
	    a. Mosaic Plot
	    b. Trellis Bar chart
	2. Two Continuous Variables
	    a. Scatter Plot
	    b. Scatter Plot Matrix
	    c. Trellis Scatter Plots
	3. Part Whole Analysis
	    a. Pie Chart
	    b. Pareto Chart
	4. One Categorical and One Continuous
	    a. Trellis Box Plot/Histogram

Figure 7.33: EDA graphs for univariate and bivariate data

Note

Because of the scope of the book, we will not be covering all the EDA techniques. Students are encouraged to explore them further.

Exercise 32: Performing Exploratory Data Analysis (EDA)

In this exercise, we will perform EDA, which includes univariate analysis and bivariate analysis on our **Churn_Modelling.csv** dataset. Continue with the same Notebook as used in the preceding exercises.

1. Let's begin with univariate analysis. Plot the distribution graph of the customers for the **EstimatedSalary**, **Age**, and **Balance** variables using the following code:

```
f, axes = plt.subplots(ncols=3, figsize=(15, 6))
sns.distplot(data.EstimatedSalary, kde=True, color="darkgreen",
ax=axes[0]).set_title('EstimatedSalary')
axes[0].set_ylabel('No of Customers')

sns.distplot(data.Age, kde=True, color="darkblue", ax=axes[1]).set_
```

```
title('Age')
axes[1].set_ylabel('No of Customers')
sns.distplot(data.Balance, kde=True, color="maroon", ax=axes[2]).set_
title('Balance')
axes[2].set_ylabel('No of Customers')
```

Your output should look as follows:

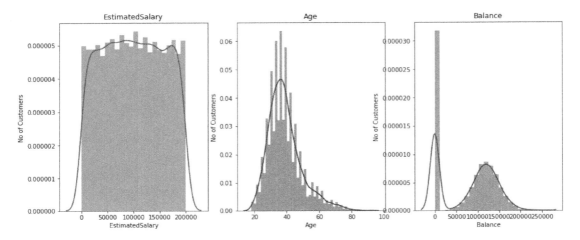

Figure 7.34: Univariate analysis

The following are the observations from the univariate analysis:

EstimatedSalary: The distribution of the estimated salary seems to be a plateau distribution.

Age: This has a normal distribution that is right skewed. Most customers lie in the range of 30-45 years of age.

Balance: This has a bimodal distribution. A considerable number of customers with a low balance are there, which seems to be an outlier.

2. Now we'll move on to bivariate analysis. Inspect whether there is a difference in churn for gender using bivariate analysis. Use the following code:

```
plt.figure(figsize=(15,4))
p=sns.countplot(y="Gender", hue='Churn', data=data,palette="Set2")
legend = p.get_legend()
legend_txt = legend.texts
legend_txt[0].set_text("No Churn")
legend_txt[1].set_text("Churn")
p.set_title('Customer Churn Distribution by Gender')
```

Your output should look as follows:

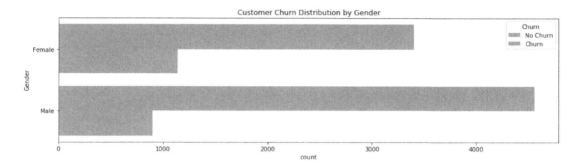

Figure 7.35: Number of customer churned by gender

You will observe that comparatively, more female customers have churned. Also, the amount of churn for customers with 3-4 products is higher.

3. Plot **Geography** versus **Churn**:

```
plt.figure(figsize=(15,4))
p=sns.countplot(x='Geography', hue='Churn',data=data, palette="Set2")
legend = p.get_legend()
legend_txt = legend.texts
legend_txt[0].set_text("No Churn")
legend_txt[1].set_text("Churn")
p.set_title('Customer Geography Distribution')
```

Your should get the following output:

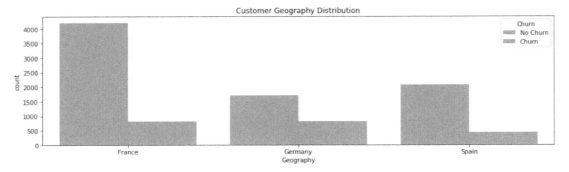

Figure 7.36: Number of customer churned by geography

Note that the difference between number of customers that churned and those that did not churn is lesser for Germany and Spain is comparison with France. Germany has the highest number of customers compared to other countries.

4. Plot **NumOfProducts** versus **Churn**:

```
plt.figure(figsize=(15,4))
p=sns.countplot(x='NumOfProducts', hue='Churn',data=data, palette="Set2")
legend = p.get_legend()
legend_txt = legend.texts
legend_txt[0].set_text("No Churn")
legend_txt[1].set_text("Churn")
p.set_title('Customer Distribution by Product')
```

Your should get the following output:

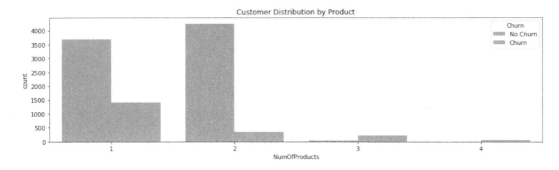

Figure 7.37: Number of customer churned by product

5. Inspect **Churn** versus **Age**:

```
plt.figure(figsize=(15,4))
ax=sns.kdeplot(data.loc[(data['Churn'] == 0),'Age'] , color=sns.color_
palette("Set2")[0],shade=True,label='no churn')
ax=sns.kdeplot(data.loc[(data['Churn'] == 1),'Age'] , color=sns.color_
palette("Set2")[1],shade=True, label='churn')
ax.set(xlabel='Customer Age', ylabel='Frequency')
plt.title('Customer Age - churn vs no churn')
```

Your should get the following output:

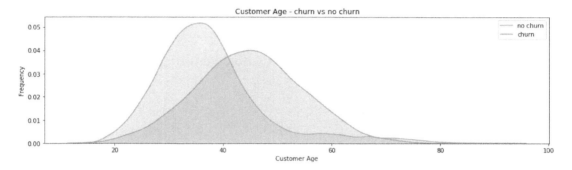

Figure 7.38: Distribution of customer age (churn versus no churn)

Customers in the 35 to 45 age group seem to churn more. As the age of the customers increases, they usually churn more.

6. Plot **Balance** versus **Churn**:

```
plt.figure(figsize=(15,4))
ax=sns.kdeplot(data.loc[(data['Churn'] == 0),'Balance'] , color=sns.color_
palette("Set2")[0],shade=True,label='no churn')
ax=sns.kdeplot(data.loc[(data['Churn'] == 1),'Balance'] , color=sns.color_
palette("Set2")[1],shade=True, label='churn')
ax.set(xlabel='Customer Balance', ylabel='Frequency')
plt.title('Customer Balance - churn vs no churn')
```

Your should get the following output:

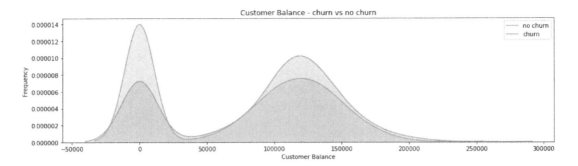

Figure 7.39: Distribution of customer balance (churn versus no churn)

Customers with a negative-to-low balance churn less than customers with a balance between 75,000–150,000.

7. Plot `CreditScore` versus `Churn`:

```
plt.figure(figsize=(15,4))
ax=sns.kdeplot(data.loc[(data['Churn'] == 0),'CreditScore'] , color=sns.
color_palette("Set2")[0],shade=True,label='no churn')
ax=sns.kdeplot(data.loc[(data['Churn'] == 1),'CreditScore'] , color=sns.
color_palette("Set2")[1],shade=True, label='churn')
ax.set(xlabel='CreditScore', ylabel='Frequency')
plt.title('Customer CreditScore - churn vs no churn')
```

Your should get the following output:

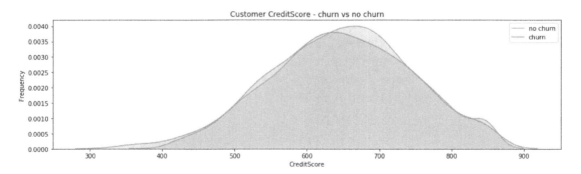

Figure 7.40: Distribution of customer credit score (churn versus no churn)

8. Plot **Balance** versus **NumOfProducts** by **Churn**:

```
plt.figure(figsize=(16,4))
p=sns.barplot(x='NumOfProducts',y='Balance',hue='Churn',data=data,
palette="Set2")
p.legend(loc='upper right')
legend = p.get_legend()
legend_txt = legend.texts
legend_txt[0].set_text("No Churn")
legend_txt[1].set_text("Churn")
p.set_title('Number of Product VS Balance')
```

Your should get the following output:

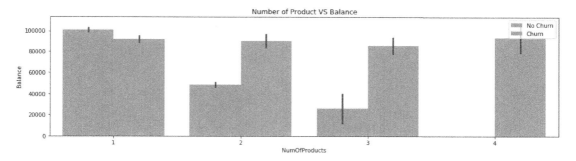

Figure 7.41: Number of product versus balance by churn

From the above figure, it appears that as the number of products increases, the balance for churned customers remains very high.

Activity 13: Performing OSE of OSEMN

You are working as a data scientist for a large telecom company. Your company's head of marketing wants to know why customers are churning, and wants to prepare a plan to reduce customer churn. For this purpose, he has provided you with some data regarding the current bill amount of customers (**Current Bill Amt**), the average calls made by each customer (**Avg Calls**), average calls made by the customers during the weekdays (**Avg Calls Weekdays**), how long the account has been active (**Account Age**), and the average number of days the customer has defaulted on bill payment (**Avg Days Delinquent**). You are asked to find the reason behind customer churn.

Your task is to explore the data and find some insights that will help the marketing head to better strategize his marketing campaign for the next quarter. Use the OSE technique from OSEMN to carry out an initial exploration of the data. Follow these steps:

1. Import the necessary libraries.

2. Read the dataset using pandas **read.csv** and look at the first few rows of the dataset. You should get the following output:

	Target Churn	Target Code	Current Bill Amt	Avg Calls	Avg Calls Weekdays	Account Age	Percent Increase MOM	Acct Plan Subtype	Complaint Code	Avg Days Delinquent	Current TechSupComplaints	Current Days OpenWorkOrders	Equipment Age
0	No Churn	0	14210	17950.000000	30297.0000	24	-0.334193	Gold	Billing Problem	6.2	0	0.0	8
1	Churn	1	14407	0.000000	0.0000	28	0.000000	Silver	Moving	1.0	0	0.0	17
2	Churn	1	12712	204.666667	10393.6667	23	0.000000	Gold	Billing Problem	17.6	0	0.0	23
3	No Churn	0	13807	15490.333300	41256.3333	39	0.148986	Silver	Billing Problem	0.0	0	0.0	17
4	No Churn	0	3805	5075.000000	12333.3333	23	-0.686047	Gold	Billing Problem	3.8	0	0.0	10

Figure 7.42: First few rows of read.csv

3. Check the length and shape of the data. The length should be 4708 and the shape should be (4708, 15).

4. Rename all the columns in a readable format. Convert all the columns containing names with a space to _, for example, rename **Target Code** to **Target_Code**. Your column names should finally look as follows:

```
Index(['Target_Churn', 'Target_Code', 'Current_Bill_Amt', 'Avg_Calls',
       'Avg_Calls_Weekdays', 'Account_Age', 'Percent_Increase_MOM',
       'Acct_Plan_Subtype', 'Complaint_Code', 'Avg_Days_Delinquent',
       'Current_TechSupComplaints', 'Current_Days_OpenWorkOrders',
       'Equipment_Age', 'Condition_of_Current_Handset',
       'Avg_Hours_WorkOrderOpenned'],
      dtype='object')
```

Figure 7.43: Column names after renaming

> Note
>
> You can use the following code for the replacement: **data.columns=data.columns.str.replace(' ','_')**

5. Check the descriptive statistics of the data and of the categorical variable.

6. Change the data type of **Target_Code**, **Condition_of_Current_Handset**, and **Current_TechSupComplaints** columns from continuous to categorical object type.

7. Check for any missing values.

> **Hint**
>
> Use count to replace missing values for categorical values and mean for continuous variables. Columns to be imputed are Complaint_Code and Condition_of_Current_Handset.

8. Perform data exploration by initially exploring the customer **Target_Churn** variable. You should get the following summary:

Target_Churn	Target_Code	Current_Bill_Amt	Avg_Calls	Avg_Calls_Weekdays	Account_Age	Percent_Increase_MOM	Avg_Days_Delinquent	Current_Days_Op
Churn	1.0	20182.709226	9348.878298	37524.030899	25.418452	-0.281309	19.075339	
No Churn	0.0	19494.510120	9194.885309	38698.530221	26.704254	0.255769	9.144444	

Figure 7.44: Summary of Target_Churn

9. Find the correlation among different variables and explain the results. You should get the following plots:

	Target_Code	Current_Bill_Amt	Avg_Calls	Avg_Calls_Weekdays	Account_Age	Percent_Increase_MOM	Avg_Days_Delinquent	C
Target_Code	1.000000	0.019995	0.007375	-0.014987	-0.089890	-0.059899	0.460092	
Current_Bill_Amt	0.019995	1.000000	0.352535	0.428040	0.003292	-0.015588	0.024285	
Avg_Calls	0.007375	0.352535	1.000000	0.727226	-0.023758	-0.040899	0.019407	
Avg_Calls_Weekdays	-0.014987	0.428040	0.727226	1.000000	0.029957	-0.044496	0.017134	
Account_Age	-0.089890	0.003292	-0.023758	0.029957	1.000000	-0.004022	-0.047542	
Percent_Increase_MOM	-0.059899	-0.015588	-0.040899	-0.044496	-0.004022	1.000000	0.049768	
Avg_Days_Delinquent	0.460092	0.024285	0.019407	0.017134	-0.047542	0.049768	1.000000	
Current_Days_OpenWorkOrders	0.002891	0.076418	0.078428	0.065318	-0.026270	-0.003013	-0.001686	
Equipment_Age	0.042373	-0.040732	-0.099348	-0.103769	0.073503	-0.003819	0.014047	
Avg_Hours_WorkOrderOpenned	0.002611	0.016852	0.013441	0.013577	0.005059	-0.008848	0.000168	

Figure 7.45: Correlation statistics of the variables

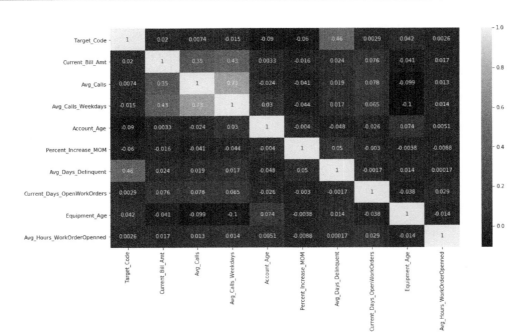

Figure 7.46: Correlation plot of different features

> **Hint**
>
> Correlation is only obtained for continuous variables, not categorical variables.

10. Perform univariate and bivariate analysis.

For univariate analysis, use the following columns: `Avg_Calls_Weekdays`, `Avg_Calls`, and `Current_Bill_Amt`. You should get the following plots:

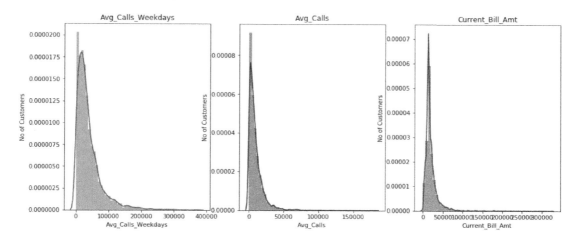

Figure 7.47: Univariate Analysis

For Bivariate Analysis, you should get the following plots:

Plot of `Complaint_Code` vs `Target_Churn`:

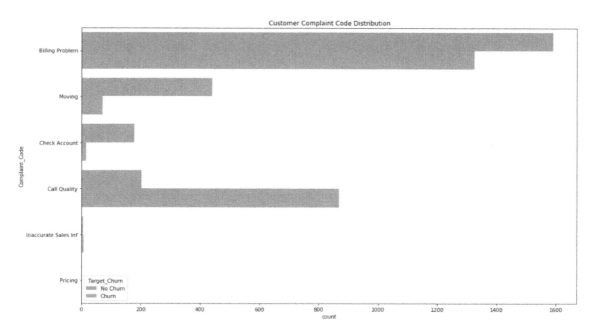

Figure 7.48: Customer complaint code distribution by churn

Plot of **Acct_Plan_Subtype** versus **Target_Churn**:

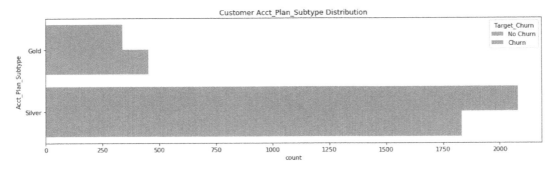

Figure 7.49: Customer account plan subtype distribution by churn

Plot of **Current_TechSupComplaints** versus **Target_Churn**:

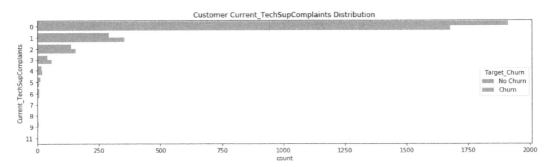

Figure 7.50: Customer technical support complaints distribution by churn

Plot of **Avg_Days_Delinquent** versus **Target_Code**:

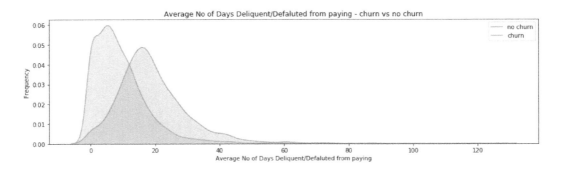

Figure 7.51: Distribution of average number of days delinquent by churn

Plot of **Account_Age** versus **Target_Code**:

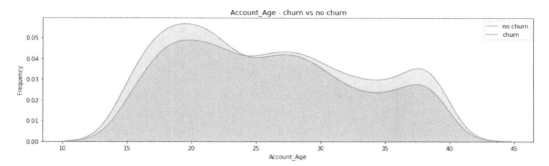

Figure 7.52: Distribution of account age by churn

Plot of **Percent_Increase_MOM** vs **Target_Code**.

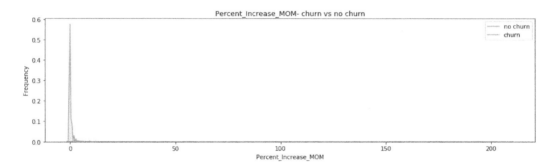

Figure 7.53: Distribution of percentage increase month on month usage by churn/no churn

> **Note**
>
> The solution for this activity can be found on page 350.

Modeling the Data

Modeling the data not only includes building your machine learning model but also selecting important features/columns that will go into your model. This section will be divided into two parts: **Feature Selection** and **Model building**.

Feature Selection

Before building our first machine learning model, we have to do some feature selection. Imagine a scenario where you have a large number of columns and you want to perform prediction. Not all the features will have an impact on your prediction model. Having irrelevant features can reduce the accuracy of your model, especially when using algorithms such as linear and logistic regression.

The benefits of feature selection are as follows:

- **Reduces training time**: Fewer columns mean less data, which in turn makes the algorithm run more quickly.

- **Reduces overfitting**: Removing irrelevant columns makes your algorithm less prone to noise, thereby reducing overfitting.

- **Improves the accuracy**: It improves the accuracy of your machine learning model.

Methods for selecting features are as follows:

- **Univariate feature selection**: This works by selecting the best feature based on the univariate statistical tests. It finds features that have the strongest relationship with the output variable.

- **Recursive feature selection**: This works by recursively removing features and building a machine learning model based on the features remaining. It then uses the model's accuracy to find the combination of features that contribute most to predicting the target.

- **Principal component analysis**: Principal component analysis is a variable reduction procedure. It uses linear algebra to transform the data into a compressed form.

- **Tree-based feature selection**: Tree-based estimators such as random forest, bagging, and boosting can be used to compute feature importance, which in turn can be used to discard irrelevant features.

> **Note**
>
> A detailed explanation of the feature selection method will be covered in the next chapter.

Exercise 33: Performing Feature Selection

In this exercise, we will be performing feature selection using a tree-based selection method that performs well on classification tasks. Ensure that you use the same Notebook as the one used for the preceding exercise:

1. Import **RandomForestClassifier** and **train_test_split** from the **sklearn** library:

```
from sklearn.ensemble import RandomForestClassifier
from sklearn.model_selection import train_test_split
```

2. Encode of the categorical variable using the following code:

```
data.dtypes
data["Geography"] = data["Geography"].astype('category').cat.codes
data["Gender"] = data["Gender"].astype('category').cat.codes
```

3. Split the data into training and testing sets as follows:

```
target = 'Churn'
X = data.drop('Churn', axis=1)
y=data[target]

X_train, X_test, y_train, y_test = train_test_split(X,y,test_size=0.15,
random_state=123, stratify=y)
```

4. Fit the model using the random forest classifier for feature selection. Use the following code:

```
forest=RandomForestClassifier(n_estimators=500,random_state=1)
forest.fit(X_train,y_train)
```

> **Note**
>
> The random forest classifier is used here for feature selection. It gives good results for classification-based problems.

5. Call the random forest **feature_importances_** attribute to find the important features and store it in a variable named **importances**:

```
importances=forest.feature_importances_
```

6. Create a variable named **features** to store all the columns, except the target variable, **Churn**. Sort the important features present in the **importances** variable using the numpy **argsort** function:

```
features = data.drop(['Churn'],axis=1).columns
indices = np.argsort(importances)[::-1]
```

7. Plot the important features obtained from the random forest using Matplotlib's **plt** attribute:

```
plt.figure(figsize=(15,4))
plt.title("Feature importances using Random Forest")
plt.bar(range(X_train.shape[1]), importances[indices],
        color="r", align="center")
plt.xticks(range(X_train.shape[1]), features[indices],
rotation='vertical',fontsize=15)
plt.xlim([-1, X_train.shape[1]])
plt.show()
```

You should get the following plot:

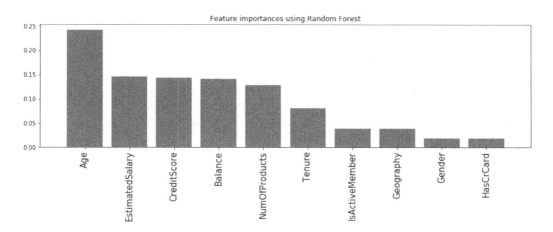

Figure 7.54: Feature importance using random forest

From the preceding figure, you can see that the five most important features selected from tree-based feature selection are **Age**, **EstimatedSalary**, **CreditScore**, **Balance**, and **NumOfProducts**.

Model Building

The next step is the OSEMN pipeline is to build a model. This includes trying out different kinds of algorithms to build our prediction model.

Exercise 34: Building a Logistic Regression Model

As a data scientist, you were able to help both your senior management and the marketing team to explain the key variables affecting customer churn. Through EDA, your marketing team understood the key reasons for customer churn. With their expectations very high, they want you to predict customer churn so that they can focus on customers who might churn.

We will be using logistic regression as the base model for our churn prediction because of its easy interpretability.

1. We will import the **statsmodel** package and select only the top five features that we got from the previous exercise to fit our model. Use the following code:

    ```
    import statsmodels.api as sm
    top5_features =
    ['Age','EstimatedSalary','CreditScore','Balance','NumOfProducts']
    logReg = sm.Logit(y_train, X_train[top5_features])
    logistic_regression = logReg.fit()
    ```

    > **Note**
    >
    > **statsmodels** is a Python module that provides classes and functions for the estimation of many different statistical models, as well as for conducting statistical tests and statistical data exploration.

2. Once the model has been fitted, obtain the summary and our parameters:

    ```
    logistic_regression.summary
    logistic_regression.params
    ```

    You will get the following output:

    ```
    Age                 0.048335
    EstimatedSalary    -0.000001
    CreditScore        -0.004470
    Balance             0.000003
    NumOfProducts      -0.361678
    dtype: float64
    ```

    Figure 7.55: Coefficients for each of the features

3. Create a function to compute the coefficients:

    ```
    coef = logistic_regression.params
    def y (coef,Age,EstimatedSalary,CreditScore,Balance,NumOfProducts) :
        return coef[0]*Age+ coef[1]*EstimatedSalary+coef[2]*
    CreditScore+coef[1]*Balance+coef[2]*NumOfProducts
    ```

4. Calculate the chance of a customer churning by inputting the following values:

Age: 50, EstimatedSalary: 100,000, CreditScore:600, Balance:100,000, NumOfProducts: 2

Use the following code

```
import numpy as np
y1 = y(coef, 50, 100000, 600,100000,2)
p = np.exp(y1) / (1+np.exp(y1))
p
```

Your output will be approximately 0.38, implying that a customer who is 50 *yrs* of Age, having an estimated salary of $100,000, a credit score of 600, balance of $100,000, and who has purchased 2 products would have a 38.23% likelihood of churning.

5. In the previous steps, we learnt how to use the **statsmodel** package. In this step, we will implement scikit-learn's **logisticRegression** to build our classifier and predict on the test data to find out the accuracy of our model:

```
from sklearn.linear_model import LogisticRegression
```

6. Fit the logistic regression model on the partitioned training data that was prepared previously.

```
clf = LogisticRegression(random_state=0, solver='lbfgs').fit(X_train[top5_
features], y_train)
```

7. Call the **predict** and **predict_proba** functions on the test data.

```
clf.predict(X_test[top5_features])
clf.predict_proba(X_test[top5_features])
```

You will get the following output:

```
array([[0.61565033, 0.38434967],
       [0.76717157, 0.23282843],
       [0.78137389, 0.21862611],
       ...,
       [0.552548  , 0.447452  ],
       [0.85311964, 0.14688036],
       [0.75851722, 0.24148278]])
```

Figure 7.56: Predicted probability of the test data with top 5 features

8. Calculate the accuracy of the model by calling the **score** function.

```
clf.score(X_test[top5_features], y_test)
```

Your output will be 0.79.

> **Note**
>
> We used **lbfgs** as an optimization algorithm that approximates Broyden–Fletcher–Goldfarb–Shanno algorithm and is recommended for a smaller dataset. More details can be found on the scikit-learn documentation: https://scikit-learn.org/stable/modules/linear_model.html.

Congratulations! You have successfully implemented logistic regression using the **statsmodel** package. The coefficients of the regression model were obtained in step 2, the logistic regression equation was created in step 3, and the probability for a customer to churn was calculated using the sigmoid function in step 4. Lastly, we used sklearn's logistic regression to predict our test data and scored an accuracy of 79%, which implied that our model was able to accurately predict 79% of the test data correctly. We will study more about how to check the accuracy of a model in the next lessson.

Interpreting the Data

The last part of our analysis is interpreting our data, which is summarizing the insights that we have obtained from our analysis:

- The number of customers that churned is 20.37% (2,037) and that number that did not churn out is 79.63% (7,963).

- Overall, the average credit score of customer who churned is 645.35 and the average age of the customers who churned is 44.83 years.

- The average balance and the estimated salary of the customers who churned are 911,108.53 and 101,465.67 respectively, which is greater than customers who didn't churn.

- The median number of products purchased by customers who churned is 1.

- Customer age and churn are 29% positively correlated.

- Balance and churn are 12% positively correlated.

- Number of products and Balance are 30% negatively correlated.

- The difference between churn and non-churn customers in Germany and Spain is less than in France.

- Comparatively, more female customers have churned. The amount of churn is greater for customers with 3-4 products.

- Customers within the 35-45 age group seem to churn more. As the age of customers increases, they usually churn more.

- The amount of churn is less with customers with a negative-to-low balance compared to customers having a balance of 75,000–150,000.

- The most important features selected from tree-based feature selection are `Age`, `EstimatedSalary`, `CreditScore`, `Balance`, and `NumOfProducts`.

Activity 14: Performing MN of OSEMN

You are working as a data scientist for a large telecoms company. Your company's head of marketing wants to know the reasons why customers are churning. He wants to prepare a plan to reduce customer churn and has given you the task of finding the reason behind customer churn.

After you have reported your initial findings to the marketing team, they want you to build a machine learning model that can predict customer churn. With your results, the marketing team can send out discount coupons to customers who might otherwise churn. Use the MN technique from OSEMN to construct your model

> **Note**
>
> We will be using the results of our previous Notebook in this activity.

1. Import the necessary libraries.

2. Encode the `Acct_Plan_Subtype` and `Complaint_Code` columns using `the.astype('category').cat.codes` command.

3. Split the data into training and testing sets.

4. Perform feature selection using the random forest classifier. You should get the following output:

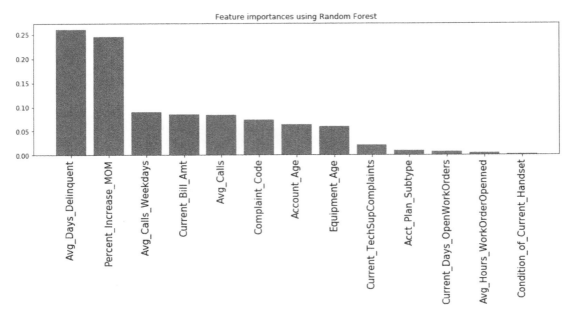

Figure 7.57: Feature importance using random forest

5. Select the top seven features and save them in a variable named **top7_features**. fit a

6. Fit a logistic regression using the **statsmodel** package.

7. Find out the probability that a customer will churn when the following data is used: **Avg_Days_Delinquent**: 40, **Percent_Increase_MOM**: 5, **Avg_Calls_Weekdays**: 39000, **Current_Bill_Amt**: 12000, **Avg_Calls**: 9000, **Complaint_Code**: 0, and **Account_Age**: 17

The given customer should have a 81.939% likelihood of churning.

> **Note**
>
> The solution for this activity can be found on page 356.

Summary

Predicting customer churn is one of the most common use cases in marketing analytics. Churn prediction not only helps marketing teams to better strategize their marketing campaigns, but also helps organizations to focus their resources wisely.

In this chapter, we explored how to use the data science pipeline for any machine learning problem. We also learned the intuition behind using logistic regression and saw how it is different from linear regression.

We looked at the structure of the data by reading it using a pandas DataFrame. We then used data scrubbing techniques such as missing value imputation, renaming columns, and datatype manipulation to prepare our data for data exploration.

We implemented various data visualization techniques, such as univariate, bivariate, and a correlation plot, which enabled us to find useful insights from the data.

Feature selection is another important part of data modeling. We used a tree-based classifier to select important features for our machine learning model. Finally, we implemented logistic regression to find out the likelihood of customer churn.

In the next chapter, we will learn how to evaluate our model, how to tune our model, and how to apply other more powerful machine learning algorithms.

8

Fine-Tuning Classification Algorithms

Learning Objectives

By the end of this chapter, you will be able to:

- Use some of the most common classification algorithms from the scikit-learn machine learning library
- Describe the logic behind tree-based models
- Choose the performance metrics required for classification problems
- Optimize and evaluate the best classification algorithm for customer churn prediction

This chapter covers other classification algorithms such as support vector machines, decision trees, random forest, and explains how to evaluate them.

Introduction

In the previous chapter, you learned about the most common data science pipeline: **OSEMN**. You also learned how to pre-process, explore, model, and finally, interpret data. In this chapter, you will learn how to evaluate the performance of the various models and choose the most appropriate one. Choosing an appropriate machine learning model is an art that requires experience, and each algorithm has its own advantages and disadvantages.

Picking the right performance metrics, optimizing, fine-tuning, and evaluating the model is an important part of building any supervised machine learning model. We will start by using the most common Python machine learning API, scikit-learn, to build our logistic regression model, then we will learn different classification algorithm, and the intuition behind them, and finally, we will learn how to optimize, evaluate, and choose the best model.

Support Vector Machines

When dealing with data that is linearly separable, the goal of the **Support Vector Machine** (**SVM**) learning algorithm is to find the boundary between classes so that there are fewer misclassification errors. However, the problem is that there could be several decision boundaries (B1, B2), as you can see in the following figure:

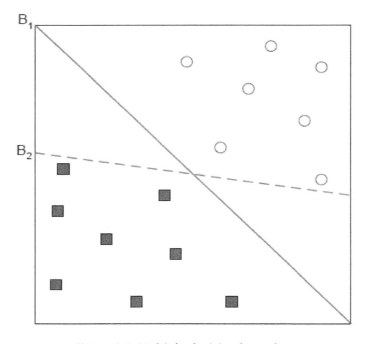

Figure 8.1: Multiple decision boundary

As a result, the question arises as to which of the boundaries is better, and how to define *better*. The solution is to use margin as the optimization objective.

The objective of the SVM algorithm is to maximize the margin. The margin of a linear classifier is to increase the width of the boundary before hitting a data point. The algorithm first finds out the width of the hyperplane and then maximizes the margin. It chooses the decision boundary that has the maximum margin. So, for instance in the above figure, it chooses B_i:

> **Note**
>
> In geometry, a hyperplane is a subspace whose dimension is one less than that of its ambient space.

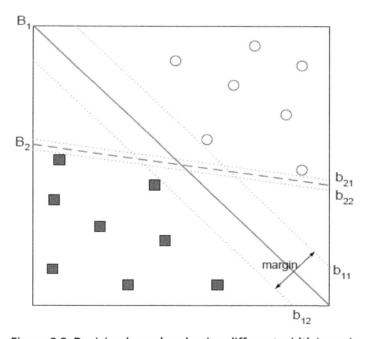

Figure 8.2: Decision boundary having different width/margin

The following are the advantages and disadvantages of the SVM algorithm:

Advantages

- SVMs are effective when dealing with high-dimensional data, where the number of dimensions is more than the number of training samples.

- SVMs are known for their use of the kernel function, making it a very versatile algorithm.

> **Note**
>
> Kernel methods owe their name to the use of kernel functions, which enable them to operate in a high-dimensional space.

Disadvantages

- SVMs do not calculate probability directly, and instead use a five-fold cross validation to calculate probability

- With high-dimensional data, it is important to choose the kernel function and regularization term, which can make the process very slow.

Intuition Behind Maximum Margin

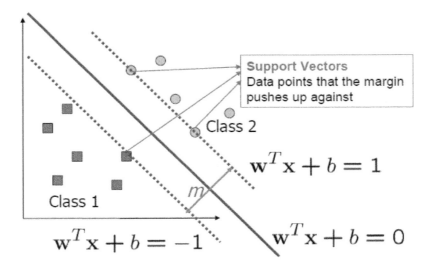

Figure 8.3: Geometrical interpretation of maximum margin

The logic behind having a large margin in the case of an SVM is that they have a lower generalization error as compared to small margins, which can result in overfitted data.

Let's consider the positive and negative hyperplane as follows:

$$w^T x_{pos} + b_0 = 1$$

$$w^T x_{neg} + b_1 = -1$$

Figure 8.4: Positive and negative hyperplane equation

Subtracting the above two equations, we get the following:

$$w^T (x_{pos} - x_{neg}) = 2$$

Figure 8.5: Combined equation of two separating hyperplane

Normalizing the equation by the vector w, we get the following:

$$||w|| = \sqrt{\sum_{i=1}^{m} w_i^2}$$

Figure 8.6: Normalized equation

We reduce the preceding equation as follows:

$$margin = \frac{w^T (x_{pos} - x_{neg})}{||w||} = \frac{2}{||w||}$$

Figure 8.7: Equation for margin m

Now, the **objective function** is obtained by maximizing the margin within the constraint that the decision boundary should classify all the points correctly.

$$w^T x_i + b_0 \geq 1 \quad if \ y_i = 1$$

$$w^T x_i + b_0 \leq -1 \quad if \ y_i = -1$$

Figure 8.8: Equation for separating the data points on a hyperplane

Linearly Inseparable Cases

With linearly inseparable cases, such as that illustrated in the following figure, we cannot use a hard-margin classifier. The solution is to introduce a new kind of classifier, known as a soft-margin classifier, using the slack variable ξ.

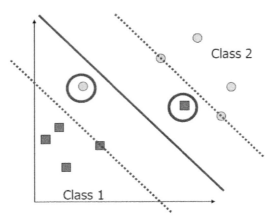

Figure 8.9: Linearly inseparable data pints

> **Note**
>
> Hard margin refers to the fitting of a model with zero errors; hence we cannot use a hard-margin classifier for the preceding figure. A soft margin, on the other hand, allows the fitting of a model with some error, as highlighted by the points circled in blue in the preceding figure.

A soft margin SVM works by:

1. Introducing the slack variable
2. Relaxing the constraints

3. Penalizing the relaxation

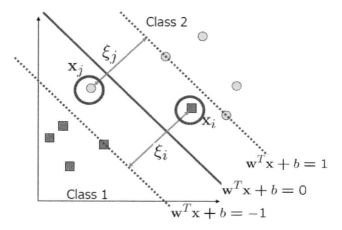

Figure 8.10: Using slack variable ξ for linearly inseparable data

The linear constraints can be changed by adding the slack variable to our equation in figure 8.x as:

$$w^T x_i + b_0 \geq 1 - \xi_i \quad if\ y_i = 1$$

$$w^T x_i + b_0 \leq -1 + \xi_i \quad if\ y_i = -1$$

$$for\ i = 1 \dots \dots N\ where\ N\ is\ the\ no\ of\ sample$$

Figure 8.11: Linear constraints for maximizing margin with slack variable ξ

The **objective function** for linearly inseparable data points is obtained by minimizing the following:

$$\frac{1}{2}||w||^2 + C\left(\sum_i \xi_i\right)$$

Figure 8.12: Objective function to be minimized

Here C is the penalty cost parameter (regularization).

Linearly Inseparable Cases Using Kernel

In the preceding example, we saw how we can use a soft margin SVM to classify our datasets using the slack variable. However, there can be scenarios where it is too hard to separate data. For example, in the following figure, it would be impossible to have a decision boundary using the slack variable and a linear hyperplane:

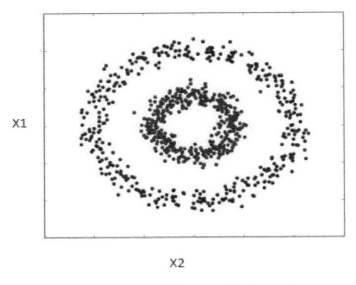

X1

X2

Figure 8.13: Linearly inseparable data points

In this scenario, we can use the concept of a kernel, which creates a nonlinear combination of original features (x_1, x_2) to project to a higher-dimensional space via a mapping function, φ, to make it linearly separable:

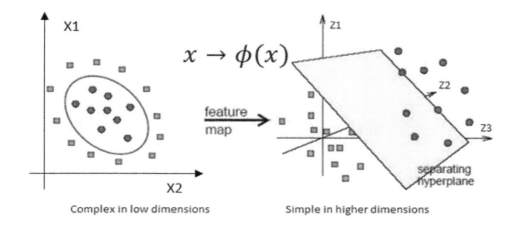

$$\phi(x_1, x_2) = (Z_1, Z_2, Z_3) = (x_1, x_2, x_1^2, x_2^2)$$

Figure 8.14: Geometric interpretation and equation for projection from low to high dimension

The problem with this explicit feature mapping is that the dimensionality of the feature can be very high, which makes it hard to represent it explicitly in memory. This is mitigated using the kernel-trick. **kernel-trick** basically replaces the dot product $x_i^T x_j$ with a kernel $\varphi\, x_i^T \varphi(x_j)$, which can be defined as follows:

$$\varkappa(x_i, x_j) = \phi(x_i)^T \phi(x_j)$$

Figure 8.15: Kernel function

There are different types of kernel functions, namely:

- Linear kernel: $\varkappa(x_i, x_j) = (x_i, x_j) = (x_i)^T(x_j)$

- Polynomial kernel (degree d): $\varkappa(x_i, x_j) = (x_i^T x_j + 1)^d$

- Gaussian kernel: $\varkappa(x_i, x_j) = exp\left(-\dfrac{\|x_i - x_j\|^2}{2\sigma^2}\right)$

  This is also represented as $\varkappa(x_i, x_j) = exp\left(-\gamma\|x_i - x_j\|^2\right)$

  Where $\gamma = \dfrac{1}{2\sigma^2}$ is a free parameter to be optimized, also known as gamma.

Figure 8.16: Different kernel functions

A kernel can also be interpreted as a similarity function and lies between 0 (an exactly dissimilar sample) and 1 (an exactly similar sample).

In scikit-learn, the following kernel functions are available:

linear: $\langle x, x'\rangle$.
polynomial: $(\gamma\langle x, x'\rangle + r)^d$. d is specified by keyword `degree`, r by `coef0`.
rbf: $exp(-\gamma\|x - x'\|^2)$. γ is specified by keyword `gamma`, must be greater than 0.
sigmoid $(\tanh(\gamma\langle x, x'\rangle + r))$, where r is specified by `coef0`.

Figure 8.17: Different kernel functions implemented in scikit-learn

Exercise 35: Training an SVM Algorithm Over a Dataset

In this exercise, we will be using the Titanic dataset named **train.csv** placed in **Lesson08** folder on GitHub. This dataset contains passenger information such as age, sex, class, and so on, and tells us whether the passenger survived. Our objective is to use this information to find out whether a given passenger is likely to survive (**0** means the passenger died and **1** means the passenger survived). We will use the SVM algorithm to build our model.

1. Import pandas, NumPy, **train_test_split**, **cross_val_score**, and **svm**, from the **sklearn** library:

```
import pandas as pd
from sklearn.model_selection import train_test_split
from sklearn import svm
from sklearn.model_selection import cross_val_score
import numpy as np
```

2. Read the dataset into a DataFrame named **titanic_data** using pandas, as shown below, and look at the first few rows of the data:

```
titanic_data=pd.read_csv(r"train.csv")
titanic_data.head()
```

Your output will look as follows:

	PassengerId	Survived	Pclass	Name	Sex	Age	SibSp	Parch	Ticket	Fare	Cabin	Embarked
0	1	0	3	Braund, Mr. Owen Harris	male	22.0	1	0	A/5 21171	7.2500	NaN	S
1	2	1	1	Cumings, Mrs. John Bradley (Florence Briggs Th...	female	38.0	1	0	PC 17599	71.2833	C85	C
2	3	1	3	Heikkinen, Miss. Laina	female	26.0	0	0	STON/O2. 3101282	7.9250	NaN	S
3	4	1	1	Futrelle, Mrs. Jacques Heath (Lily May Peel)	female	35.0	1	0	113803	53.1000	C123	S
4	5	0	3	Allen, Mr. William Henry	male	35.0	0	0	373450	8.0500	NaN	S

Figure 8.18: First few rows of titanic data

3. Check the data types, as follows:

```
titanic_data.dtypes
```

You'll get the following output:

```
PassengerId      int64
Survived         int64
Pclass           int64
Name            object
Sex             object
Age            float64
SibSp            int64
Parch            int64
Ticket          object
Fare           float64
Cabin           object
Embarked        object
dtype: object
```

Figure 8.19: Data type of titanic data set

4. Look for any missing values using the following code:

```
titanic_data.isnull().sum()
```

You should get the following output:

```
PassengerId       0
Survived          0
Pclass            0
Name              0
Sex               0
Age             177
SibSp             0
Parch             0
Ticket            0
Fare              0
Cabin           687
Embarked          2
dtype: int64
```

Figure 8.20: Checking for missing values

5. Convert the data in the **sex** and **embarked** columns to categorical type using the **cat.codes** function and look at the data types again. Use the following code:

```
titanic_data["Sex"] = titanic_data["Sex"].astype('category').cat.codes
titanic_data["Embarked"] = titanic_data["Embarked"].astype('category').
cat.codes
titanic_data.dtypes
```

Your output should now appear as follows:

```
PassengerId       int64
Survived          int64
Pclass            int64
Name             object
Sex                int8
Age             float64
SibSp             int64
Parch             int64
Ticket           object
Fare            float64
Cabin            object
Embarked           int8
dtype: object
```

Figure 8.21: Encoding column Sex and Embarked

6. Perform missing value imputation on the **Age** and **Cabin** columns. Replace the missing values in the **Age** column with the mean and those in **Cabin** column with 0 if no value is present and with 1 if some value is present. Use the following code:

```
mean_value=titanic_data['Age'].mean()
titanic_data['Age']=titanic_data['Age'].fillna(mean_value)
titanic_data[['Cabin']]=np.where(titanic_data[['Cabin']].isnull(), 0, 1)
```

7. Split the data into train and test sets and save them as **X_train**, **X_test**, **y_train**, and **y_test** as shown:

```
target = 'Survived'
X = titanic_data.drop(['PassengerId','Survived','Name','Ticket'],axis=1)
y=titanic_data[target]
X_train, X_test, y_train, y_test = train_test_split(X.values,y,test_
size=0.50,random_state=123, stratify=y)
```

8. Fit a linear svm with **C=1**:

> **Note**
>
> **C** is the penalty cost parameter for regularization. Please refer to the objective function for linearly inseparable data points in SVM algorithm.

```
clf_svm=svm.SVC(kernel='linear', C=1)
clf_svm.fit(X_train,y_train)
```

9. Predict on the test data:

```
clf_svm.predict(X_test)
```

10. Calculate the accuracy score using the following code:

```
clf_svm.score(X_test, y_test)
```

For the Titanic dataset, the SVM classifier will score an accuracy of around 76.6%. This implies it can predict 76.6% of the test data accurately.

Decision Trees

Decision trees are mostly used for classification tasks. They are a non-parametric form of supervised learning method. Decision trees work on the concept of finding out the target variable by learning simple decision rules from data. They can be used for both classification and regression tasks. The following are the advantages and disadvantages of using decision tress for classification:

Advantages

- Decision trees are very simple to understand and can be visualized.

- They can handle both numeric and categorical data.

- The requirement for data cleaning in the case of decision trees is very low since it is able to handle missing data.

- It's a non-parametric machine learning algorithm that makes no assumption of space distribution and classifier structures.

- It's a white box model rather than a black box model like neural networks, and is able to explain the logic of split using Boolean values.

Disadvantages

- Decision trees tend to overfit data very easily, and pruning is required to prevent overfitting of the model.

- They are not suitable for imbalanced data, where we may have a decision tree that is biased. A decision tree would try to split the node based on the majority class and therefore doesn't generalize very well. The remedy is to balance your data before applying decision trees.

Exercise 36: Implementing a Decision Tree Algorithm Over a Dataset

In this exercise, we will use decision trees to build our model over the same Titanic dataset that we used in the previous exercise.

> **Note**
>
> Ensure that you use the same Jupyter Notebook as the one used for the preceding exercise.

1. Import **tree**, **graphviz**, **stringIO**, **image**, **export_graphviz**, and **pydotplus**:

```
import graphviz
from sklearn import tree
from sklearn.externals.six import StringIO
from IPython.display import Image
from sklearn.tree import export_graphviz
import pydotplus
```

2. Fit the decision tree classifier using the following code:

```
clf_tree = tree.DecisionTreeClassifier()
clf_tree = clf_tree.fit(X_train, y_train)
```

3. Plot the decision tree using a graph. In this plot, we will be using **export_graphviz** to visualize our decision tree. We will use the output of our decision tree classifier as our input **clf**. The target variable will be the **class_names**, that is **Died** or **Survived**.

```
dot_data = StringIO()
export_graphviz(clf_tree, out_file=dot_data,
                filled=True, rounded=True,
                class_names=['Died','Survived'],max_depth = 3,
                special_characters=True,feature_names=X.columns.values)
graph = pydotplus.graph_from_dot_data(dot_data.getvalue())
Image(graph.create_png())
```

The output of the above snippet will be a graphic visualization of the decision tree till a depth of 3.

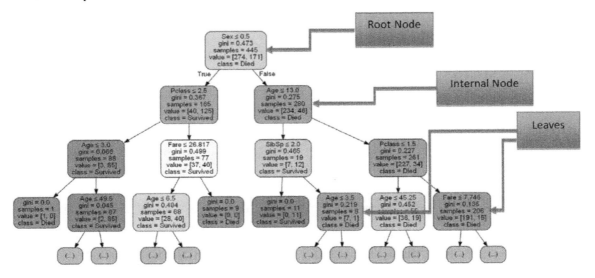

Figure 8.22: Graphic visualization of the decision tree

4. Calculate the accuracy score using the following code:

```
clf.score(X_test, y_test)
```

You should get an output of 0.775, which implies that our decision tree classifier scores an accuracy of around 77.5%. Hence our classifier is able to predict 77.5% of the test data correctly.

Important Terminology of Decision Trees

A decision tree is so called because the predictive model can be represented in a tree-like structure. A decision tree is read from the top down starting at the **root node**. Each internal node represents a split based on the values of one of the inputs. The inputs can appear in any number of splits throughout the tree. Cases move down the branch that contains its input value. A case moves left if the inequality is true and right otherwise. The **terminal nodes** of the tree are called **leaves**. The leaves represent the predicted target.

Decision Tree Algorithm Formulation

Decision trees use multiple algorithms to split at the root node or sub-node. A decision tree goes through all of the features and picks the feature on which it can get the most homogeneous sub-nodes. For classification tasks, it decides the most homogeneous sub-nodes based on the information gained. This information can be calculated using either of these three algorithms:

- Gini Impurity

- Entropy

- Misclassification rate

In short, each of the nodes in a decision tree represents a feature, each of the branches represent a decision rule, and each of the leaves represent an outcome. It is a flow-like structure.

Information Gain

It gives details on how much "information" a feature will hold about the class. Features that are perfectly separable or partitioned will give us maximum information, while features that are not perfectly separable or partitioned will give us less information:

$$IG(D_p, f) = I(D_p) - \frac{N_{left}}{N_p} I(D_{left}) - \frac{N_{right}}{N_p} I(D_{right})$$

Figure 8.23: Information gain formula

Here, IG=Information gain, I=Impurity, f=Feature, D_p=Parent dataset, D_{left}=Left child dataset, D_{right}=Right child dataset, N_p=Total number of samples in the parent dataset, N_{left}=Number of samples in the left child dataset, and N_{right}=Number of samples in the right child dataset.

The impurity can be calculated using either of the following three criteria:

Gini Impurity

The Gini index can be defined as the criteria that would minimize the probability of misclassification.

$$I_g(t) = \sum_{i=1}^{k} p(i|t)(1 - p(i|t)) = 1 - \sum_{i=1}^{k} p(i|t)^2$$

Figure 8.24: Gini impurity

Where, k=number of classes and p(i | t)=proportion of samples that belong to class k for a particular node t.

For a two-class problem, we can simplify the preceding equation as:

$$I_g(t) = 1 - (p^2 + q^2)$$

Where

$$p = probability\ of\ success$$

$$q = probability\ of\ failure$$

Figure 8.25: Simplified Gini impurity formula for binary classification

Entropy

Entropy can be defined as the criteria that maximizes mutual information.

$$I_h(t) = - \sum_{i=1}^{k} p(i|t) \log_2 p(i|t)$$

Figure 8.26: Entropy formula

Here, p(i | t)=proportion of samples that belong to class k for a particular node t. The entropy is 0 if all the samples belong to the same class, where as it is maximum if we have uniform class distribution.

For a two class problem, we can simplify the preceding equation as:

$$I_g(t) = -p \log_2 p - q \log_2 q$$

Where $p = probability\ of\ success$

$q = probability\ of\ failure$

Figure 8.27: Simplified equation

Misclassification error

This measures the misclassification error which can be defined as:

$$I_e(t) = 1 - max\{p(i|t)\}$$

Figure 8.28: Misclassification formula

Gini impurity and entropy typically give the same results, and either one of them can be used to calculate the impurity. To prune the tree, we can use the misclassification error.

Example: Referring to the Titanic dataset, we want to divide the node to find out whether a person survived or died based on features such as **Sex** and **Embarked**.

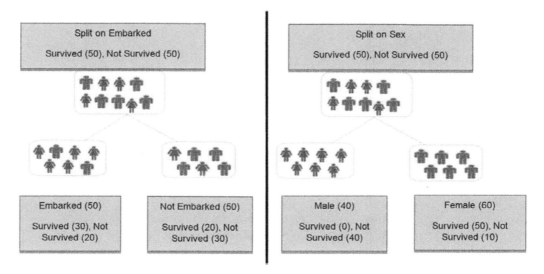

Figure 8.29: Visual representation of tree split

Gini index impurity for embarked:

$$I_g(D_p) = 1 - (0.5^2 + 0.5^2) = 0.5$$

$$I_g(D_{left/embarked}) = 1 - \left(\left(\frac{30}{50}\right)^2 + \left(\frac{20}{50}\right)^2\right) = 0.48$$

$$I_g(D_{right/Not\ embarked}) = 1 - \left(\left(\frac{20}{50}\right)^2 + \left(\frac{30}{50}\right)^2\right) = 0.48$$

$$IG(D_p, embarked) = I(D_p) - \frac{N_{left}}{N_p}I(D_{left}) - \frac{N_{right}}{N_p}I(D_{right}) = 0.5 - \frac{50}{100}0.48 - \frac{50}{100}0.48 = 0.02$$

Figure 8.30: Information gain calculated using Gini impurity (Embarked)

Gini index impurity for gender:

$$I_g(D_p) = 1 - (0.5^2 + 0.5^2) = 0.5$$

$$I_g(D_{left/male}) = 1 - \left(\left(\frac{0}{40}\right)^2 + \left(\frac{40}{40}\right)^2\right) = 0$$

$$I_g(D_{right/fenale}) = 1 - \left(\left(\frac{50}{60}\right)^2 + \left(\frac{10}{60}\right)^2\right) = 0.28$$

$$IG(D_p, sex) = I(D_p) - \frac{N_{left}}{N_p}I(D_{left}) - \frac{N_{right}}{N_p}I(D_{right}) = 0.5 - \frac{40}{100}*0 - \frac{60}{100}*0.28 = 0.33$$

Figure 8.31: Information gain calculated using Gini impurity (Gender)

From the information gain calculated, the decision tree will split based on the gender/sex feature, which is 0.33.

> **Note**
>
> Similarly, information gain can be calculated using entropy and misclassification. Students are encouraged to try these two calculations on their own.

Random Forest

The decision tree algorithm that we saw earlier faced the problem of overfitting. Since we fit only one tree on the training data, there is a high chance that the tree will overfit the data without proper pruning. The **random forest** algorithm reduces variance/ overfitting by averaging multiple decision trees, which individually suffer from high variance.

Random forest is an ensemble method of supervised machine learning. Ensemble methods combine predictions obtained from multiple base estimators/classifiers to improve the overall prediction/robustness. Ensemble methods are divided into the following two types:

- **Bagging**: The data is randomly divided into several subsets and the model is trained over each of these subsets. Several estimators are built independently from each other and then the predictions are averaged together, which ultimately helps to reduce variance (overfitting).

- **Boosting**: In the case of boosting, base estimators are built sequentially and each model built is very weak. The objective therefore is to build models in sequence, where the latter models try to reduce the error from the previous model and thereby reduce bias (underfitting).

The random forest algorithm works as follows:

1. A random bootstrap sample (a sample drawn with replacement) of size n is chosen from the training data.

2. Decision trees are grown on each instance of the bootstrap.

3. d features are chosen randomly without replacement.

4. Each node is split using the d features selected based on objective functions, which could be information gain.

5. Steps 1-4 are repeated k times.

6. Each of the predictions by multiple trees are aggregated and assigned a class label by majority vote.

The following diagram illustrates how the random forest algorithm works:

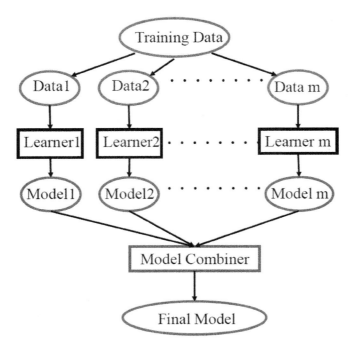

Figure 8.32: Working of a random forest model

The following are the advantages and disadvantages of a random forest algorithm:

Advantages

- It does not suffer from overfitting, since we take the average of all the predictions
- It can be used to get feature importance
- It can be used for both regression and classification tasks
- It can be used for highly imbalanced datasets
- It is able to handle missing data

Disadvantages

- It suffers from bias, although it reduces variance
- It's mostly a black box model and is difficult to explain

Exercise 37: Implementing a Random Forest Model Over a Dataset

In this exercise, we will be using a random forest to build our model over the same Titanic dataset used previously. Ensure that you use the same Jupyter Notebook as the one used for the preceding exercise.

1. Import the random forest classifier:

    ```
    from sklearn.ensemble import RandomForestClassifier
    ```

2. Fit the random forest classifier to the training data using the following code:

    ```
    clf = RandomForestClassifier(n_estimators=20, max_depth=None,
        min_samples_split=7, random_state=0)
    clf.fit(X_train,y_train)
    ```

3. Predict on the test data:

    ```
    clf.predict(X_test)
    ```

4. Calculate the accuracy score:

    ```
    clf.score(X_test, y_test)
    ```

    You should get an output close to 0.79, which implies that the random forest classifier scores an accuracy of around 79.1%.

So far, we've implemented different classical algorithms such as SVM, decision tree, and random forest. We understood the mathematics behind this algorithm and the advantages and disadvantages of each of these algorithms. Let's now perform an activity to implement these in practice.

Activity 15: Implementing Different Classification Algorithms

In this activity, we will continue working with the telecom dataset (**Telco_Churn_Data. csv**) that we used in the previous chapter and build different models over this dataset using the scikit-learn API. Your marketing team was impressed with the initial findings and they now want you to build a machine learning model that can predict customer churn. This model will be used by the marketing team to send out discount coupons to customers who may churn. In order to build the best prediction model, it is important to try different algorithms and come up with the best performing algorithm that the management can use.

In this activity, you will use the logistic regression, SVM, and random forest algorithms.

> **Note**
>
> In Activity 14, we saved our 7 most important features to the variable **top7_features**. We will use these features to build our machine learning model.

Follow the steps below:

1. Import the libraries for the logistic regression, decision tree, SVM, and random forest algorithms.

2. Fit individual models to **clf_logistic**, **clf_svm**, **clf_decision**, and **clf_random** variables.

   Use the following parameters: For the logistic regression model, use **random_state=0**, **solver='lbfgs'**; for the SVM, use **kernel='linear'**, **C=1**; and for the random forest model, use **n_estimators=20**, **max_depth=None**, **min_samples_split=7**, **random_state=0**.

3. Use the **score** function to get the accuracy for each of the algorithms.

You should get the following accuracy scores for each of the models at the end of this activity:

Algorithm	Accuracy
Logistic Regression	0.745
SVM	0.765
Decision Tree	0.748
Random Forest	0.810

Figure 8.33: Comparison of Different Algorithm Accuracy on Titanic Dataset

> **Note**
>
> The solution for this activity can be found on page 358.

Preprocessing Data for Machine Learning Models

Preprocessing data before applying any machine learning model can improve the accuracy of the model to a large extent. Therefore, it is important to preprocess data before applying a machine learning algorithm. Preprocessing data consists of the following methods: Standardization, Scaling, and Normalization

Standardization

Most machine learning algorithms assume that all features are centered at zero and have variance in the same order. In the case of linear models such as logistic and linear regression, some of the parameters used in the objective function assume that all the features are centered around zero and have unit variance. If the values of a feature are much higher than some of the other features, then that feature might dominate the objective function and the estimator may not be able to learn from other features. In such cases, standardization can be used to rescale features such that they have a mean of 0 and variance of 1. The following formula is used for standardization.

$$x^i(std) = \frac{x^i - \mu_x}{\sigma_x}$$

Figure 8.34: Standardization

Here, x^i is the input data, μ^x is the mean, and σ^x is the standard deviation. Standardization is most useful for optimization algorithms such as gradient descent. The scikit-learn API has the `StandardScalar` utility class.

Exercise 38: Standardizing Data

For this exercise, we will use the bank churn prediction data that was used in Chapter 7. In the previous chapter, we performed feature selection using random forest. The features selected for our bank churn prediction data are: `Age`, `EstimatedSalary`, `CreditScore`, `Balance`, and `NumOfProducts`.

In this exercise, our objective will be to standardize data after we have carried out feature selection. On exploring the previous chapter, it was clear that data is not standardized; therefore in this exercise, we will implement standard scalar to standardize the data to zero mean and unit variance. Ensure that you use the same Notebook as the one used for the preceding two exercises.

1. Import the **preprocessing** library:

```
from sklearn import preprocessing
```

2. Take the features **Age**, **EstimatedSalary**, **CreditScore**, **Balance**, and **NumOfProducts**:

```
X_train[top5_features].head()
```

You will get the following output:

	Age	Estimated Salary	CreditScore	Balance	NumOfProducts
490	29.0	196356.17	591	97541.24	1
5555	39.0	164018.98	614	0.00	2
9235	27.0	80587.27	462	176913.52	1
6594	40.0	57817.84	747	0.00	1
6671	49.0	187811.71	677	0.00	2

Figure 8.35: First few rows of top5_features

3. Fit the **StandardScalar** function on the **X_train** data using the following code:

```
scaler = preprocessing.StandardScaler().fit(X_train[top5_features])
```

4. Check the mean and scaled values. Use the following code to check the mean:

```
scaler.mean_
```

```
array([3.89098824e+01, 1.00183902e+05, 6.49955882e+02, 7.61412119e+04,
       1.52882353e+00])
```

Figure 8.36: Mean values

This prints the mean of the five columns. Now check the scaled values:

```
scaler.scale_
```

```
array([1.03706201e+01, 5.74453373e+04, 9.64815072e+01, 6.24292333e+04,
       5.80460085e-01])
```

Figure 8.37: Scaled values

The above output shows the scaled values of the five columns.

> **Note**
>
> You can read more about the preceding two functions at https://scikit-learn.org/
> stable/modules/generated/sklearn.preprocessing.StandardScaler.html.

5. Apply the **transform** function to the **X_train** data. This function performs standardization by centering and scaling the training data

```
X_train_scalar=scaler.transform(X_train[top5_features])
```

6. Next, apply the **transform** function to the **X_test** data and check the output:

```
X_test_scalar=scaler.transform(X_test[top5_features])
X_train_scalar
```

You will get the following output on checking the scalar transform data:

```
array([[-0.95557279,  1.67415272, -0.61105889,  0.34278858, -0.91104202],
       [ 0.00868971,  1.11123166, -0.37267123, -1.21964035,  0.81172932],
       [-1.14842529, -0.3411353 , -1.94810268,  1.61418462, -0.91104202],
       ...,
       [-0.56986779, -0.72635385,  0.36322108, -1.21964035, -0.91104202],
       [-0.37701529, -1.47154105,  0.91254915, -1.21964035, -0.91104202],
       [-0.08773654, -0.55862971, -1.11892823, -0.16336821, -0.91104202]])
```

Figure 8.38: Scalar transformed data

Scaling

Scaling is another method for preprocessing your data. Scaling your data cause the features to lie between a certain minimum and maximum value, mostly between zero and one. As a result, the maximum absolute value of each feature is scaled. Scaling can be effective for some of the machine learning algorithms that use the Euclidean distance such as the KNN (K-Nearest Neighbors) or k-means clustering:

$$x^i(norm) = \frac{x^i - x_{min}}{x_{max} - x_{min}}$$

Figure 8.39: Equation for scaling data

Here, x^i is the input data, x_{min} is the minimum value of the feature, and x_{max} is the maximum value of the feature. In scikit-learn, we use **MinMaxScaler** or **MaxAbsScaler**.

> **Note**
>
> You can read more about the **MinMaxScaler** and **MaxAbsScaler** at https://scikit-learn.org/stable/modules/generated/sklearn.preprocessing.MinMaxScaler.html and https://scikit-learn.org/stable/modules/generated/sklearn.preprocessing.MaxAbsScaler.html.

Exercise 39: Scaling Data After Feature Selection

In this exercise, our objective is to scale data after feature selection. We will use the same bank churn prediction data to perform scaling. Ensure that you continue using the same Jupyter Notebook.

1. Fit the **minmax** scaler on the training data:

```
min_max = preprocessing.MinMaxScaler().fit(X_train[top5_features])
```

2. Check the min and scaled value:

```
min_max.min_
```

You will get the following mean values.

```
array([-2.43243243e-01, -5.79055300e-05, -7.00000000e-01,  0.00000000e+00,
        -3.33333333e-01])
```

Figure 8.40: Mean values

Now check the scaled values:

```
min_max.scale_
```

You will get the following scaled values.

```
array([1.35135135e-02, 5.00047755e-06, 2.00000000e-03, 3.98568200e-06,
        3.33333333e-01])
```

Figure 8.41: Scaled values

3. Transform the train and test data using `min_max`:

```
X_train_min_max=min_max.transform(X_train[top5_features])
X_test_min_max=min_max.transform(X_test[top5_features])
```

Normalization

In normalization, individual training samples are scaled to have a unit norm. (The norm of a vector is the size or length of the vector. Hence, each of the training samples' vector length will be scaled to 1.) This method is mostly used when we want to use a quadratic form such as the dot-product or any kernel to quantify sample similarity. It's mostly effective in clustering and text classification.

We use either the L1 norm or the L2 norm for normalization:

L1 Norm:

$$\|x\|_1 = \sum_i |x_i|$$

L2 Norm:

$$\|x\|_2 = \sqrt{\sum_i |x_i|^2}$$

Figure 8.42: Normalization

xi is the input training samples.

> **Note**
>
> In scikit-learn, we use the **Normalize** and **Normalizer** utility classes. The difference between the two normalizations is out of the scope of this chapter.

Exercise 40: Performing Normalization on Data

In this exercise our objective will be to normalize data after feature selection. We will use the same bank churn prediction data for normalizing. Continue using the same Jupyter Notebook as the one used in the preceding exercise.

1. Fit the Normalizer() on the training data:

```
normalize = preprocessing.Normalizer().fit(X_train[top5_features])
```

2. Check the **normalize** function, that is, whether L1 or L2 Norm:

```
normalize
```

This will give you the following output, indicating an L2 norm:

$$Normalizer(copy=True, norm='l2')$$

Figure 8.43: Checking the normalize function

3. Transform the training and testing data using normalize:

```
X_train_normalize=normalize.transform(X_train[top5_features])
X_test_normalize=normalize.transform(X_test[top5_features])
```

Model Evaluation

When we train our model, we usually split our data into a training and testing datasets. This is to ensure that the model doesn't overfit. **Overfitting** refers to a phenomena where a model performs very well on the training data, but fails to give good results on testing data, or in other words, the model fails to generalize.

In scikit learn, we have a function known as **train_test_split** that splits the data into training and testing sets randomly.

When evaluating our model, we start by changing the parameters to improve the accuracy as per our test data. There is a high chance of leaking some of the information from the testing set to our training set if we optimize our parameters using only the testing set data. In order to avoid this, we can split data into three parts—training, testing, and validation sets. However, the disadvantage of this technique is that we will be further reducing our training dataset.

The solution is to use **cross-validation**. In this process, we do not need a separate validation dataset; we split dataset into training and testing data only. However, the training data is split into k smaller sets using a technique called k-fold CV, which can be explained using the following figure:

Figure 8.44: k-fold cross validation

The algorithm is as follows:

1. The entire training data is divided into k fold, in this case it's 10.

2. The model is trained on k-1 portions (blue blocks highlighted in the preceding figure)

3. Once the model is trained, the classifier is evaluated on the remaining 1 portion (red blocks highlighted in the preceding figure).

   Steps 2 and 3 are repeated k times.

4. Once the classifier has carried out the evaluation, an overall average score is taken.

This method doesn't work well if we have **class imbalance**, and therefore we use a method known as **stratified K fold**.

> **Note**
>
> In many real-world classification problems, classes are not equally distributed. One class may be highly represented, that is, 90%, while another class may consist of only 10% of the samples. We will cover how to deal with imbalanced datasets in the next chapter.

We use stratified K fold to deal with datasets where there is class imbalance. In datasets where there is class imbalance, during splitting, care must be taken to maintain class proportions. In the case of stratified K fold, it maintains class ratio in each portion.

Exercise 41: Implementing Stratified k-fold

In this exercise, we will fit the stratified k-fold function of scikit-learn to the bank churn prediction data and use the logistic regression classifier from the previous exercise to fit our k-fold data. Along with that, we will also implement the scikit-learn k-fold cross-validation scorer function. Continue using the same Notebook as the one used for the preceding exercise:

1. Import **StratifiedKFold** from **sklearn**:

   ```
   from sklearn.model_selection import StratifiedKFold
   ```

2. Fit the classifier on the training and testing data with **n_splits=10**, and **random_state=1**:

   ```
   skf = StratifiedKFold(n_splits=10,random_state=1).split(X_train[top5_
   features].values,y_train.values)
   ```

3. Calculate the k-cross fold validation score:

   ```
   results=[]
   for i, (train,test) in enumerate(skf):
       clf.fit(X_train[top5_features].values[train],y_train.values[train])

   fit_result=clf.score(X_train[top5_features].values[test],y_train.
   values[test])
       results.append(fit_result)
       print('k-fold: %2d, Class Ratio: %s, Accuracy: %.4f' % (i,np.
   bincount(y_train.values[train]),fit_result))
   ```

4. Find out the accuracy:

```
print('accuracy for CV is:%.3f' % np.mean(results))
```

You will get an output showing the accuracy as 0.790.

5. Import the scikit-learn cross_val_score:

```
from sklearn.model_selection import cross_val_score
```

6. Fit the classifier and print the accuracy:

```
results_cross_val_score=cross_val_score(estimator=clf,X=X_train[top5_
features].values,y=y_train.values,cv=10,n_jobs=1)
print('accuracy for CV is:%.3f' % np.mean(results_cross_val_score))
```

You will get an output showing the accuracy as 0.790.

In this exercise, we implemented k-fold cross validation using two methods, one where we used a **for** loop and another where we used the **cross_val_score** function of **sklearn**. We used logistic regression as our base classifier present in the variable **clf** from *Exercise 34*, *Chapter 7*. From the cross validation our logistic regression gave an accuracy of around 79% overall.

Fine-Tuning of the Model

In the case of a machine learning model, there are two types of parameter tuning that can be performed.

- The first one is the parameters that the model learns from itself, such as the *coefficients* in case of linear regression or the *margin* in case of SVM.

- The second one are parameters that must be optimized separately, and are known as **hyperparameters**, for example, the *alpha* value in case of lasso linear regression or the *number of leaf nodes* in case of decision trees. In the case of a machine learning model, there can be a number of hypermeters and hence it becomes difficult for someone to tune the model by adjusting each of the hyperparameters manually.

There are two methods for performing hypermeter search operations in scikit-learn, which are described below:

Grid search: In the case of grid search, it uses brute force exhaustive search to permute all combinations of hyperparameters, which are provided to it as a list of values.

Randomized Grid Search: Randomized grid search is a faster alternative to grid search, which can be very slow due to the use of brute force. In this method, parameters are randomly chosen from a distribution that the user provides. Additionally, the user can provide a sampling iteration specified by **n_iter**, which is used as a computational budget.

Exercise 42: Fine-Tuning a Model

In this exercise, we will implement a grid search to find out the best parameters for an SVM on the bank churn prediction data. We will continue using the same Notebook as in our preceding exercise.

1. Import **SVM**, **GridSearchCV**, and **StratifiedKfold**:

    ```
    from sklearn import svm
    from sklearn.model_selection import GridSearchCV
    from sklearn.model_selection import StratifiedKFold
    ```

2. Specify the parameters for grid search as follows:

    ```
    parameters = [ {'kernel': ['linear'], 'C':[0.1, 1, 10]}, {'kernel':
    ['rbf'], 'gamma':[0.5, 1, 2], 'C':[0.1, 1, 10]}]
    ```

3. Fit the grid search with **StratifiedKFold** having parameter as **n_splits = 10**:

    ```
    clf = GridSearchCV(svm.SVC(), parameters, cv = StratifiedKFold(n_splits =
    10))
    clf.fit(X_train[top5_features], y_train)
    ```

4. Print the best score and the best parameters:

    ```
    print('best score train:', clf.best_score_)
    print('best parameters train: ', clf.best_params_)
    ```

You will get the following output:

```
best score train: 0.7963529411764706
best parameters train:  {'C': 0.1, 'gamma': 0.5, 'kernel': 'rbf'}
```

Figure 8.45: Best score and parameters obtained from grid search

> **Note**
>
> Grid search takes a lot of time to find out the optimum parameters, and hence, the search parameters given should be wisely chosen.

From the exercise, we can conclude that the best parameters chosen from grid search were `C:0.1`, `Gamma:0.5`, and `kernel:rbf`

From the exercise, we saw how model tuning helps to achieve higher accuracy. Firstly, we implemented data preprocessing, which is the first step to improve the accuracy of the model. Later, we learned how cross-validation and grid search enable us to further tune the machine learning model and improve the accuracy.

Activity 16: Tuning and Optimizing the Model

The models you built in the previous activity produced good results, especially the random forest model, which produced an accuracy score of more than 80%. You now need to improve the accuracy of the random forest model and generalize it. Tuning the model using different pre-processing steps, cross validation, and grid search will improve the accuracy of the model. We will be using the same Jupyter notebook as the one used in the preceding activity. Follow these steps:

1. Store five out of seven features, that is, `Avg_Calls_Weekdays`, `Current_Bill_Amt`, `Avg_Calls`, `Account_Age`, and `Avg_Days_Delinquent` in a variable `top5_features`. Store the other two features, `Percent_Increase_MOM` and `Complaint_Code`, in a variable `top5_features`. These features have values in the range of –1 to 7, whereas the other five features have values in the range of 0 to 374457. Hence we can leave these features and standardize rest of the five features.

2. Use **StandardScalar** to standardize the five features.

3. Create a variable **X_train_scalar_combined**, combine the standardized five features with the two features (**Percent_Increase_MOM** and **Complaint_Code**), which were not standardized.

4. Apply the same scalar standardization to the test data (**X_test_scalar_combined**).

5. Fit the random forest model.

6. Score the random forest model. You should get a value close to 0.81.

7. Import the library for grid search and use the following parameters:

```
parameters = [ {'min_samples_split': [4,5,7,9,10], 'n_
estimators':[10,20,30,40,50,100,150,160,200,250,300],'max_depth':
[2,5,7,10]}]
```

8. Use grid search CV with stratified k-fold to find out the best parameters. Use **StratifiedKFold(n_splits = 10)** and **RandomForestClassifier()**.

9. Print the best score and the best parameters. You should get the following values:

```
best score train: 0.8022994251437141
best parameters train:  {'max_depth': 7, 'min_samples_split': 10, 'n_estimators': 100}
```

Figure 8.46: Best score and best parameters

10. Score the model using the test data. You should get a score close to 0.82.

Combining the results of the accuracy score obtained in Activity 15 and Activity 16, here are the results for random forest:

Algorithm	Accuracy
Random Forest (Default)	0.810
Random Forest (Pre-Processing)	0.811
Random Forest (Grid Search and CV)	0.824

Figure 8.47: Comparing the accuracy of random forest using different methods

We can conclude that data pre-processing and model tuning methods can greatly improve model accuracy.

> **Note**
>
> The solution for this activity can be found on page 359.

Performance Metrics

In the case of classification algorithms, we use a confusion matrix, which gives us the performance of the learning algorithm. It is a square matrix that counts the number of true positive (TP), true negative (TN), false positive (FP), and false negative (FN) outcomes.

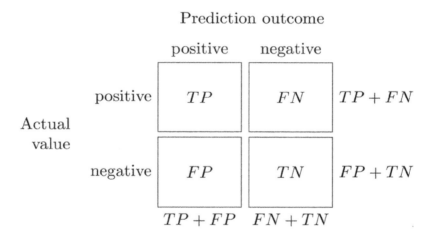

Figure 8.48: Confusion matrix

True positive: The number of cases that were observed and predicted as 1.

False negative: The number of cases that were observed as 1 but predicted as 0.

False positive: The number of cases that were observed as 0 but predicted as 1.

True negative: The number of cases that were observed as 1 but predicted as 0.

Precision

It is the ability of a classifier to not label a sample that is negative as positive. The precision for an algorithm is calculated using the following formula:

$$precision = \frac{t_p}{t_p + f_p}$$

Figure 8.49: Precision

This is useful in the case of email spam detection. In this scenario, we do not want any important emails to be detected as spam.

Recall

It refers to the ability of a classifier to correctly identify all the positive samples, that is, out of the total pool of positive (t_p + f_n) how many were correctly identified. This is also known as **True Positive Rate** (**TPR**) or **sensitivity** and is given by the following formula:

$$Recall = \frac{t_p}{t_p + f_n}$$

Figure 8.50: Recall

This is useful in scenarios where, for example, we want to detect whether a tumor is malignant or benign. In that scenario, we can use the recall score, since our main objective is to detect all the malignant cases. Even if the classifier picks up a case that is benign as malignant, the patient could get a second screening.

F1 Score

This is the harmonic mean of precision and recall. It is given by the following formula.

$$F1 = \frac{precision * Recall}{precision + Recall}$$

Figure 8.51: F1 Score

The F1 score can be useful when we want to have an optimal blend of precision and recall.

Exercise 43: Evaluating the Performance Metrics for a Model

In the previous exercise, we used the scikit-learn **score** function to find out the model performance. However, it is not the right way to find out the accuracy or performance of a model. In this exercise, we will calculate the F1 score and the accuracy of our random forest model for the bank churn prediction dataset. Continue using the same Notebook as the one used in the preceding exercise.

1. Import **RandomForestClassifier**, **metrics**, **classification_report**, **confusion matrix**, and **accuracy_score**:

    ```
    from sklearn.ensemble import RandomForestClassifier
    from sklearn.metrics import classification_report,confusion_
    matrix,accuracy_score
    from sklearn import metrics
    ```

2. Fit the random forest classifier using the following code over the training data:

    ```
    clf_random = RandomForestClassifier(n_estimators=20, max_depth=None,
        min_samples_split=7, random_state=0)
    clf_random.fit(X_train[top5_features],y_train)
    ```

3. Predict on the test data the classifier:

    ```
    y_pred=clf_random.predict(X_test[top5_features])
    ```

4. Print the classification report:

    ```
    target_names = ['No Churn', 'Churn']
    print(classification_report(y_test, y_pred, target_names=target_names))
    ```

    Your output will look as follows:

	precision	recall	f1-score	support
No Churn	0.86	0.94	0.90	1194
Churn	0.65	0.40	0.49	306
micro avg	0.83	0.83	0.83	1500
macro avg	0.75	0.67	0.70	1500
weighted avg	0.82	0.83	0.82	1500

    Figure 8.52: Classification Report

5. Fit the confusion matrix and save it into a pandas DataFrame named **cm_df**:

```
cm = confusion_matrix(y_test, y_pred)
cm_df = pd.DataFrame(cm,
                      index = ['No Churn','Churn'],
                      columns = ['No Churn','Churn'])
```

6. Plot the confusion matrix using the following code:

```
plt.figure(figsize=(8,6))
sns.heatmap(cm_df, annot=True,fmt='g',cmap='Blues')
plt.title(Random Forest \nAccuracy:{0:.3f}'.format(accuracy_score(y_test,
y_pred)))
plt.ylabel('True Values')
plt.xlabel('Predicted Values')
plt.show()
```

You should get the following output:

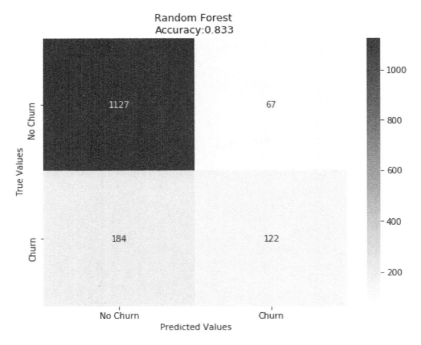

Figure 8.53: Confusion Matrix

From this exercise, we can conclude that our random forest model has an overall F1 score of 0.82. However, the F1 score of the customers who have churned is less than 50%.This is due to highly imbalanced data, as a result of which the model fails to generalize. You will learn how to make the model more robust and improve the F1 Score for imbalanced data in the next chapter.

ROC Curve

The **ROC curve** is a graphical method used to inspect the performance of binary classification models by shifting the decision threshold of the classifier. It is plotted based on **TPR** and **FPR**. We saw what TPR is in the last section. FPR is given by the following equation:

$$FPR = \frac{f_p}{f_p + t_n}$$

Figure 8.54: False positive rate (1–specificity)

This is equivalent to 1–*specificity*.

Specificity is defined as –*ve Recall*.

–*ve Recall* is the ability of a classifier to correctly find all the negative samples, that is, out of the total pool of negative (*tn* + *fp*) how many were correctly identified as negative. It is given by the following equation.

$$-ve\ Recall = \frac{t_n}{t_n + f_p}$$

Figure 8.55: –ve Recall

The following diagram illustrates how an ROC curve is plotted:

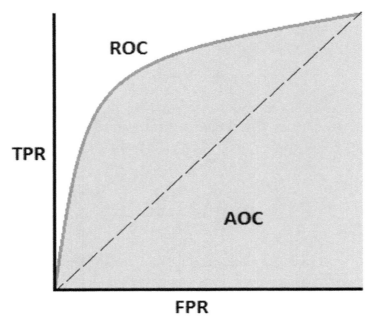

Figure 8.56: ROC curve

The diagonal of the ROC curve represents random guessing. Classifiers that lie below the diagonal are considered to perform worse than random guessing. A perfect classifier would have its ROC curve at the top left corner, having a TPR of 1 and FPR of 0.

Exercise 44: Plotting the ROC Curve

In this exercise, we will plot the ROC curve for the random forest model from the previous exercise on the bank churn prediction data. Continue with the same Jupyter Notebook as the one used in the preceding exercise.

1. Import **roc_curve,auc**:

```
from sklearn.metrics import roc_curve,auc
```

2. Calculate the TPR, FPR, and threshold using the following code:

```
fpr, tpr, thresholds = roc_curve(y_test, y_pred, pos_label=1)
roc_auc = metrics.auc(fpr, tpr)
```

3. Plot the ROC curve using the following code:

```
plt.figure()
plt.title('Receiver Operating Characteristic')
plt.plot(fpr, tpr, label='%s AUC = %0.2f' % ('Random Forest', roc_auc))
plt.plot([0, 1], [0, 1],'r--')
plt.xlim([0.0, 1.0])
plt.ylim([0.0, 1.05])
plt.ylabel('Sensitivity(True Positive Rate)')
plt.xlabel('1-Specificity(False Positive Rate)')
plt.title('Receiver Operating Characteristic')
plt.legend(loc="lower right")
plt.show()
```

Your plot should appear as follows:

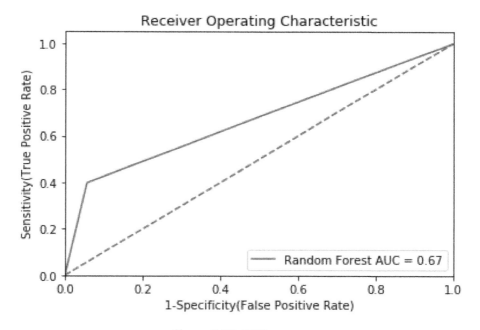

Figure 8.57: ROC curve

From our exercise, it can be concluded that the model has an area under the curve of 0.67. Even though the F1 score of the model was calculated to be 0.82, from our classification report, the AUC score is much less. The FPR is closer to 0, however the TPR is closer 0.4. The AUC curve and the overall F1 score can be greatly improved by pre-processing the data and fine-tuning the model using techniques that we implemented in the previous exercise.

In the previous activity, we saw how using fine-tuning techniques greatly improved our model accuracy. In the next activity, we will find out the performance of our random forest model and compare the ROC curve of all the models.

Activity 17: Comparison of the Models

In our previous activity, we improved the accuracy score of our random forest model score to 0.82. However, we were not using the correct performance metrics. In this activity, we would find out the F1 score of our random forest model and also compare the ROC curve of different machine learning models created in Activity 15. Ensure that you use the same Jupyter Notebook as the one used in the preceding activity. Follow these steps:

1. Import the required libraries.

2. Fit the random forest classifier with the parameters obtained from grid search in the preceding activity. Use the variable `clf_random_grid`.

3. Predict on the standardized scalar test data `X_test_scalar_combined`.

4. Fit the classification report. You should get the following output:

	precision	recall	f1-score	support
No Churn	0.85	0.80	0.82	364
Churn	0.80	0.85	0.82	343
micro avg	0.82	0.82	0.82	707
macro avg	0.82	0.82	0.82	707
weighted avg	0.82	0.82	0.82	707

Figure 8.58: Classification report

5. Plot the confusion matrix. Your output should be as follows:

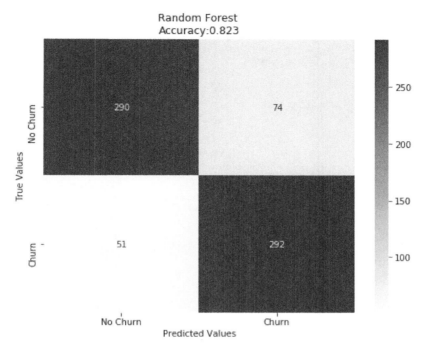

Figure 8.59: Confusion matrix

6. Import the library for auc and roc curve.

7. Use the classifiers that were created in Activity 15, that is, **clf_logistic**, **clf_svm**, **clf_decision**, and **clf_random_grid**. Create a dictionary of all these models.

8. Plot the ROC curve. The following **for** loop can be used as a hint:

```
for m in models:
    model = m['model']
    ------ FIT THE MODEL
    ------ PREDICT
    ------ FIND THE FPR, TPR AND THRESHOLD
    roc_auc =FIND THE AUC
    plt.plot(fpr, tpr, label='%s AUC = %0.2f' % (m['label'], roc_auc))
plt.plot([0, 1], [0, 1],'r--')
```

```
plt.xlim([0.0, 1.0])
plt.ylim([0.0, 1.05])
plt.ylabel('Sensitivity(True Positive Rate)')
plt.xlabel('1-Specificity(False Positive Rate)')
plt.title('Receiver Operating Characteristic')
plt.legend(loc="lower right")
plt.show()
```

You plot should look as follows:

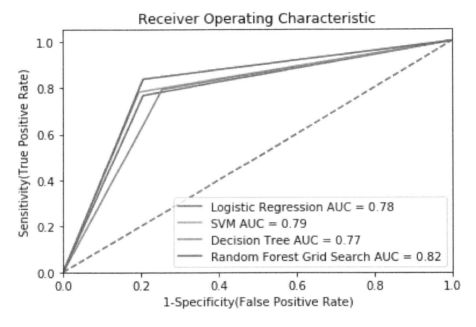

Figure 8.60: ROC curve

Summary

In this chapter, you learnt how to perform classification using some of the most commonly used algorithms. You also understood the advantage and disadvantage of each algorithm. You also learned in depth how a tree-based model works.

You got to grips with why the pre-processing of data using techniques such as standardization is necessary, and implemented various fine-tuning techniques for optimizing a machine learning model. You were able to choose the right performance metrics for your classification problems and explored the concept behind the confusion matrix. You also learned how to compare different models and choose the best performing models.

In the next chapter, you will learn about multi-classification problems and how to tackle imbalanced data.

Modeling Customer Choice

Learning Objectives

By the end of this chapter, you will be able to:

- Describe the logic behind multiclass classification problems
- Create a multiclass classification classifier
- Use different sampling techniques to solve the problem of imbalanced data

This chapter covers different types of multiclass classification problems and explains how to calculate performance metrics and deal with imbalanced data.

Introduction

In the previous chapters, you learned about common classification algorithms such as logistic regression, SVM, decision tree, and random forest. You also learned the advantages and disadvantages of each of these algorithms. You implemented these algorithms using the most popular machine learning API, scikit-learn, and fine-tuned, optimized, and evaluated different machine learning models.

In this chapter, you will start by exploring multiclass classification. Then, you will deep dive into the intuition behind multiclass classification problems and see how to tackle class-imbalanced data. Finally, you will create a multiclass classification classifier.

Understanding Multiclass Classification

The classification algorithms that we discussed earlier were mostly binary classifiers, where the target variable can have only two categorical values or classes. However, there can be scenarios where we have more than two classes to classify samples into. For instance, given data on customer transactions, the marketing team may be tasked with identifying the credit card product most suitable for a customer, such as cashback, air miles, gas station, or shopping.

Multiclass classification can be broadly divided into the following three categories:

1. **Multiclass classification**: Multiclass classification problems involve classifying instances or samples into one class out of multiple classes (more than two). Each sample is assigned only one label and cannot be assigned more than one label at a time. For example, an image can be classified as that of a cat, dog, or rabbit, and not more than one of them at the same time.

2. **Multilabel classification**: In the case of multilabel classification, each sample is assigned a set of target labels. For example, given some news articles, we may want to assign multiple labels to each of these articles to know what kind of topics they cover.

3. **Multioutput Regression**: In the case of multioutput regression, each sample is assigned several target variables with different properties. For instance, the target could be to predict the wind direction, humidity, and temperature.

Classifiers in Multiclass Classification

Multiclass classification can be implemented by scikit-learn in the following two ways:

1. **One-vs-all classifier**: Here, one classifier is fitted against one class. For each of the classifiers, the class is then fitted against all the other classes, producing a real-valued decision confidence score, instead of class labels. From the decision confidence score, the maximum value is picked up to get the final class label. The advantage of one-vs-all is its interpretability and efficiency. The following figure illustrates how this classifier works:

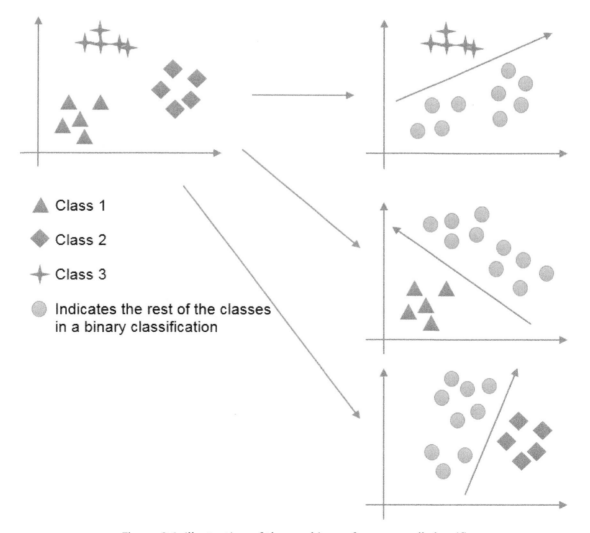

Figure 9.1: Illustration of the workings of a one-vs-all classifier

2. **One-vs-one classifier**: This constructs one classifier per pair of classes. The intuitive idea is to develop a binary classifier for each possible pair of classes, derive the decision boundary between these two classes, and build an ensemble. During prediction, the label is assigned by majority voting and in the event of a tie, the class with the highest aggregate classification confidence (obtained by summing the pair-wise confidence levels that were calculated earlier) is selected.

Exercise 45: Implementing a Multiclass Classification Algorithm on a Dataset

For this exercise, we will be using the wine dataset from UCI. The dataset comprises data on the quantities of 13 constituents of three different wine cultivars grown in the same region of Italy. Given the chemical composition, you need to classify which variety of wine each sample belongs to. The target variable for the wines consists of three classes, causing this to become a multiclass classification problem. You need to implement a multiclass classification algorithm to classify these three different varieties of wine and observe the difference between `OneVsRestClassifier` and `OneVsOneClassifier`:

1. Import the `load_wine` dataset from `sklearn.datasets`, the `OneVsRestClassifier`, `OneVsOneClassifier`, and `LinearSVC`. We will be using a linear SVC, which is good for multiclass classification:

   ```
   from sklearn.datasets import load_wine
   from sklearn.multiclass import OneVsRestClassifier,OneVsOneClassifier
   from sklearn.svm import LinearSVC
   ```

   > **Note**
   >
   > Linear SVC is similar to SVC with the **kernel='linear'** parameter but is implemented as **liblinear** rather than **libsvm**, so it has more flexibility in the choice of penalties and loss functions and should scale better to large numbers of samples.

2. Load the **wine** dataset to a variable named **wine**, and use **wine.data** and **wine.target** to load all the features and the target to variables **X** and **y**, respectively:

   ```
   wine = load_wine()
   X, y = wine.data, wine.target
   ```

3. Fit and predict using the one-vs-all classifier. Use the following code:

```
OneVsRestClassifier(LinearSVC(random_state=0)).fit(X, y).predict(X)
```

You will receive the following array as output:

```
array([0, 0, 0, 0, 0, 0, 0, 0, 0, 0, 0, 0, 0, 0, 0, 0, 0, 0, 0, 0, 0,
       0, 0, 0, 0, 0, 0, 0, 0, 0, 0, 0, 0, 0, 0, 0, 0, 0, 0, 0, 0, 0,
       0, 0, 0, 0, 0, 0, 1, 1, 1, 1, 1, 1, 1, 1, 1, 1, 1, 1, 1, 1, 1, 1,
       1, 1, 1, 1, 2, 1, 1, 1, 1, 1, 1, 1, 1, 1, 1, 1, 1, 2, 2, 1, 1, 1,
       1, 1, 1, 1, 1, 1, 1, 1, 1, 1, 1, 1, 2, 2, 2, 2, 2, 2, 2, 2, 2, 2,
       2, 2, 2, 2, 2, 2, 2, 2, 2, 2, 2, 2, 2, 2, 2, 2, 2, 2, 1, 2, 2,
       2, 1, 2, 2, 2, 2, 2, 2, 2, 2, 2, 2, 2, 2, 2, 2])
```

Figure 9.2: Output of the one-vs-all classifier

4. Fit and predict using the one-vs-one classifier. Use the following code:

```
OneVsOneClassifier(LinearSVC(random_state=0)).fit(X, y).predict(X)
```

You will receive the following array as output:

```
array([0, 0, 0, 0, 0, 0, 0, 0, 0, 0, 0, 0, 0, 0, 0, 0, 0, 0, 0, 0, 0,
       0, 0, 0, 0, 0, 0, 0, 0, 0, 0, 0, 0, 0, 0, 0, 0, 0, 0, 0, 0, 0,
       0, 0, 0, 0, 0, 0, 1, 1, 1, 1, 1, 1, 1, 1, 1, 1, 1, 1, 1, 1, 1, 1,
       1, 1, 1, 1, 2, 1, 2, 1, 1, 1, 1, 1, 1, 1, 1, 1, 1, 2, 1, 1, 1, 1,
       1, 1, 1, 1, 1, 1, 1, 1, 1, 1, 1, 1, 2, 2, 2, 2, 2, 2, 2, 2, 2, 2,
       2, 2, 2, 2, 2, 2, 2, 2, 2, 2, 2, 2, 2, 2, 2, 2, 2, 2, 2, 2, 2,
       2, 2, 2, 2, 2, 2, 2, 2, 2, 2, 2, 2, 2, 2, 2])
```

Figure 9.3: Output of the one-vs-one classifier

From the preceding outputs, you will observe that both the classifiers give the same results. The difference between both, however, is the computation time. The one-vs-one classifier fits $k * (k - 1) / 2$ classifiers, resulting in a greater number of pairs, which leads to an increase in computation time.

Performance Metrics

The performance metrics in the case of multiclass classification would be the same as what we used for binary classification in the previous chapter, that is, precision, recall, and F1-score obtained using a confusion matrix.

In the case of a multiclass classification problem, we average out the metrics to find out the **micro-average** or **macro-average** of the precision, recall, and F1 score in a k-class system, where k is the number of classes. Averaging is useful in the case of multiclass classification since we have multiple class labels:

- **Micro-average**: This weighs each instance or prediction equally. It aggregates the contributions of all classes to compute the average metric. If our dataset is not balanced and we want our classifiers to be biased toward the least frequent classes, then we use the micro-average. The micro-average for precision, recall, and F1 metrics is calculated by summing up the individual true positives (TPs), false positives (FPs), and false negatives (FNs) as follows:

$$PRE_{micro} = \frac{TP_1 + TP_2 + \ldots + TP_k}{TP_1 + TP_2 + \ldots + TP_k + FP_1 + FP_2 + \ldots + FP_k}$$

$$Recall_{micro} = \frac{TP_1 + TP_2 + \ldots + TP_k}{TP_1 + TP_2 + \ldots + TP_k + FN_1 + FN_2 + \ldots + FN_k}$$

$$F1_{micro} = 2 \times \frac{PRE_{micro}}{Recall_{micro}}$$

Figure 9.4: Equation for calculating the micro-average of various performance metrics

- **Macro-average**: In the case of macro-averaging, all classes are equally weighted to evaluate the overall performance of a classifier with respect to the most frequent class labels. It computes the metric independently for each class and then takes the average (hence, treating all classes equally). If our dataset is not balanced and we want our classifiers to be biased toward the most frequent classes, then we use macro-average. The macro-average for the various performance metrics can be calculated as follows:

$$PRE_{macro} = \frac{PRE_1 + PRE_2 + \ldots + PRE_k}{k}$$

$$Recall_{macro} = \frac{Recall_1 + Recall_2 + \ldots + Recall_k}{k}$$

$$F1_{macro} = 2 \times \frac{PRE_{macro}}{Recall_{macro}}$$

Figure 9.5: Equation for calculating the macro-average of various performance metrics

Exercise 46: Evaluating Performance Using Multiclass Performance Metrics

In this exercise, we will evaluate the performance of our model using different metrics and observe the difference between the performance metrics:

1. Import the **load_wine** dataset, **numpy**, **svm**, **train_test_split**, **precision_recall_fscore_support**, **classification_report**, **confusion_matrix**, and **accuracy_score**:

```
from sklearn.metrics import precision_recall_fscore_support
import numpy as np
from sklearn.datasets import load_wine
from sklearn import svm
from sklearn.model_selection import train_test_split
from sklearn.metrics import classification_report,confusion_matrix,accuracy_score
```

2. Load the **wine** dataset and store it in a **wine_data** variable, as follows:

```
wine_data=load_wine()
```

3. Check the features and target:

```
wine_data['feature_names']
wine_data['target_names']
```

You will get the following output for the features:

```
['alcohol',
 'malic_acid',
 'ash',
 'alcalinity_of_ash',
 'magnesium',
 'total_phenols',
 'flavanoids',
 'nonflavanoid_phenols',
 'proanthocyanins',
 'color_intensity',
 'hue',
 'od280/od315_of_diluted_wines',
 'proline']
```

Figure 9.6: Features of the wine_data

You will get the following output for the target:

```
array(['class_0', 'class_1', 'class_2'], dtype='<U7')
```

Figure 9.7: Target names of wine_data

4. Split the data into training and testing sets and store it in the **X_train, X_test, y_train**, and **y_test** variables, as follows:

```
X_train, X_test, y_train, y_test = train_test_split(wine_
data['data'],wine_data['target'],test_size=0.20, random_state=123,
stratify=wine_data['target'])
```

5. Store the SVM linear model in the **model** variable and fit the SVM classifier to the training set. Store the fitted model in the **clf** variable:

```
model = svm.SVC(kernel='linear')
clf = model.fit(X_train,y_train)
```

6. Use the **predict** function of the classifier to predict on the test data and store the results in **y_pred**:

```
y_pred=clf.predict(X_test)
```

7. Fit the macro-averaging and the micro-averaging using the **precision_recall_fscore_support** function. The **precision_recall_fscore_support** function can directly calculate the metrics for micro- and macro-averages, as follows:

```
precision_recall_fscore_support(y_test, y_pred, average='macro')
precision_recall_fscore_support(y_test, y_pred, average='micro')
```

You will get approximately the following values as output for macro- and micro-averages respectively: **0.974, 0.976, 0.974, None** and **0.972, 0.972, 0.972, None**. These values represent the precision, recall, F1 score, and support metrics, respectively.

8. You can also calculate more detailed metrics statistics using the **classification_
    report** function. Store the target names of the wine data in the **target_names**
    variable. Generate the classification report using the **y_test** and **y_pred** variables:

```
target_names = wine_data['target_names']
print(classification_report(y_test, y_pred,target_names=target_names))
```

	precision	recall	f1-score	support
class_0	0.92	1.00	0.96	12
class_1	1.00	0.93	0.96	14
class_2	1.00	1.00	1.00	10
micro avg	0.97	0.97	0.97	36
macro avg	0.97	0.98	0.97	36
weighted avg	0.97	0.97	0.97	36

Figure 9.8: Output of the classification_report function

From the preceding classification report, we can see that when using micro-averaging, since each of the classes are equally weighted, we get similar scores for precision, recall, and f1, whereas macro-averaging gives weightage to the most frequent class labels, resulting in different scores.

Activity 18: Performing Multiclass Classification and Evaluating Performance

You have been provided with data on the annual spend amount of each of the 20,000 customers of a major retail company. The marketing team of the company used different channels to sell their goods and has segregated customers based on the purchases made using different channels, which are as follows: 0-Retail, 1-Road Show, 2-Social Media, and 3-Televison. As a data scientist, you are tasked with building a machine learning model that will be able to predict the most effective channel that can be used to target a customer based on the annual spend on the following seven products (features) sold by the company: fresh produce, milk, grocery, frozen products, detergents, paper, and delicatessen.

1. Import the required libraries.

2. Load the marketing data into a DataFrame named **data** using pandas and look at the first few rows of the DataFrame. It should appear as follows:

	Fresh	Milk	Grocery	Frozen	Detergents_Paper	Delicassen	Channel
0	6623.613537	5513.093240	6019.057354	5669.568008	5898.660607	5179.234947	2
1	5642.542497	5829.866565	3960.339943	4270.020548	3498.818262	4327.423268	2
2	5292.078175	6634.370556	4444.335138	4888.286021	3265.391352	4887.560190	2
3	5595.227928	4754.860698	2977.856511	3462.490957	3609.264559	4268.641413	0
4	5126.693267	6009.649079	3811.569943	4744.115976	3829.516831	5097.491872	2

Figure 9.9: The first five rows of the data DataFrame

3. Check the shape and the missing values, and show the summary report of the data.

The shape should be (20000,7), and there should be no null values in the data. The summary of the data should be as follows:

	Fresh	Milk	Grocery	Frozen	Detergents_Paper	Delicassen	Channel
count	20000.000000	20000.000000	20000.000000	20000.000000	20000.000000	20000.000000	20000.000000
mean	5853.350191	5267.873868	4873.362341	4899.477763	4786.331781	5613.672184	1.499350
std	1128.370297	1177.563192	1265.579790	1220.923393	1154.682284	1343.743103	1.118464
min	1.000000	1.000000	1.000000	1.000000	1.000000	1.000000	0.000000
25%	5155.249455	4438.167387	3983.317183	4071.997222	3877.943500	4705.582182	0.000000
50%	5988.720207	5337.741327	4828.100401	5048.099489	4857.070488	5425.888761	1.000000
75%	6573.895741	6081.755179	5784.992859	5684.876863	5602.146034	6574.281056	3.000000
max	10000.000000	10000.000000	10000.000000	10000.000000	10000.000000	10000.000000	3.000000

Figure 9.10: Summary of the data

4. Check the target variable, **Channel**, for the number of transactions for each of the channels. You should get the following output:

```
0    5007
3    5002
1    5001
2    4990
Name: Channel, dtype: int64
```

Figure 9.11: The number of transactions for each channel

5. Split the data into training and testing sets.

6. Fit a random forest classifier and store the model in a **clf_random** variable. Take the number of estimators as 20, the maximum depth as **None**, the number of samples as 7, and use **random_state=0**.

7. Predict on the test data and store the predictions in **y_pred**.

8. Find out the micro- and macro-average report using the **precision_recall_fscore_support** function.

9. Print the classification report. It should look as follows:

	precision	recall	f1-score	support
Retail	0.90	0.90	0.90	1002
RoadShow	0.87	0.85	0.86	1000
SocialMedia	0.93	0.92	0.92	998
Televison	0.87	0.89	0.88	1000
micro avg	0.89	0.89	0.89	4000
macro avg	0.89	0.89	0.89	4000
weighted avg	0.89	0.89	0.89	4000

Figure 9.12: Classification report for the Random Forest classifier

10. Plot the confusion matrix. It will appear as follows:

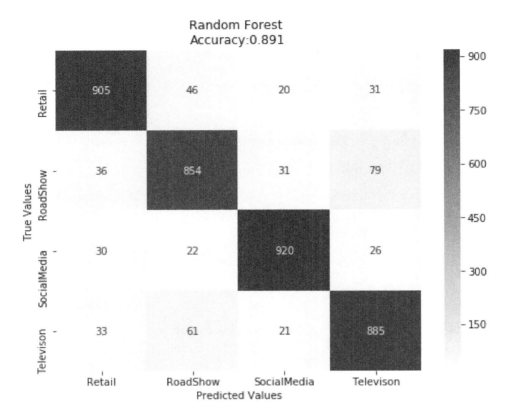

Figure 9.13: Confusion matrix for the Random Forest classifier

> **Note**
> The solution for this activity can be found on page 362.

Class Imbalanced Data

Class imbalance is the most common problem that a data scientist can encounter. Most real-world classification tasks involve classifying data, where one class or multiple classes are over-represented. This is called **class imbalance**. Common examples where class-imbalanced data is encountered is in fraud detection, anti-money laundering, spam detection, and cancer detection.

Exercise 47: Performing Classification on Imbalanced Data

For this exercise, we are going to use the mammography dataset from UCI. The dataset contains some attributes of patients, using which we need to build a model that can predict whether a patient will have cancer (that is, a malignant outcome, indicated by 1) or not (that is, a benign outcome, indicated by –1). 70% of the dataset has benign outcomes; hence, it is a highly imbalanced dataset. In this exercise, we will observe how imbalanced data affects the performance of a model:

1. Import **fetch_datasets**, **pandas**, **RandomForestClassifier**, **train_test_split**, **classification_report**, **confusion_matrix**, **accuracy_score**, **metrics**, **seaborn**, and **svm**:

    ```
    from imblearn.datasets import fetch_datasets
    import pandas as pd
    from sklearn.ensemble import RandomForestClassifier
    from sklearn.model_selection import train_test_split
    from sklearn.metrics import classification_report,confusion_
    matrix,accuracy_score
    from sklearn import metrics
    import matplotlib.pyplot as plt
    import seaborn as sns
    from sklearn import svm
    ```

2. Fetch the **mammography** dataset from **fetch_datasets** using the following code:

    ```
    mammography=fetch_datasets()['mammography']
    ```

3. Check the number of benign and malignant cases:

    ```
    pd.DataFrame(mammography['target'])[0].value_counts()
    ```

    The number of benign cases should be 10,923 and the number of malignant cases should be 260.

4. Split the data into training and testing sets, as shown here:

    ```
    X_train, X_test, y_train, y_test = train_test_
    split(mammography['data'],mammography['target'],test_size=0.20, random_
    state=123, stratify=mammography['target'])
    ```

5. Check the number of benign and malignant cases in both the training and testing data:

    ```
    pd.DataFrame(y_train)[0].value_counts()
    ```

    In the training data, the number of benign cases will be 8,738 and the number of malignant cases will be 208. Similarly, check for the testing data:

    ```
    pd.DataFrame(y_test)[0].value_counts()
    ```

    In the testing data, the number of benign cases will be 2,185 and the number of malignant cases will be 52.

6. Now, fit a random forest classifier using the following code and save the model to a **clf_random** variable:

    ```
    clf_random = RandomForestClassifier(n_estimators=20, max_depth=None,
        min_samples_split=7, random_state=0)
    clf_random.fit(X_train,y_train)
    ```

7. Predict on the test data and save the predictions to **y_pred**:

    ```
    y_pred=clf_random.predict(X_test)
    ```

8. Generate the classification report as shown here:

    ```
    target_names = ['Benign', 'Malignant']
    print(classification_report(y_test, y_pred,target_names=target_names))
    ```

    Your output will appear as follows:

    ```
                   precision    recall  f1-score   support

          Benign        0.99      1.00      0.99      2185
       Malignant        0.81      0.48      0.60        52

       micro avg        0.99      0.99      0.99      2237
       macro avg        0.90      0.74      0.80      2237
    weighted avg        0.98      0.99      0.98      2237
    ```

Figure 9.14: Output of the classification_report function

9. Finally, plot the confusion matrix:

```
cm = confusion_matrix(y_test, y_pred)
cm_df = pd.DataFrame(cm,
                     index = ['Benign', 'Malignant'],
                     columns = ['Benign', 'Malignant'])
plt.figure(figsize=(8,6))
sns.heatmap(cm_df, annot=True,fmt='g',cmap='Blues')
plt.title('Random Forest \nAccuracy:{0:.3f}'.format(accuracy_score(y_test,
y_pred)))
plt.ylabel('True Values')
plt.xlabel('Predicted Values')
plt.show()
```

Your output should appear as follows:

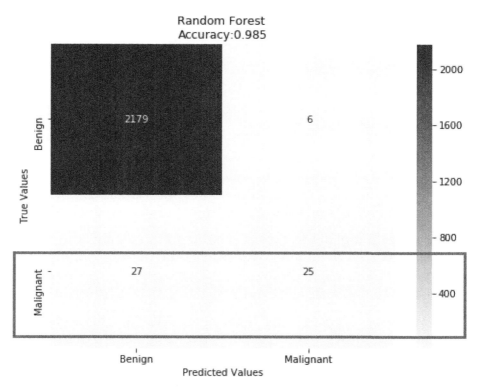

Figure 9.15: Confusion matrix for Random Forest classifier

From the preceding confusion matrix, we can say that our model classified 27 cases out of 52 cases as **Benign**; however, they were actually **Malignant**. Similarly, the model classified 6 cases as **Malignant**, when the cases were actually **Benign**.

It's therefore clear that class imbalance influenced the machine learning model to be more biased toward the majority class, which is **Benign**. This is because the machine learning algorithm learns by implicitly optimizing predictions depending on the most abundant class in the dataset to minimize the cost function during training. As a result, the classifier failed to correctly predict the malignant cases, which can be very dangerous in cancer detection, although the accuracy of the model is 98%. If we see the recall score for malignant cases, then it's less than 50%.

Dealing with Class-Imbalanced Data

One way of dealing with the imbalanced dataset is to assign a penalty to every wrong prediction on the minority class. This can be done using the `class_weight` parameter available in scikit-learn.

Therefore, the code in step 6 of the preceding exercise can be changed as shown here:

```
clf_random = RandomForestClassifier(n_estimators=20, max_depth=None,
    min_samples_split=7, random_state=0,class_weight='balanced')
```

There are other strategies to deal with imbalanced data as well. Some of them are as follows:

- **Random Undersampling**: In the case of random undersampling, the majority class samples are randomly eliminated to maintain class balance. The advantage of using this method is that it reduces the number of training samples, and hence the training time decreases; however, it may lead to underfitted models.

- **Random Oversampling**: In the case of random oversampling, the minority class samples are replicated randomly to represent a higher representation of the minority class in the training sample. The advantage of using this method is that there is no information loss; however, it may lead to overfitting of the data.

- **Synthetic Minority Oversampling Technique** (**SMOTE**): This technique is used to mitigate the problems we faced in random oversampling. In this method, a subset of the minority class data is taken, and a similar replica of the data is created, which is added to the main datasets. The advantage of using this method is that it reduces overfitting of the data and does not lead to any loss of information. However, it is not very effective for high-dimensional data.

Exercise 48: Visualizing Sampling Techniques

In this exercise, we will use the same mammography dataset from the previous exercise and see how each of the sampling strategies covered in the preceding section behaves. We will continue from our previous Jupyter Notebook, used in *Exercise 47*:

1. Import **RandomOverSampler**, **RandomUnderSampler**, **SMOTE**, **counter**, and **NumPy** library:

```
from imblearn.over_sampling import RandomOverSampler
from imblearn.under_sampling import RandomUnderSampler
from imblearn.over_sampling import SMOTE
from collections import Counter
import numpy as np
```

2. Create a **make_meshgrid** function. This function creates a rectangular grid out of an array of *x* and *y* values. The *x* and *y* values can be any of the two columns of the dataset that we want to plot. **meshgrid** is very useful to evaluate functions on a grid. Use the following code:

```
def make_meshgrid(x, y, h=.02):
    x_min, x_max = x.min() - 1, x.max() + 1
    y_min, y_max = y.min() - 1, y.max() + 1
    xx, yy = np.meshgrid(np.arange(x_min, x_max, h), np.arange(y_min, y_
max, h))
    return xx, yy
```

3. Create a **plot_contours** function for plotting the decision boundary and contours, respectively. This function will be used to plot the results of the classifier in terms of contours that it has predicted on the mesh grid that we built in the previous step. Use the following code:

```
def plot_contours(ax, clf, xx, yy, **params):
    Z = clf.predict(np.c_[xx.ravel(), yy.ravel()])
    Z = Z.reshape(xx.shape)
    out = ax.contourf(xx, yy, Z, **params)
    return out
```

4. We will take the first two columns from our mammography dataset and assign it to variable **X** and the target is assigned to variable **Y**, as follows:

```
X=mammography['data'][:,[0,1]]
y=mammography['target']
```

> **Note**
>
> You can use either of the two columns in the preceding snippet. Depending upon the columns used, the prediction results and contours may vary. For the best results, take the most important features or columns.

5. Check the number of samples present in the target variable for benign (−1) and malignant (1) cases:

```
print(sorted(Counter(y).items()))
```

Your output will show 10,923 benign cases and 260 malignant cases. Therefore, the target variable is highly imbalanced, as we saw previously as well.

6. We will use the same random forest classifier as we used in our previous exercise to fit our data. We will be using X and Y where we haven't used any sampling techniques on y to perform class imbalance. Fit an SVM model with an RBF kernel. We will start by fitting our original data, X and y, without using any kind of sampling techniques:

```
clf = clf_random.fit(X,y)
```

7. Use the **make_meshgrid** function that we created earlier to pass the first two column values (**X0** and **X1**) of the dataset and assign it to **xx** and **yy**:

```
fig, ax = plt.subplots()
# title for the plots
title = (' Decision surface of Random Forest using Original Data ')
# Set-up grid for plotting.
X0, X1 = X[:, 0], X[:, 1]
xx, yy = make_meshgrid(X0, X1)
```

8. Use the **plot_contour** function to pass the result of the subplot, the prediction from the classifier, and the meshgrid results (xx,yy) for plotting the prediction contours or the decision surface of the SVM classifier:

```
plot_contours(ax, clf, xx, yy, cmap=plt.cm.coolwarm, alpha=0.8)
ax.scatter(X0, X1, c=y, cmap=plt.cm.coolwarm, s=20, edgecolors='k')
ax.set_ylabel('y')
ax.set_xlabel('x')
ax.set_xticks(())
ax.set_yticks(())
ax.set_title(title)
plt.show()
```

You will get the following plot:

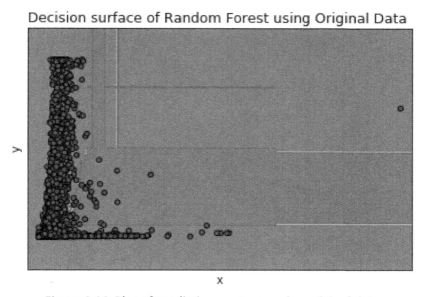

Figure 9.16: Plot of prediction contours using original data

Note

From this figure, we can see that only a few of the malignant cases are picked up by the classifier and many of the malignant cases are misclassified as **Benign**.

9. Let's now perform undersampling. Call the **RandomUnderSampler** function and store it in the **rus** variable, as shown:

```
rus = RandomUnderSampler(random_state=0)
```

10. Use the **fit_resample** method of **RandomUnderSampler** to resample our data and target variable and store the results in **X_resampled** and **y_resampled**, respectively:

```
X_resampled, y_resampled = rus.fit_
resample(mammography['data'],mammography['target'])
```

11. Once we have performed under sampling, check the class distribution using the **counter** function on **y_resampled** and print the results:

```
print(sorted(Counter(y_resampled).items()))
```

Your output will now show 260 benign cases and 260 malignant cases, implying that the target variable has been undersampled.

12. Fit the random forest classifier on the undersampled data, **X_resampled[:[0,1]]** and **y_resampled**. Use the **make_meshgrid** function to generate the meshgrid, as follows:

```
X=X_resampled[:,[0,1]]
y=y_resampled

clf = clf_random.fit(X,y)

fig, ax = plt.subplots()
# title for the plots
title = ('Decision surface of Random Forest using Under Sample')
# Set-up grid for plotting.
X0, X1 = X[:, 0], X[:, 1]
xx, yy = make_meshgrid(X0, X1)
```

13. Then, plot the prediction contours using the **plot_contours** function, as shown:

```
plot_contours(ax, clf, xx, yy, cmap=plt.cm.coolwarm, alpha=0.8)
ax.scatter(X0, X1, c=y, cmap=plt.cm.coolwarm, s=20, edgecolors='k')
ax.set_ylabel('y')
ax.set_xlabel('x')
ax.set_xticks(())
ax.set_yticks(())
ax.set_title(title)
plt.show()
```

Your plot should look as follows:

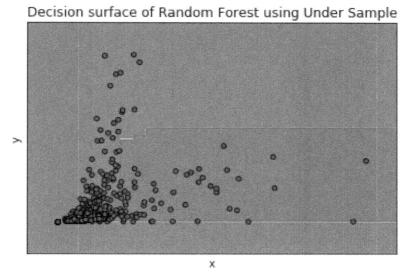

Figure 9.17: Plot of prediction contours using undersampling

From the preceding figure, we can see that many of the malignant cases are picked up by the classifier. However, we also have many less benign cases (260), which was originally 10,293. Due to the undersampling, our overall dataset has reduced.

14. Let's now perform oversampling. Call the **RandomOverSampler** function and store it in the **ros** variable, as shown:

```
ros = RandomOverSampler(random_state=0)
```

15. Use the **fit_resample** method of **RandomOverSampler** to resample our data and target variable and store the results in **X_resampled** and **y_resampled**, as follows:

```
X_resampled, y_resampled = ros.fit_
resample(mammography['data'],mammography['target'])
```

16. Once we have performed oversampling, check the class distribution using the **counter** function on **y_resampled**:

```
print(sorted(Counter(y_resampled).items()))
```

Your output will now show 10,923 benign and malignant cases, implying that the target variable has been oversampled.

17. Fit the SVM classifier on the oversampled data, **X_resampled[:[0,1]]** and **y_resampled**. Use **make_meshgrid** to generate the meshgrid, as follows:

```
X=X_resampled[:,[0,1]]
y=y_resampled

clf = clf_random.fit(X,y)

fig, ax = plt.subplots()
# title for the plots
title = ('Decision surface of Random Forest using sample')
# Set-up grid for plotting.
X0, X1 = X[:, 0], X[:, 1]
xx, yy = make_meshgrid(X0, X1)
```

18. Plot the prediction contours using the **plot_contours** function:

```
plot_contours(ax, clf, xx, yy, cmap=plt.cm.coolwarm, alpha=0.8)
ax.scatter(X0, X1, c=y, cmap=plt.cm.coolwarm, s=20, edgecolors='k')
ax.set_ylabel('y')
ax.set_xlabel('x')
ax.set_xticks(())
ax.set_yticks(())
ax.set_title(title)
#ax.legend()
plt.show()
```

The plot will look as follows:

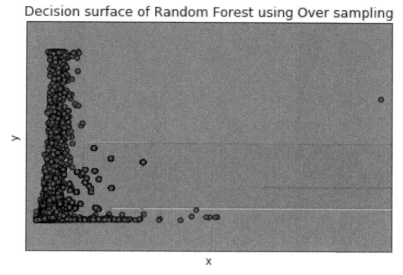

Figure 9.18: Plot pf prediction contours using oversampling

From the preceding figure, you will observe that many of the malignant cases are picked up by the classifier. However, we have oversampled our malignant cases by replicating data points, which increased from 260 to 10,923, and this may lead to an overfitted model.

19. Finally, let's perform SMOTE. Use the **fit_resample** method of the **SMOTE()** function to resample the data and store it in a variable, **x_resampled** and **y_resampled**, as shown:

```
X_resampled, y_resampled = SMOTE().fit_
resample(mammography['data'],mammography['target'])
```

20. Once we have performed SMOTE, check the class distribution using the **counter** function on **y_resampled**:

```
print(sorted(Counter(y_resampled).items()))
```

Your output will now show 10,923 benign and malignant cases.

21. Fit the random forest classifier on the data, **X_resampled[:[0,1]]** and **y_resampled**. Use the **make_meshgrid** function to generate the meshgrid, as follows:

```
X=X_resampled[:,[0,1]]
y=y_resampled

clf = clf_random.fit(X,y)

fig, ax = plt.subplots()
# title for the plots
title = ('Decision surface of Random Forest using SMOTE')
# Set-up grid for plotting.
X0, X1 = X[:, 0], X[:, 1]
xx, yy = make_meshgrid(X0, X1)
```

22. Plot the prediction contours using the **plot_contours** function:

```
plot_contours(ax, clf, xx, yy, cmap=plt.cm.coolwarm, alpha=0.8)
ax.scatter(X0, X1, c=y, cmap=plt.cm.coolwarm, s=20, edgecolors='k')
ax.set_ylabel('y')
ax.set_xlabel('x')
ax.set_xticks(())
ax.set_yticks(())
ax.set_title(title)
#ax.legend()
plt.show()
```

Your plot will appear as follows:

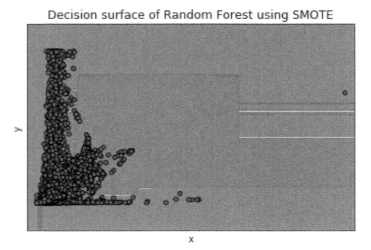

Figure 9.19: Plot of prediction contours using SMOTE

From the preceding figure, we can see that some of the malignant cases are not picked up by the classifier. Although by using SMOTE, our malignant cases increased from 260 to 10,923, unlike random oversampling, SMOTE doesn't simply duplicate the data; it generates a similar replica of the minority class and hence helps in generalizing the model.

Exercise 49: Fitting a Random Forest Classifier Using SMOTE and Building the Confusion Matrix

In *Exercise 47*, we noticed that our model was not able to generalize because of imbalanced data and our recall score was less than 50%. Out of 52 malignant cases, the model was able to pick only 25 cases correctly. In this exercise, we will build a model using SMOTE that will be able to correctly detect all the malignant cases and improve the recall score.

> **Note**
>
> Use the same Jupyter Notebook as the one used for the preceding two exercises.

1. We will use SMOTE for sampling our **X_train** and **y_train** data to build our classifier:

   ```
   X_resampled, y_resampled = SMOTE().fit_resample(X_train,y_train)
   ```

2. Fit the random forest classifier on the sampled data:

   ```
   clf_random.fit(X_resampled,y_resampled)
   ```

3. Predict on the test data:

   ```
   y_pred=clf_random.predict(X_test)
   ```

4. Generate the classification report, as follows:

   ```
   target_names = ['Benign', 'Malignant']
   print(classification_report(y_test, y_pred,target_names=target_names))
   ```

Your output will be as follows:

	precision	recall	f1-score	support
Benign	0.99	0.98	0.99	2185
Malignant	0.50	0.71	0.59	52
micro avg	0.98	0.98	0.98	2237
macro avg	0.75	0.85	0.79	2237
weighted avg	0.98	0.98	0.98	2237

Figure 9.20: Output of the classification_report function

5. Plot the confusion matrix using the following code:

```
cm = confusion_matrix(y_test, y_pred)

cm_df = pd.DataFrame(cm,
                index = ['Benign', 'Malignant'],
                columns = ['Benign', 'Malignant'])
plt.figure(figsize=(8,6))
sns.heatmap(cm_df, annot=True,fmt='g',cmap='Blues')
plt.title('Random Forest \nAccuracy:{0:.3f}'.format(accuracy_score(y_test,
y_pred)))
plt.ylabel('True Values')
plt.xlabel('Predicted Values')
plt.show()
```

It will appear as follows:

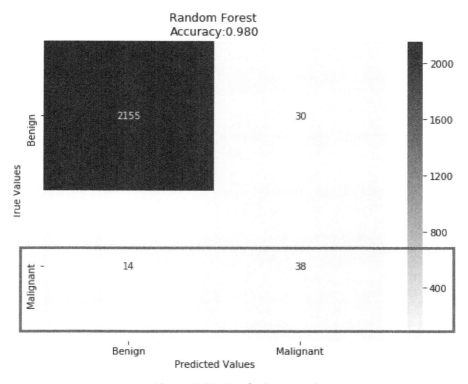

Figure 9.21: Confusion matrix

In the last two exercises, we implemented different techniques to deal with imbalanced datasets. However, it must be noted that there is no single method that can effectively deal with all imbalanced datasets. Each of these methods must be tried to find out the best possible method for a dataset. In *Exercise* 3, we saw that, without using class imbalance, our classifier was able to identify only 25 malignant cases, whereas using sampling techniques (SMOTE), the classifier identified 38 malignant cases. From the classification report, we can see that our recall score went up to 71% from 48%.

Activity 19: Dealing with Imbalanced Data

For this activity, we will be using the **bank.csv** dataset present in the **Lesson09** folder on GitHub. This dataset contains data related to the direct marketing campaigns (that were based on phone calls) of a Portuguese banking institution. Often, more than one contact for the same client was required, in order to access whether the product (bank term deposit) would be subscribed (**yes**) or not (**no**). The dataset contains some customer information (such as age, job, and so on) and campaign-related information (such as contact or communication type, day, month, and duration of the contact, and so on).

For the next marketing campaign, your company wants to use this data and only contact potential customers who will subscribe to the term deposit, thereby reducing the effort needed to contact those customers who are not interested. For this, you need to create a model that will be able predict whether customers will subscribe to the term deposit (variable **y**). Follow the steps given here:

1. Import all the necessary libraries.

2. Read the dataset into a pandas DataFrame named **bank** and look at the first few rows of the data. Your output should be as follows:

	age	job	marital	education	default	balance	housing	loan	contact	day	month	duration	campaign	pdays	previous	poutcome	y
0	30	unemployed	married	primary	no	1787	no	no	cellular	19	oct	79	1	-1	0	unknown	no
1	33	services	married	secondary	no	4789	yes	yes	cellular	11	may	220	1	339	4	failure	no
2	35	management	single	tertiary	no	1350	yes	no	cellular	16	apr	185	1	330	1	failure	no
3	30	management	married	tertiary	no	1476	yes	yes	unknown	3	jun	199	4	-1	0	unknown	no
4	59	blue-collar	married	secondary	no	0	yes	no	unknown	5	may	226	1	-1	0	unknown	no

Figure 9.22: The first few rows of bank data

3. Rename the **y** column as **Target**.

4. Replace the values **no** with **0** and **yes** with **1**.

5. Check the shape and missing values in the data. The shape should be (4334,17) and there should be no missing values.

6. Use the **describe** function to check the continuous and categorical values:

	age	balance	day	duration	campaign	pdays	previous	Target
count	4334.000000	4334.000000	4334.000000	4334.000000	4334.000000	4334.000000	4334.000000	4334.000000
mean	40.991924	1410.637517	15.913936	264.544301	2.806876	39.670974	0.544070	0.115828
std	10.505378	3010.612091	8.216673	260.642141	3.129682	99.934062	1.702219	0.320056
min	19.000000	-3313.000000	1.000000	4.000000	1.000000	-1.000000	0.000000	0.000000
25%	33.000000	67.000000	9.000000	104.000000	1.000000	-1.000000	0.000000	0.000000
50%	39.000000	440.000000	16.000000	186.000000	2.000000	-1.000000	0.000000	0.000000
75%	48.000000	1464.000000	21.000000	329.000000	3.000000	-1.000000	0.000000	0.000000
max	87.000000	71188.000000	31.000000	3025.000000	50.000000	871.000000	25.000000	1.000000

Figure 9.23: Output for continuous variables

> **Note**
>
> Specify **(include=['O'])** to get a summary of the categorical variables.

	job	marital	education	default	housing	loan	contact	month	poutcome
count	4334	4334	4334	4334	4334	4334	4334	4334	4334
unique	12	3	3	2	2	2	3	12	4
top	management	married	secondary	no	yes	no	cellular	may	unknown
freq	942	2680	2306	4261	2476	3650	2801	1339	3555

Figure 9.24: Output for categorical variables

7. Check the count of the class labels present in the target variable. You should get the following output:

```
0      3832
1       502
Name: Target, dtype: int64
```

Figure 9.25: Count of class labels

8. Use the **cat.codes** function to encode the **job**, **marital**, **default**, **housing**, **loan**, **contact**, and **poutcome** columns. Since **education** and **month** are ordinal columns, convert them as follows:

```
bank['education'].replace({'primary': 0, 'secondary': 1,'tertiary':2})
bank['month'].replace(['jan', 'feb', 'mar','apr','may','jun','jul','aug','
sep','oct','nov','dec'], [1,2,3,4,5,6,7,8,9,10,11,12], inplace = True)
```

9. Check the **bank** data after the conversion. You will get the following output:

	age	job	marital	education	default	balance	housing	loan	contact	day	month	duration	campaign	pdays	previous	poutcome	Target
0	30	10	1	0	10	1787	1	0	0	19	10	79	1	-1	0	3	0
1	33	7	1	1	7	4789	1	1	0	11	5	220	1	339	4	0	0
2	35	4	2	2	4	1350	2	0	0	16	4	185	1	330	1	0	0
3	30	4	1	2	4	1476	1	1	2	3	6	199	4	-1	0	3	0
4	59	1	1	1	1	0	1	0	2	5	5	226	1	-1	0	3	0

Figure 9.26: The first few rows of bank data after conversion

10. Split the data into training and testing sets using **train_test_split**.

11. Check the number of classes in **y_train** and **y_test**. You will get the output [(0,3256, (1, 427)] for **y_train** and [(0, 576), (1, 75)] for **y_test**.

12. Use the **standard_scalar** function to transform the **X_train** and **X_test** data. Assign it to the **X_train_sc** and **X_test_sc** variables.

13. Call the random forest classifier with parameters **n_estimators=20**, **max_depth=None**, **min_samples_split=7**, and **random_state=0**.

14. Fit the random forest model.

15. Predict on the test data using the random forest model.

16. Get the classification report:

```
               precision    recall  f1-score   support

          No        0.92      0.98      0.95       576
         Yes        0.67      0.32      0.43        75

   micro avg        0.90      0.90      0.90       651
   macro avg        0.79      0.65      0.69       651
weighted avg        0.89      0.90      0.89       651
```

Figure 9.27: Classification report

17. Get the confusion matrix:

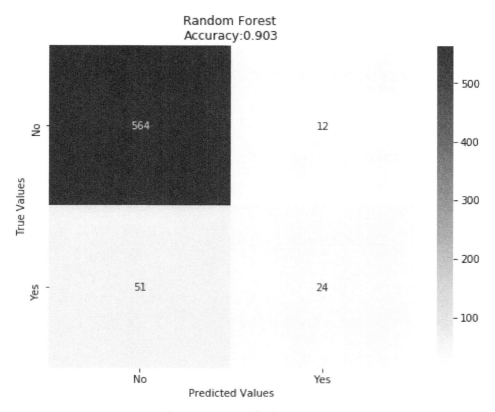

Figure 9.28: Confusion matrix

18. Use the `smote()` function on **x_train** and **y_train**. Assign it to the **x_resampled** and **y_resampled** variables, respectively.

19. Use **standard_scalar** to fit on **x_resampled** and **x_test**. Assign it to the **X_train_sc_resampled** and **X_test_sc** variables.

20. Fit the random forest classifier on **X_train_sc_resampled** and **y_resampled**.

21. Predict on **X_test_sc**.

22. Generate the classification report. It should look as follows:

	precision	recall	f1-score	support
No	0.95	0.90	0.92	576
Yes	0.45	0.61	0.52	75
micro avg	0.87	0.87	0.87	651
macro avg	0.70	0.76	0.72	651
weighted avg	0.89	0.87	0.88	651

Figure 9.29: Classification report of the random forest classifier

23. Plot the confusion matrix. It should appear as follows:

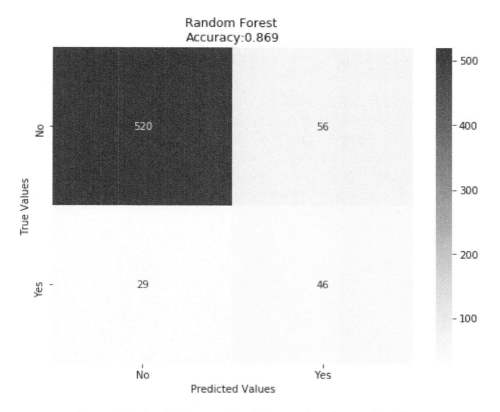

Figure 9.30: Confusion matrix of the random forest classifier

Note

The solution for this activity can be found on page 364.

Summary

In this chapter, we understood the logic behind multiclass classification problems. We created a multiclass classifier to predict the most suitable channel to be used to target customers. Through different examples and exercises, we tackled imbalanced datasets. This chapter also gave us an idea of how using different sampling methods can be useful in tackling imbalanced data.

In this book, we have covered several topics that are fundamental to marketing analytics. Beginning with data manipulation and visualization in Python, we covered customer segmentation using unsupervised methods such as clustering, predicted customer spend, and developed ideas for both regression and classification problems using a variety of use cases. Finally, we evaluated and tuned different machine learning models and learned how to handle imbalanced datasets. Following these chapters, you should now be able to think like a data scientist and apply these skills to different marketing scenarios.

Appendix

About

This section is included to assist the students to perform the activities in the book.
It includes detailed steps that are to be performed by the students to achieve the objectives of the activities.

Chapter 1: Data Preparation and Cleaning

Activity 1: Addressing Data Spilling

1. Import **pandas** and **copy** into the console, as follows:

    ```
    import pandas as pd
    import copy
    ```

2. Use the **read_excel** function to read the xlsx file and the **head** function to look at the first few rows:

    ```
    sales = pd.read_excel("sales.xlsx")
    sales.head()
    ```

3. Look at the data types of **sales** and see if they make more sense:

    ```
    sales.dtypes
    ```

    You should get the following output:

    ```
    Year              int64
    Product          object
    line             object
    Product.1        object
    type             object
    Product.2        object
    Order            object
    method           object
    type.1           object
    Retailer         object
    country          object
    Revenue          object
    Planned          object
    revenue          object
    Product.3        object
    cost            float64
    Quantity        float64
    Unit            float64
    cost.1          float64
    Unit.1          float64
    price           float64
    Gross           float64
    profit          float64
    Unit.2          float64
    sale            float64
    price.1         float64
    dtype: object
    ```

Figure 1.57: Looking at the datatype of sales.xlsx

4. We can iterate through the DataFrame rows to understand how the data is in the first row and how it should be:

```
forlabel,content in sales.iteritems():
    print label, content[1]
```

This gives the following output:

```
Year 2004
Product Camping
line Equipment
Product.1 Cooking
type Gear
Product.2 TrailChef
Order Water
method Bag
type.1 Telephone
Retailer Canada
country 13444.68
Revenue 14313.48
Planned 6298.8
revenue 2172
Product.3 2.9
cost 6.59
Quantity 7145.88
Unit 6.19
cost.1 nan
Unit.1 nan
price nan
Gross nan
profit nan
Unit.2 nan
sale nan
price.1 nan
```

Figure 1.58: Iterating through the first row

5. From the preceding output, you can infer that the data should actually contain column names starting with a capital letter. Add the following code to get an overview of what the data should actually look like:

```
d = {"Year": 2004, "Product line": "Camping Equipment", "Product
type":"Cooking Gear", "Product":"TrailChef Water Bag",
    "Order method type":"Telephone", "Retailer Country":"Canada",
"Revenue":13444.68, "Planned revenue":14313.48,
    "Product cost":6298.8, "Quantity":2172, "Unit cost":2.9, "Unit
price":6.59, "Gross Profit":7145.88, "Unit sale price":6.19}
```

You should get the following output:

```
pd.DataFrame(d, index = ["0"])
```

	Gross Profit	Order method type	Planned revenue	Product	Product cost	Product line	Product type	Quantity	Retailer Country	Revenue	Unit cost	Unit price	Unit sale . price	Year
0	7145.88	Telephone	14313.48	TrailChef Water Bag	6298.8	Camping Equipment	Cooking Gear	2172	Canada	13444.68	2.9	6.59	6.19	2004

Figure 1.59: Looking at how the data should be structured

6. The **Year** column seems to be in its right place, so we can start by creating the **Product line** column. Let's see how many values it has leaked into:

```
sales.groupby(['Product','line'])['Year'].count()
```

Your output will be as follows:

```
Product        line
Camping        Equipment      20112
Golf           Equipment       6615
Mountaineering Equipment       9261
Outdoor        Protection      6615
Personal       Accessories    22932
Name: Year, dtype: int64
```

Figure 1.60: Seeing how values are distributed across the columns

7. We are not sure whether the spillage is only restricted to these two columns, so let's look at the next column too, to be sure:

```
sales.groupby(['Product','line', 'Product.1'])['Year'].count()
```

Your output will be as follows:

```
Product          line          Product.1
Camping          Equipment     Cooking      5880
                               Lanterns     5292
                               Packs        2646
                               Sleeping     3087
                               Tents        3207
Golf             Equipment     Golf         1764
                               Irons        1764
                               Putters      1323
                               Woods        1764
Mountaineering   Equipment     Climbing     3087
                               Rope         1764
                               Safety       1764
                               Tools        2646
Outdoor          Protection    First        2205
                               Insect       2205
                               Sunscreen    2205
Personal         Accessories   Binoculars   2646
                               Eyewear      7056
                               Knives       3087
                               Navigation   4410
                               Watches      5733
Name: Year, dtype: int64
```

Figure 1.61: Looking at data to get the number of columns required

8. Let's resolve the **Product line** column and see if we were able to do anything:

```
sales['Product line'] = sales.apply(lambda x: x['Product'] +''+ x['line'],
axis = 1)
sales = sales.drop(['Product', 'line'], axis = 1)
sales.head()
```

The DataFrame should now look as follows:

type	Product.2	Order	method	type.1	Retailer	country	Revenue	...	Unit	cost.1	Unit.1	price	Gross	profit	Unit.2	sale	price.1	Product line
Gear	TrailChef	Water	Bag	Telephone	United	States	315044	...	156672.570	5.195714	NaN	NaN	NaN	NaN	NaN	NaN	NaN	Camping Equipment
Gear	TrailChef	Water	Bag	Telephone	Canada	13444.7	14313.5	...	6.190	NaN	NaN	NaN	NaN	NaN	NaN	NaN	NaN	Camping Equipment
Gear	TrailChef	Water	Bag	Telephone	Mexico	NaN	NaN	...	NaN	NaN	NaN	NaN	NaN	NaN	NaN	NaN	NaN	Camping Equipment
Gear	TrailChef	Water	Bag	Telephone	Brazil	NaN	NaN	...	NaN	NaN	NaN	NaN	NaN	NaN	NaN	NaN	NaN	Camping Equipment
Gear	TrailChef	Water	Bag	Telephone	Japan	181120	235237	...	5.488	NaN	NaN	NaN	NaN	NaN	NaN	NaN	NaN	Camping Equipment

Figure 1.62: Collecting data from multiple columns into the correct field

9. Instead of directly changing the sales DataFrame, let's create a copy of it, called **tmp**, and make changes to it. Once we have finalized the filtering procedure, we don't want to lose the original DataFrame. Let's continue looking at the next column of interest, that is, **Product type**:

```
tmp = copy.deepcopy(sales)
tmp.groupby(['Product.1','type', 'Product.2'])['Year'].count()
```

This gives the following output:

```
Product.1    type         Product.2
Binoculars   Opera        Vision        441
             Ranger       Vision        441
             Seeker       35            441
                          50            441
                          Extreme       441
                          Mini          441
Climbing     Accessories  Firefly      1323
                          Granite      1764
Cooking      Gear         TrailChef    5880
Eyewear      Bella        E-mail         63
                          Fax            63
                          Mail           63
                          Sales          63
                          Special        63
                          Telephone      63
                          Web            63
             Capri        E-mail         63
                          Fax            63
                          Mail           63
                          Sales          63
                          Special        63
                          Telephone      63
                          Web            63
             Cat          Eye           441
             Dante        E-mail         63
```

Figure 1.63: Seeing variation in number of words required to represent product type

We can see that some fields are not the fields we are interested in. Let's limit our view to only those that we are interested in.

10. As we are only interested in the **Climbing Accessories**, **Cooking Gear**, **First Aid**, **Golf Accessories**, **Insect Repellents**, and **Sleeping Bags** product types, so let's filter them out. Using a similar logic as before, we store these columns in a new DataFrame, **tmp1**:

```
tmp1 = copy.deepcopy(tmp[tmp['Product.1'].isin(['Climbing', 'Cooking',
'First', 'Golf', 'Insect', 'Sleeping'])])
tmp1.head()
```

This gives the following output:

	Year	Product.1	type	Product.2	Order	method	type.1	Retailer	country	Revenue	...	Unit	cost.1	Unit.1	price	Gross	profit	Unit.2
0	2004	Cooking	Gear	TrailChef	Water	Bag	Telephone	United	States	315044	...	156672.570	5.195714	NaN	NaN	NaN	NaN	NaN
1	2004	Cooking	Gear	TrailChef	Water	Bag	Telephone	Canada	13444.7	14313.5	...	6.190	NaN	NaN	NaN	NaN	NaN	NaN
2	2004	Cooking	Gear	TrailChef	Water	Bag	Telephone	Mexico	NaN	NaN	...	NaN	NaN	NaN	NaN	NaN	NaN	NaN
3	2004	Cooking	Gear	TrailChef	Water	Bag	Telephone	Brazil	NaN	NaN	...	NaN	NaN	NaN	NaN	NaN	NaN	NaN
4	2004	Cooking	Gear	TrailChef	Water	Bag	Telephone	Japan	181120	235237	...	5.488	NaN	NaN	NaN	NaN	NaN	NaN

5 rows × 25 columns

Figure 1.64: Filtering out the categories we need

Then perform the following **groupby** operations as well:

```
tmp1.groupby(['Product.1')['Year'].count()
tmp1.groupby(['Product.1', 'type', 'Product.2'])['Year'].count()
```

This gives the following output:

```
tmp1.groupby(['Product.1'])['Year'].count()

Product.1
Climbing    3087
Cooking     5880
First       2205
Golf        1764
Insect      2205
Sleeping    3087
Name: Year, dtype: int64
```

```
tmp1.groupby(['Product.1','type', 'Product.2'])['Year'].count()

Product.1  type         Product.2
Climbing   Accessories  Firefly      1323
                        Granite      1764
Cooking    Gear         TrailChef    5880
First      Aid          Aloe          441
                        Calamine      441
                        Compact       441
                        Deluxe        441
                        Insect        441
Golf       Accessories  Course       1764
Insect     Repellents   BugShield    2205
Sleeping   Bags         Hibernator   3087
Name: Year, dtype: int64
```

Figure 1.65: Looking for the variation in the required product types categories

We can see that—because of our choice of fields—luckily, we only have to append two columns to get the attribute we need.

11. Now that we know **tmp1** requires only two words for **Product type**, we are done:

```
tmp1['Product type'] = tmp1['Product.1'] + ''+ tmp1['type']
tmp1 = tmp1.drop(['Product.1', 'type'], axis = 1)
tmp1.head()
```

This gives the following output:

Order	method	type.1	Retailer	country	Revenue	Planned revenue	...	cost.1	Unit.1	price	Gross	profit	Unit.2	sale	price.1	Product line	Product type
Water	Bag	Telephone	United	States	315044	437477	158372 ...	5.195714	NaN	NaN	NaN	NaN	NaN	NaN	NaN	Camping Equipment	Cooking Gear
Water	Bag	Telephone	Canada	13444.7	14313.5	6298.8	2172 ...	NaN	NaN	NaN	NaN	NaN	NaN	NaN	NaN	Camping Equipment	Cooking Gear
Water	Bag	Telephone	Mexico	NaN	NaN	NaN	NaN ...	NaN	NaN	NaN	NaN	NaN	NaN	NaN	NaN	Camping Equipment	Cooking Gear
Water	Bag	Telephone	Brazil	NaN	NaN	NaN	NaN ...	NaN	NaN	NaN	NaN	NaN	NaN	NaN	NaN	Camping Equipment	Cooking Gear
Water	Bag	Telephone	Japan	181120	235237	89413.1	35696 ...	NaN	NaN	NaN	NaN	NaN	NaN	NaN	NaN	Camping Equipment	Cooking Gear

Figure 1.66: Joining data with these required categories

12. The next column we have to worry about is **Product**. Let's see how many columns we need for that:

```
tmp1.groupby(['Product.2', 'Order'])['Year'].count()
```

This gives the following output:

```
Product.2   Order
Aloe        Relief          441
BugShield   Extreme         441
            Lotion          882
            Natural         441
            Spray           441
Calamine    Relief          441
Compact     Relief          441
Course      Pro            1764
Deluxe      Family          441
Firefly     Charger         441
            Climbing        441
            Rechargeable    441
Granite     Belay           441
            Carabiner       441
            Chalk           441
            Pulley          441
Hibernator  Camp            441
            E-mail           63
            Extreme         441
            Fax              63
            Lite            441
            Mail             63
            Pad             441
            Pillow          441
            Sales            63
            Self            441
```

Figure 1.67: Looking at the variation in the product category

This column has some values that are one word and some that are more than that.

13. Let's create another variable, **tmp2**, for values containing more than one word:

```
tmp2 = copy.deepcopy(tmp1[~tmp1['Order'].isin(['E-mail', 'Fax', 'Mail',
'Sales', 'Special', 'Telephone', 'Web'])])
tmp2.head()
```

This gives the following output:

	Year	Product.2	Order	method	type.1	Retailer	country	Revenue	Planned	revenue	...	cost.1	Unit.1	price	Gross	profit	Unit.2	sale	price.1
0	2004	TrailChef	Water	Bag	Telephone	United	States	315044	437477	158372	...	5.195714	NaN	NaN	NaN	NaN	NaN	NaN	NaN
1	2004	TrailChef	Water	Bag	Telephone	Canada	13444 7	14313.5	6298.8	2172	...	NaN	NaN	NaN	NaN	NaN	NaN	NaN	NaN
2	2004	TrailChef	Water	Bag	Telephone	Mexico	NaN	NaN	NaN	NaN	...	NaN	NaN	NaN	NaN	NaN	NaN	NaN	NaN
3	2004	TrailChef	Water	Bag	Telephone	Brazil	NaN	NaN	NaN	NaN	...	NaN	NaN	NaN	NaN	NaN	NaN	NaN	NaN
4	2004	TrailChef	Water	Bag	Telephone	Japan	181120	235237	89413.1	35696	...	NaN	NaN	NaN	NaN	NaN	NaN	NaN	NaN

5 rows × 24 columns

Figure 1.68: Filtering out observations with values containing more than one word

14. We look at the variation in **tmp2** and see that, while most of the columns have two words, some columns have more than two words:

```
tmp2.groupby(['Product.2','Order', 'method'])['Year'].count()
```

This gives the following output:

```
Calamine      Relief        E-mail        63
                            Fax           63
                            Mail          63
                            Sales         63
                            Special       63
                            Telephone     63
                            Web           63
Compact       Relief        Kit           441
Course        Pro           Gloves        441
                            Golf          882
                            Umbrella      441
Deluxe        Family        Relief        441
Firefly       Charger       E-mail        63
                            Fax           63
                            Mail          63
                            Sales         63
                            Special       63
                            Telephone     63
                            Web           63
              Climbing      Lamp          441
              Rechargeable  Battery       441
Granite       Belay         E-mail        63
                            Fax           63
                            Mail          63
                            Sales         63
                            Special       63
                            Telephone     63
                            Web           63
```

Figure 1.69: Distribution in the next few fields

15. We keep on performing this procedure of repeatedly storing values that have more leakage into another variable, until we have exhausted all the columns and got a structured dataset by the last step:

```
tmp8 = copy.deepcopy(tmp7[tmp7['Product.3'].isin(['Kingdom', 'States'])])
tmp8.head()
```

This gives the following output:

Year	revenue	Product.3	cost	Quantity	Unit	cost.1	Unit.1	price	Gross	profit	Unit.2	sale	price.1	Product line	Product type	Product	Order method type
2004	United	States	5819.70	6586.16	1733.2	619.0	2.8	10.64	4086.50	5.105	NaN	NaN	NaN	Golf Equipment	Golf Accessories	Course Pro Golf and Tee Set	Sales visit
2004	United	Kingdom	NaN	NaN	NaN	NaN	NaN	NaN	NaN	NaN	NaN	NaN	NaN	Golf Equipment	Golf Accessories	Course Pro Golf and Tee Set	Sales visit
2005	United	States	10904.28	11363.52	2990.4	1068.0	2.8	10.64	7913.88	10.210	NaN	NaN	NaN	Golf Equipment	Golf Accessories	Course Pro Golf and Tee Set	Sales visit
2005	United	Kingdom	27987.84	28855.68	7593.6	2712.0	2.8	10.64	20394.24	10.320	NaN	NaN	NaN	Golf Equipment	Golf Accessories	Course Pro Golf and Tee Set	Sales visit
2006	United	States	NaN	NaN	NaN	NaN	NaN	NaN	NaN	NaN	NaN	NaN	NaN	Golf Equipment	Golf Accessories	Course Pro Golf and Tee Set	Sales visit

Figure 1.70: Distribution after structuring the longest parts

After structuring the fields with the longest names for **Products**, **Order method type**, and **Retailer country**, we can see that there is no spillage in the columns containing numerical values. Let's handle the remaining cases directly.

16. We finish structuring the last part of the data directly and store the final structured data separately:

```
tmp8['Retail country'] = tmp8['revenue'] + '' + tmp8['Product.3']
tmp8 = tmp8.drop(['revenue', 'Product.3'], axis = 1)
tmp8["Revenue"] = tmp8['cost']
tmp8 = tmp8.drop(['cost'], axis = 1)
tmp8["Planned revenue"] = tmp8['Quantity']
tmp8 = tmp8.drop(['Quantity'], axis = 1)
tmp8["Product cost"] = tmp8['Unit']
tmp8 = tmp8.drop(['Unit'], axis = 1)
tmp8["Quantity"] = tmp8['cost.1']
tmp8 = tmp8.drop(['cost.1'], axis = 1)
tmp8["Unit cost"] = tmp8['Unit.1']
tmp8 = tmp8.drop(['Unit.1'], axis = 1)
tmp8["Unit price"] = tmp8['price']
```

```
tmp8 = tmp8.drop(['price'], axis = 1)
tmp8["Gross profit"] = tmp8['Gross']
tmp8 = tmp8.drop(['Gross'], axis = 1)
tmp8["Unit sale price"] = tmp8['profit']
tmp8 = tmp8.drop(['profit', 'Unit.2', 'sale', 'price.1'], axis = 1)
tmp8.head()
```

This gives the following output:

	Year	Product line	Product type	Product	Order method type	Retail country	Revenue	Planned revenue	Product cost	Quantity	Unit cost	Unit price	Gross profit	Unit sale price
17514	2004	Golf Equipment	Golf Accessories	Course Pro Golf and Tee Set	Sales visit	United States	5819.70	6586.16	1733.2	619.0	2.8	10.64	4086.50	5.105
17529	2004	Golf Equipment	Golf Accessories	Course Pro Golf and Tee Set	Sales visit	United Kingdom	NaN	NaN	NaN	NaN	NaN	NaN	NaN	NaN
38682	2005	Golf Equipment	Golf Accessories	Course Pro Golf and Tee Set	Sales visit	United States	10904.28	11363.52	2990.4	1068.0	2.8	10.64	7913.88	10.210
38697	2005	Golf Equipment	Golf Accessories	Course Pro Golf and Tee Set	Sales visit	United Kingdom	27987.84	28855.68	7593.6	2712.0	2.8	10.64	20394.24	10.320
59850	2006	Golf Equipment	Golf Accessories	Course Pro Golf and Tee Set	Sales visit	United States	NaN	NaN	NaN	NaN	NaN	NaN	NaN	NaN

Figure 1.71: Fully structuring the data for the longest data

We store the structured dataset separately as **str1**:

```
str1 = tmp8
```

17. Once we structure the last layer of the data completely like this, it is easier for us to structure the layer just before it, as we can use the knowledge of the previous layer and reduce structuring the current layer to a problem we have already solved before:

```
temp = copy.deepcopy(tmp7[~tmp7.index.isin(tmp8.index.values)])
temp.head()
```

You should get the following output:

	Year	revenue	Product.3	cost	Quantity	Unit	cost.1	Unit.1	price	Gross profit	Unit.2	sale	price.1	Product line	Product type	Product
17515	2004	Canada	NaN	NaN	NaN	NaN	NaN	NaN	NaN	NaN	NaN	NaN	NaN	NaN	Golf Equipment	Golf Accessories	Course Pro Golf and Tee Set
17516	2004	Mexico	13497.6	14598.08	3841.6	1372.0	2.8	10.64	9656.02	6.806667	NaN	NaN	NaN	NaN	Golf Equipment	Golf Accessories	Course Pro Golf and Tee Set
17517	2004	Brazil	NaN	NaN	NaN	NaN	NaN	NaN	NaN	NaN	NaN	NaN	NaN	NaN	Golf Equipment	Golf Accessories	Course Pro Golf and Tee Set
17518	2004	Japan	NaN	NaN	NaN	NaN	NaN	NaN	NaN	NaN	NaN	NaN	NaN	NaN	Golf Equipment	Golf Accessories	Course Pro Golf and Tee Set
17519	2004	Korea	8433.46	8788.64	2312.8	826.0	2.8	10.64	6120.66	10.210000	NaN	NaN	NaN	NaN	Golf Equipment	Golf Accessories	Course Pro Golf and Tee Set

Figure 1.72: Structuring data with the second longest data fields

18. Now, we keep on going backward and structure the entire dataset with the help of the correctly structured preceding layers:

```
temp1['Retailer country'] = temp1['method']
temp1 = temp1.drop(['method'], axis = 1)
\temp1["Planned revenue"] = temp1['Retailer']
temp1 = temp1.drop(['Retailer'], axis = 1)
temp1["Product cost"] = temp1['country']
temp1 = temp1.drop(['country'], axis = 1)
temp1["Unit cost"] = temp1['Planned']
temp1 = temp1.drop(['Planned'], axis = 1)
temp1["Unit price"] = temp1['revenue']
temp1 = temp1.drop(['revenue'], axis = 1)
temp1["Gross profit"] = temp1['Product.3']
temp1 = temp1.drop(['Product.3'], axis = 1)
temp1["Unit sale price"] = temp1['cost']
temp1 = temp1.drop(['cost'], axis = 1)
```

```
temp1["Quantity"]  = temp1['Revenue']
temp1 = temp1.drop(['Revenue'], axis = 1)
temp1['Revenue'] = temp1['type.1']
temp1 = temp1.drop('type.1', axis = 1)
temp1 = temp1[['Year', 'Product line', 'Product type', 'Product', 'Order
method type', 'Retailer country', 'Revenue',
'Planned revenue', 'Product cost', 'Quantity', 'Unit cost', 'Unit price',
'Gross profit', 'Unit sale price']]


temp1.head()
```

This gives the following output:

	Year	Product line	Product type	Product	Order method type	Retailer country	Revenue	Planned revenue	Product cost	Quantity	Unit cost	Unit price	Gross profit	Unit sale price
2500	2004	Camping Equipment	Sleeping Bags	Hibernator	Telephone	Canada	NaN	NaN	NaN	NaN	NaN	NaN	NaN	NaN
2501	2004	Camping Equipment	Sleeping Bags	Hibernator	Telephone	Mexico	26627.2	28631.8	16770	195	86	146.83	9857.25	136.550
2502	2004	Camping Equipment	Sleeping Bags	Hibernator	Telephone	Brazil	NaN	NaN	NaN	NaN	NaN	NaN	NaN	NaN
2503	2004	Camping Equipment	Sleeping Bags	Hibernator	Telephone	Japan	624589	720054	421744	4904	86	146.83	202845	130.823
2504	2004	Camping Equipment	Sleeping Bags	Hibernator	Telephone	Korea	NaN	NaN	NaN	NaN	NaN	NaN	NaN	NaN

Figure 1.73: Iteratively going backward while stabilizing the longest fields

19. Finally, we just make sure to combine our data and we are done:

```
df = pd.concat([str1, str2, str3, str4, str5, str6, str7, str8, str9,
str10, str11, str12, str13, str14,
               str15, str16, str17, str18, str19, str20, str21, str22],
sort = True)[['Year', 'Product line',
'Product type', 'Product', 'Order method type', 'Retailer country',
'Revenue', 'Planned revenue',
'Product cost', 'Quantity', 'Unit cost', 'Unit price', 'Gross profit',
'Unit sale price']]
df.groupby('Product type').count()
```

This gives the following output:

Product type	Year	Product line	Product	Order method type	Retailer country	Revenue	Planned revenue	Product cost	Quantity	Unit cost	Unit price	Gross profit	Unit sale price
Climbing Accessories	3087	3087	3087	3087	3087	729	729	729	729	729	729	729	729
Cooking Gear	5880	5880	5880	5880	5880	2059	2059	2059	2053	2059	2059	2059	2059
First Aid	2205	2205	2205	2205	2205	812	812	812	809	812	812	812	812
Golf Accessories	1764	1764	1764	1764	1323	619	619	619	615	619	619	619	619
Insect Repellents	2205	2205	2205	2205	2205	795	795	795	795	795	795	795	795
Sleeping Bags	3087	3087	3087	3087	3087	1216	1190	1189	1017	1189	1189	1189	1189

Figure 1.74: Combining Data Sources

Chapter 2: Data Exploration and Visualization

Activity 2: Analyzing Advertisements

1. Import pandas and seaborn using the following code:

```
import pandas as pd
import seaborn as sns
sns.set()
```

2. Read the **Advertising.csv** file and look at the first few rows:

```
ads = pd.read_csv("Advertising.csv", index_col = 'Date')
ads.head()
```

3. Look at the memory and other internal information about the DataFrame:

```
ads.info
```

This gives the following output:

```
<class 'pandas.core.frame.DataFrame'>
Index: 200 entries, 2018-01-01 to 2018-07-19
Data columns (total 4 columns):
TV          200 non-null float64
newspaper   200 non-null float64
radio       200 non-null float64
sales       200 non-null float64
dtypes: float64(4)
memory usage: 7.8+ KB
```

Figure 2.63: The result of ads.info()

4. As all the attributes are numeric, it is enough to understand the distribution of the data with **describe()**:

```
ads.describe()
```

This gives the following output:

	TV	newspaper	radio	sales
count	200.000000	200.000000	200.000000	200.000000
mean	147042.500000	30554.000000	23264.000000	14022.500000
std	85854.236315	21778.620839	14846.809176	5217.456566
min	700.000000	300.000000	0.000000	1600.000000
25%	74375.000000	12750.000000	9975.000000	10375.000000
50%	149750.000000	25750.000000	22900.000000	12900.000000
75%	218825.000000	45100.000000	36525.000000	17400.000000
max	296400.000000	114000.000000	49600.000000	27000.000000

Figure 2.64: The result of ads.describe()

5. See how the values in the column are spread:

```
ads.quantile([0.1, 0.2, 0.3, 0.4, 0.5, 0.6, 0.7, 0.8, 0.9, 1.0])
```

As all values are within a reasonable range, we don't need to filter out any data and can directly proceed.

6. Look at the histograms of individual features and understand the values better:

```
sns.distplot(ads['TV'], kde = False)
sns.distplot(ads['newspaper'], kde = False)
sns.distplot(ads['radio'], kde = False)
sns.distplot(ads['sales'], kde = False)
```

Looking at the data, it is clear that we are interested in analyzing behaviors that drive an increase in sales. Therefore, **sales** is the KPI we need to look at.

7. Understand the relationships between columns with this command:

```
sns.pairplot(ads)
```

This should give the following output:

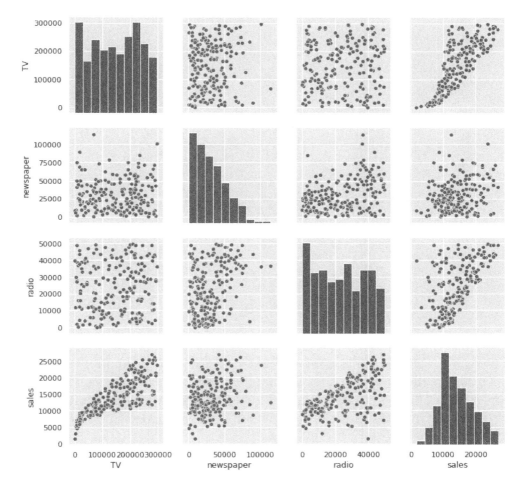

Figure 2.65: Output of pairplot of the ads feature

You can derive the following insights from the data: Both **TV** and **radio** have a clear positive correlation with **sales**. The correlation with **newspaper** is not that direct, but as the distribution of newspapers is low, we can't make a claim about no or negative correlation.

8. You can also try to find unknown or hidden relationships in the data. Let's analyze the relationship between **newspaper** and **sales**:

```
ads[['newspaper', 'sales']].plot()
```

```
<matplotlib.axes._subplots.AxesSubplot at 0x7f1939231410>
```

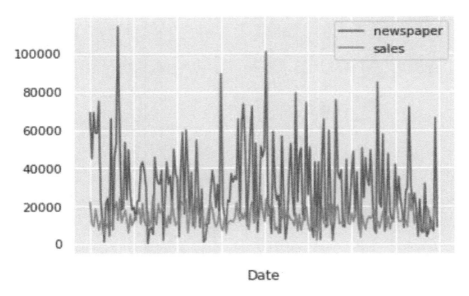

Date

Figure 2.66: pandas plot of the relationship between newpaper and sales

There seems to be a trend in the sales values preceding the newspaper value. We can look at this relationship in detail in further analysis. Anyway, the data seems to be fully explored now. The data from 1st Jan 2018 to 19th July 2018 has **TV** and **radio** in direct correlation with **sales**, but the relationship between **sales** and **newspaper** can be explored further using different techniques.

Chapter 3: Unsupervised Learning: Customer Segmentation

Activity 3: Loading, Standardizing, and Calculating Distance with a Dataset

1. Load the data from the **customer_interactions.csv** file into a pandas DataFrame and look at the first five rows of data:

```
import pandas as pd
df = pd.read_csv('customer_interactions.csv')
df.head()
```

2. Calculate the Euclidean distance between the first two data points in the DataFrame using the following code:

```
import math
math.sqrt((df.loc[0, 'spend'] - df.loc[1, 'spend'])**2 + (df.loc[0,
'interactions'] - df.loc[1, 'interactions'])**2)
```

> **Note**
>
> There are other, more concise methods for calculating distance, including using the SciPy package. Since we are doing it here for pedagogical reasons, we have used the most explicit method.

3. Calculate the standardized values of the variables and store them in new columns named **z_spend** and **z_interactions**. Use **df.head()** to look at the first five rows of data:

```
df['z_spend'] = (df['spend'] - df['spend'].mean())/df['spend'].std()
df['z_interactions'] = (df['interactions'] - df['interactions'].mean())/
df['interactions'].std()
df.head()
```

4. Calculate the distance between the first two data points using the standardized values:

```
math.sqrt((df.loc[0, 'z_spend'] - df.loc[1, 'z_spend'])**2 + (df.loc[0,
'z_interactions'] - df.loc[1, 'z_interactions'])**2)
```

Activity 4: Using k-means Clustering on Customer Behavior Data

1. Read in the data in the **customer_offers.csv** file, and set the **customer_name** column to the index:

```
import pandas as pd

customer_offers = pd.read_csv('customer_offers.csv')
customer_offers = customer_offers.set_index('customer_name')
```

2. Perform k-means clustering with three clusters, and save the cluster each data point is assigned to:

```
from sklearn import cluster

model = cluster.KMeans(n_clusters=3, random_state=10)
cluster = model.fit_predict(customer_offers)
offer_cols = customer_offers.columns
customer_offers['cluster'] = cluster
```

3. Use PCA to visualize the clusters:

```
from sklearn import decomposition
import matplotlib.pyplot as plt
%matplotlib inline

pca = decomposition.PCA(n_components=2)
customer_offers['pc1'], customer_offers['pc2'] = zip(*pca.fit_
transform(customer_offers[offer_cols]))

colors = ['r', 'b', 'k', 'g']
markers = ['^', 'o', 'd', 's']

for c in customer_offers['cluster'].unique():
  d = customer_offers[customer_offers['cluster'] == c]
  plt.scatter(d['pc1'], d['pc2'], marker=markers[c], color=colors[c])

plt.show()
```

4. For each cluster, investigate how they differ from the average in each of our features. In other words, find how much customers in each cluster differ from the average proportion of times they responded to an offer. Plot these differences in a bar chart:

```
total_proportions = customer_offers[offer_cols].mean()
for i in range(3):
  plt.figure(i)
  cluster_df = customer_offers[customer_offers['cluster'] == i]
  cluster_proportions = cluster_df[offer_cols].mean()

  diff = cluster_proportions - total_proportions
  plt.bar(range(1, 33), diff)
```

5. Load the information about what the offers were from **offer_info.csv**. For each cluster, find the five offers where the cluster differs most from the mean, and print out the varietal of those offers:

```
offer_info = pd.read_csv('offer_info.csv')
for i in range(3):
  cluster_df = customer_offers[customer_offers['cluster'] == i]
  cluster_proportions = cluster_df[offer_cols].mean()

  diff = cluster_proportions - total_proportions
  cluster_rep_offers = list(diff.sort_values(ascending=False).index.
astype(int)[0:5])
  print(offer_info.loc[offer_info['offer_id'].isin(cluster_rep_
offers),'varietal'])
```

From Figure 3.24 (which shows the top five offers for each cluster), you will notice that most of the wines in the first list are champagne, and the one that isn't is Prosecco, a type of sparkling wine closely related to champagne. Similarly, the last cluster contains mostly Pinot Noir, and one Malbec, which is a red wine similar to Pinot Noir. The second cluster might contain customers who care less about the specific type of wine, since it contains a white, a red, and three sparkling wines. This might indicate that the first group would be a good target in the future for offers involving champagne, and the second group might be a good target for offers involving red wines.

Chapter 4: Choosing the Best Segmentation Approach

Activity 5: Determining Clusters for High-End Clothing Customer Data Using the Elbow Method with the Sum of Squared Errors

1. Read in the data from **four_cols.csv**:

```
import pandas as pd
df = pd.read_csv('four_cols.csv')
```

2. Inspect the data using the **head** function:

```
df.head()
```

3. Standardize all columns:

```
cols = df.columns
zcols = []
for col in cols:
    df['z_' + col] = (df[col] - df[col].mean())/df[col].std()
    zcols.append('z_' + col)
```

4. Plot the data, using dimensionality reduction (principal component analysis):

```
from sklearn import decomposition
import matplotlib.pyplot as plt
%matplotlib inline

pca = decomposition.PCA(n_components=2)
df['pc1'], df['pc2'] = zip(*pca.fit_transform(df[zcols]))

plt.scatter(df['pc1'], df['pc2'])
plt.show()
```

5. Visualize clustering with two and seven clusters:

```
from sklearn import cluster

colors = ['r', 'b', 'k', 'g', 'm', 'y', 'c']
markers = ['^', 'o', 'd', 's', 'P', 'X', 'v']

plt.figure(figsize=(12,16))
```

```
for n in range(2,8):
  model = cluster.KMeans(n_clusters=n, random_state=10)
  df['cluster'] = model.fit_predict(df[zcols])

  plt.subplot(3, 2, n-1)
  for c in df['cluster'].unique():
    d = df[df['cluster'] == c]
    plt.scatter(d['pc1'], d['pc2'], marker=markers[c], color=colors[c])

plt.show()
```

6. Create a plot of the sum of squared errors and look for an elbow:

```
import numpy as np

ss = []
krange = list(range(2,11))
X = df[zcols].values
for n in krange:
  model = cluster.KMeans(n_clusters=n, random_state=10)
  model.fit_predict(X)
  cluster_assignments = model.labels_
  centers = model.cluster_centers_
  ss.append(np.sum((X - centers[cluster_assignments]) ** 2))

plt.plot(krange, ss)
plt.xlabel("$K$")
plt.ylabel("Sum of Squares")
plt.show()
```

Activity 6: Using Different Clustering Techniques on Customer Behavior Data

1. Read in the data from **customer_offers.csv**:

```
import pandas as pd
df = pd.read_csv('customer_offers.csv').set_index('customer_name')
```

2. Use mean-shift clustering (with quantile = 0.1) to cluster the data:

```
from sklearn import cluster

X = df.as_matrix()
bandwidth = cluster.estimate_bandwidth(X, quantile=0.1, n_samples=500)
ms = cluster.MeanShift(bandwidth=bandwidth, bin_seeding=True)

df['ms_cluster'] = ms.fit_predict(X)
```

3. Use k-modes clustering (with **k=4**) to cluster the data:

```
from kmodes.kmodes import KModes

km = KModes(n_clusters=4)
df['kmode_cluster'] = km.fit_predict(X)
```

4. Use k-means clustering (with **k=4** and **random_state=100**) to cluster the data:

```
model = cluster.KMeans(n_clusters=4, random_state=100)
df['kmean_cluster'] = model.fit_predict(X)
```

5. Using dimensionality reduction (principal component analysis), visualize the resulting clustering of each method:

```
from sklearn import decomposition
import matplotlib.pyplot as plt
%matplotlib inline

colors = ['r', 'b', 'k', 'g']
markers = ['^', 'o', 'd', 's']

pca = decomposition.PCA(n_components=2)
df['pc1'], df['pc2'] = zip(*pca.fit_transform(X))

plt.figure(figsize=(8,12))
```

```
ax = plt.subplot(3, 1, 1)
for c in df['ms_cluster'].unique():
  d = df[df['ms_cluster'] == c]
  plt.scatter(d['pc1'], d['pc2'], marker=markers[c], color=colors[c])
ax.set_title('mean-shift')
ax = plt.subplot(3, 1, 2)
for c in df['kmode_cluster'].unique():
  d = df[df['kmode_cluster'] == c]
  plt.scatter(d['pc1'], d['pc2'], marker=markers[c], color=colors[c])
ax.set_title('kmode')

ax = plt.subplot(3, 1, 3)
for c in df['kmean_cluster'].unique():
  d = df[df['kmean_cluster'] == c]
  plt.scatter(d['pc1'], d['pc2'], marker=markers[c], color=colors[c])
ax.set_title('kmean')

plt.show()
```

Activity 7: Evaluating Clustering on Customer Behavior Data

1. Import the data from **customer_offers.csv**:

```
import pandas as pd
df = pd.read_csv('customer_offers.csv').set_index('customer_name')
```

2. Perform a train-test split using **random_state = 100**:

```
from sklearn import model_selection

X_train, X_test = model_selection.train_test_split(df, random_state = 100)
```

> **Note**
>
> This is a relatively small dataset, with only 100 data points, so it is pretty sensitive to how the data is split up. When datasets are small like this, it might make sense to use other cross-validation methods, which you can read about here: https://scikit-learn.org/stable/modules/cross_validation.html.

3. Plot the silhouette scores for k-means clustering using *k* ranging from 2 to 10:

```
from sklearn import cluster
from sklearn import metrics
import matplotlib.pyplot as plt
%matplotlib inline

krange = list(range(2,11))
avg_silhouettes = []
for n in krange:
  model = cluster.KMeans(n_clusters=n, random_state=100)
  model.fit(X_train)
  cluster_assignments = model.predict(X_test)
  silhouette_avg = metrics.silhouette_score(X_test, cluster_assignments)
  avg_silhouettes.append(silhouette_avg)

plt.plot(krange, avg_silhouettes)
plt.xlabel("$K$")
plt.ylabel("Average Silhouette Score")
plt.show()
```

From the plot, you will observe that the maximum silhouette score is obtained at **k=3**.

4. Use the *k* found in the previous step, and print out the silhouette score on the test set:

```
model = cluster.KMeans(n_clusters=3, random_state=100)
model.fit(X_train)

km_labels = model.predict(X_test)
km_silhouette = metrics.silhouette_score(X_test, km_labels)

print('k-means silhouette score: ' + str(km_silhouette))
```

5. Perform mean-shift clustering and print out its silhouette score on the test set:

```
bandwidth = cluster.estimate_bandwidth(X_train, quantile=0.1, n_
samples=500)
ms = cluster.MeanShift(bandwidth=bandwidth, bin_seeding=True)

ms.fit(X_train)

ms_labels = ms.predict(X_test)

ms_silhouette = metrics.silhouette_score(X_test, ms_labels)
print('mean-shift silhouette score: ' + str(ms_silhouette))
```

6. Perform k-modes clustering and print out its silhouette score on the test set:

```
from kmodes.kmodes import KModes

km = KModes(n_clusters=4)
km.fit(X_train)

kmode_labels = km.predict(X_test)

kmode_silhouette = metrics.silhouette_score(X_test, kmode_labels)

print('k-mode silhouette score: ' + str(kmode_silhouette))
```

Chapter 5: Predicting Customer Revenue Using Linear Regression

Activity 8: Examining Relationships between Storefront Locations and Features about their Area

1. Load the data from **location_rev.csv** and then take a look at it:

```
import pandas as pd

df = pd.read_csv('location_rev.csv')
df.head()
```

2. Use seaborn's **pairplot** function to visualize the data and its relationships:

    ```
    import seaborn as sns
    %matplotlib inline
    ```

    ```
    sns.pairplot(df)
    ```

3. Use correlations to investigate the relationship between the different variables and the location revenue:

    ```
    df.corr()
    ```

The resulting correlations should make sense. The more competitors in the area, the lower the revenue of a location, while the median income, loyalty members, and population density are all positively related. A location's age is also positively correlated with revenue, indicating that the longer a location is open, the better known it is and the more customers it attracts (or perhaps, only locations that do well last a long time).

Activity 9: Building a Regression Model to Predict Storefront Location Revenue

1. Import the data from **location_rev.csv** and view the first few rows:

    ```
    import pandas as pd
    df = pd.read_csv('location_rev.csv')
    df.head()
    ```

2. Create a variable, **X**, with the predictors in it, and store the outcome (revenue) in a separate variable, **y**:

    ```
    X = df[['num_competitors',
            'median_income',
            'num_loyalty_members',
            'population_density',
            'location_age'
            ]]
    y = df['revenue']
    ```

3. Split the data into training and test sets. Use **random_state = 100**:

```
from sklearn.model_selection import train_test_split

X_train, X_test, y_train, y_test = train_test_split(X, y, random_state =
100)
```

4. Create a linear regression model and fit it on the training data:

```
from sklearn.linear_model import LinearRegression

model = LinearRegression()
model.fit(X_train,y_train)
```

5. Print out the model coefficients:

```
model.coef_
```

6. Print out the model intercept:

```
model.intercept_
```

7. Produce a prediction for a location that has 3 competitors; a median income of 30,000; 1,200 loyalty members; a population density of 2,000; and a location age of 10:

```
single_location = pd.DataFrame({
    'num_competitors': [3],
    'median_income': [30000],
    'num_loyalty_members': [1200],
    'population_density': [2000],
    'location_age': [10]
})

model.predict(single_location)
```

8. Plot the model predictions versus the true values on the test data:

```
import matplotlib.pyplot as plt
%matplotlib inline

plt.scatter(model.predict(X_test),y_test)
plt.xlabel('Model Predictions')
plt.ylabel('True Value')
plt.plot([0, 100000], [0, 100000], 'k-', color = 'r')
plt.show()
```

9. Calculate the correlation between the model predictions and the true values of the test data:

```
from scipy.stats.stats import pearsonr

pearsonr(model.predict(X_test),y_test)
```

The first number shows an extremely high correlation value (just over 0.9, where 1.0 would be a perfect correlation). The second number shows an extremely small p-value, indicating that it's very unlikely that this correlation is due to chance. Taken together, this indicates that our model is working very well on the test data.

Chapter 6: Other Regression Techniques and Tools for Evaluation

Activity 10: Testing Which Variables are Important for Predicting Responses to a Marketing Offer

1. Import **pandas**, read in the data from **offer_responses.csv**, and use the **head** function to view the first five rows of the data:

```
import pandas as pd

df = pd.read_csv('offer_responses.csv')
df.head()
```

2. Import **train_test_split** from **sklearn** and use it to split the data into a training and test set, using responses as the **y** variable and all others as the predictor (**X**) variables. Use **random_state=10** for **train_test_split**:

```
from sklearn.model_selection import train_test_split

X = df[['offer_quality',
        'offer_discount',
        'offer_reach'
       ]]

y = df['responses']

X_train, X_test, y_train, y_test = train_test_split(X, y, random_state = 10)
```

3. Import **LinearRegression** and **mean_squared_error** from **sklearn**. Fit a model to the training data (using all of the predictors), get predictions from the model on the test data, and print out the calculated RMSE on the test data:

```
from sklearn.linear_model import LinearRegression
from sklearn.metrics import mean_squared_error


model = LinearRegression()
model.fit(X_train,y_train)


predictions = model.predict(X_test)


print('RMSE with all variables: ' + str(mean_squared_error(predictions,
y_test)**0.5))
```

4. Create **X_train2** and **X_test2** by dropping **offer_quality** from **X_train** and **X_test**. Train and evaluate the RMSE of the model using **X_train2** and **X_test2**:

```
X_train2 = X_train.drop('offer_quality',axis=1)
X_test2 = X_test.drop('offer_quality',axis=1)


model = LinearRegression()
model.fit(X_train2,y_train)


predictions = model.predict(X_test2)


print('RMSE without offer quality: ' + str(mean_squared_error(predictions,
y_test)**0.5))
```

5. Perform the same sequence of steps from step 4, but this time dropping **offer_discount** instead of **offer_quality**:

```
X_train3 = X_train.drop('offer_discount',axis=1)
X_test3 = X_test.drop('offer_discount',axis=1)


model = LinearRegression()
model.fit(X_train3,y_train)


predictions = model.predict(X_test3)


print('RMSE without offer discount: ' + str(mean_squared_
error(predictions, y_test)**0.5))
```

6. Perform the same sequence of steps, but this time dropping **offer_reach**:

```
X_train4 = X_train.drop('offer_reach',axis=1)
X_test4 = X_test.drop('offer_reach',axis=1)

model = LinearRegression()
model.fit(X_train4,y_train)

predictions = model.predict(X_test4)

print('RMSE without offer reach: ' + str(mean_squared_error(predictions,
y_test)**0.5))
```

You should notice that the RMSE went up when **offer_reach** or **offer_discount** was removed from the model, but remained about the same when **offer_quality** was removed. This suggests that **offer_quality** isn't contributing to the accuracy of the model and could be safely removed to simplify the model.

Activity 11: Using Lasso Regression to Choose Features for Predicting Customer Spend

1. Import **pandas**, use it to read the data in **customer_spend.csv**, and use the **head** function to view the first five rows of data:

```
import pandas as pd

df = pd.read_csv('customer_spend.csv')
df.head()
```

2. Use **train_test_split** from **sklearn** to split the data into training and test sets, with **random_state=100** and **cur_year_spend** as the **y** variable:

```
from sklearn.model_selection import train_test_split

cols = df.columns[1:]
X = df[cols]

y = df['cur_year_spend']

X_train, X_test, y_train, y_test = train_test_split(X, y, random_state =
100)
```

3. Import **Lasso** from **sklearn** and fit a lasso model (with **normalize=True** and **random_state=10**) to the training data:

```
from sklearn.linear_model import Lasso

lasso_model = Lasso(normalize=True, random_state=10)
lasso_model.fit(X_train,y_train)
```

4. Get the coefficients from the lasso model, and store the names of the features that have non-zero coefficients along with their coefficient values in the **selected_features** and **selected_coefs** variables, respectively:

```
coefs = lasso_model.coef_
selected_features = cols[coefs > 0]
selected_coefs = coefs[coefs > 0]
```

5. Print out the names of the features with non-zero coefficients and their associated coefficient values using the following code:

```
for coef, feature in zip(selected_coefs, selected_features):
    print(feature + ' coefficient: ' + str(coef))
```

From the output, we can see not only which variables are important, but also the effect that they have. For example, for each dollar a customer spent in the previous year, we can expect a customer to spend approximately $0.80 this year, everything else being equal.

Activity 12: Building the Best Regression Model for Customer Spend Based on Demographic Data

1. Import pandas, read the data in **spend_age_income_ed.csv** into a DataFrame, and use the **head** function to view the first five rows of the data:

```
import pandas as pd

df = pd.read_csv('spend_age_income_ed.csv')
df.head()
```

2. Perform a train-test split, with **random_state=10**:

```
from sklearn.model_selection import train_test_split

X = df[['age','income','years_of_education']]
y = df['spend']

X_train, X_test, y_train, y_test = train_test_split(X, y, random_state =
10)
```

3. Fit a linear regression model to the training data:

```
from sklearn.linear_model import LinearRegression

model = LinearRegression()
model.fit(X_train,y_train)
```

4. Fit two regression tree models to the data, one with **max_depth=2** and one with **max_depth=5**:

```
from sklearn.tree import DecisionTreeRegressor

max2_tree_model = DecisionTreeRegressor(max_depth=2)
max2_tree_model.fit(X_train,y_train)

max5_tree_model = DecisionTreeRegressor(max_depth=5)
max5_tree_model.fit(X_train,y_train)
```

5. Fit two random forest models to the data, one with **max_depth=2**, one with **max_depth=5**, and **random_state=10** for both:

```
from sklearn.ensemble import RandomForestRegressor

max2_forest_model = RandomForestRegressor(max_depth=2, random_state=10)
max2_forest_model.fit(X_train,y_train)

max5_forest_model = RandomForestRegressor(max_depth=5, random_state=10)
max5_forest_model.fit(X_train,y_train)
```

6. Calculate and print out the RMSE on the test data for all five models:

```
from sklearn.metrics import mean_squared_error

linear_predictions = model.predict(X_test)
print('Linear model RMSE: ' + str(mean_squared_error(linear_predictions,
y_test)**0.5))

max2_tree_predictions = max2_tree_model.predict(X_test)
print('Tree with max depth of 2 RMSE: ' + str(mean_squared_error(max2_
tree_predictions, y_test)**0.5))

max5_tree_predictions = max5_tree_model.predict(X_test)
print('Tree with max depth of 5 RMSE: ' + str(mean_squared_error(max5_
tree_predictions, y_test)**0.5))

max2_forest_predictions = max2_forest_model.predict(X_test)
print('Random Forest with max depth of 2 RMSE: ' + str(mean_squared_
error(max2_forest_predictions, y_test)**0.5))

max5_forest_predictions = max5_forest_model.predict(X_test)
print('Random Forest with max depth of 5 RMSE: ' + str(mean_squared_
error(max5_forest_predictions, y_test)**0.5))
```

We can see that, with this particular problem, a random forest with a max depth of 5 does best out of the models we tried. In general, it's good to try a few different types of models and values for hyperparameters to make sure you get the model that captures the relationships in the data well.

Chapter 7: Supervised Learning: Predicting Customer Churn

Activity 13: Performing OSE from OSEMN

1. Import the necessary libraries.

    ```
    import pandas as pd
    import numpy as np
    import matplotlib.pyplot as plt
    import seaborn as sns
    ```

    Read the dataset using pandas **read.csv**. and look at the first few rows of the DataFrame:

    ```
    data= pd.read_csv(r'Telco_Churn_Data.csv')
    data.head(5)
    ```

2. Check the length and shape of the data.

    ```
    len(data)
    data.shape
    ```

    The length should be 4708 and the shape should be (4708, 15).

3. Check for any missing values present in the data set and use the **info** method to check missing values in each of the columns.

    ```
    data.isnull().values.any()
    ```

    This will return **True**, implying that missing values are present.

    ```
    data.info()
    ```

This gives the following output:

```
<class 'pandas.core.frame.DataFrame'>
RangeIndex: 4708 entries, 0 to 4707
Data columns (total 15 columns):
Target Churn                 4708 non-null object
Target Code                  4708 non-null int64
Current Bill Amt             4708 non-null int64
Avg Calls                    4708 non-null float64
Avg Calls Weekdays           4708 non-null float64
Account Age                  4708 non-null int64
Percent Increase MOM         4708 non-null float64
Acct Plan Subtype            4708 non-null object
Complaint Code               4701 non-null object
Avg Days Delinquent          4708 non-null float64
Current TechSupComplaints    4708 non-null int64
Current Days OpenWorkOrders  4708 non-null float64
Equipment Age                4708 non-null int64
Condition of Current Handset 4264 non-null float64
Avg Hours WorkOrderOpenned   4708 non-null float64
dtypes: float64(7), int64(5), object(3)
memory usage: 551.8+ KB
```

Figure 7.58: Output of data.info

4. Rename all the columns in a readable format. Convert all the columns names with a space to _, for example, rename **Target Code** to **Target_Code**.

    ```
    data.columns=data.columns.str.replace(' ','_')
    data.columns
    ```

5. Check the descriptive statistics of the data

    ```
    data.describe()
    ```

6. Check the descriptive statistics of Categorical variable

    ```
    data.describe(include='object')
    ```

7. Change the data type of **Target_Code**, **Condition_of_Current_Handset**, and **Current_TechSupComplaints** columns from continuous to categorical object type:

    ```
    data['Target_Code']=data.Target_Code.astype('object')
    data['Condition_of_Current_Handset']=data.Condition_of_Current_Handset.astype('object')
    data['Current_TechSupComplaints']=data.Current_TechSupComplaints.astype('object')
    data['Target_Code']=data.Target_Code.astype('int64')
    data.describe(include='object')
    ```

    This gives the following output:

	Target_Churn	Acct_Plan_Subtype	Complaint_Code	Current_TechSupComplaints	Condition_of_Current_Handset
count	4708	4708	4701	4708	4264.0
unique	2	2	6	11	3.0
top	No Churn	Silver	Billing Problem	0	1.0
freq	2421	3914	2908	3589	4186.0

    Figure 7.59: Output of describe function for categorical variables

8. Check the percentage of missing values and then impute the values of both **Complaint_Code** and **Condition_of_Current_Handset** with the most occurring values:

    ```
    round(data.isnull().sum()/len(data)*100,2)
    ```

    ```
    Target_Churn                    0.00
    Target_Code                     0.00
    Current_Bill_Amt                0.00
    Avg_Calls                       0.00
    Avg_Calls_Weekdays              0.00
    Account_Age                     0.00
    Percent_Increase_MOM            0.00
    Acct_Plan_Subtype               0.00
    Complaint_Code                  0.15
    Avg_Days_Delinquent             0.00
    Current_TechSupComplaints       0.00
    Current_Days_OpenWorkOrders     0.00
    Equipment_Age                   0.00
    Condition_of_Current_Handset    9.43
    Avg_Hours_WorkOrderOpenned      0.00
    dtype: float64
    ```

    Figure 7.60: Checking percentage of missing values

```
data.Complaint_Code.value_counts()
```

```
Billing Problem          2908
Call Quality             1070
Moving                    511
Check Account             195
Inaccurate Sales Inf       13
Pricing                     4
Name: Complaint_Code, dtype: int64
```

Figure 7.61: Checking missing values in Complaint_Code

```
data.Condition_of_Current_Handset.value_counts()
```

```
1.0    4186
2.0      74
3.0       4
Name: Condition_of_Current_Handset, dtype: int64
```

Figure 7.62: Checking missing values in Condition_of_Current_Handset

```
data['Complaint_Code']=data['Complaint_Code'].fillna(value='Billing
Problem')
data['Condition_of_Current_Handset']=data['Condition_of_Current_Handset'].
fillna(value=1)
data['Condition_of_Current_Handset']=data.Condition_of_Current_Handset.
astype('object')
```

9. Perform data exploration by initially exploring the customer **Target_Churn** variable:

```
data['Target_Churn'].value_counts(0)
data['Target_Churn'].value_counts(1)*100
summary_churn = data.groupby('Target_Churn')
summary_churn.mean()
```

10. Find the correlation among different variables:

```
corr = data.corr()
plt.figure(figsize=(15,8))
sns.heatmap(corr,
            xticklabels=corr.columns.values,
            yticklabels=corr.columns.values,annot=True)
corr
```

From the plots, you will observe that `Avg_Calls_Weekdays` and `Avg_Calls` are highly correlated, which makes sense since they represent the same thing–average calls. `Current_Bill_Amt` seems to be correlated with both variables, which is as expected, since the more you talk the higher your bill will be.

11. Perform univariate and bivariate analysis.

    Here's the univariate analysis:

    ```
    f, axes = plt.subplots(ncols=3, figsize=(15, 6))
    sns.distplot(data.Avg_Calls_Weekdays, kde=True,  color="darkgreen",
    ax=axes[0]).set_title('Avg_Calls_Weekdays')
    axes[0].set_ylabel('No of Customers')
    sns.distplot(data.Avg_Calls, kde=True,color="darkblue", ax=axes[1]).set_
    title('Avg_Calls')
    axes[1].set_ylabel('No of Customers')
    sns.distplot(data.Current_Bill_Amt, kde=True, color="maroon", ax=axes[2]).
    set_title('Current_Bill_Amt')
    axes[2].set_ylabel('No of Customers')
    ```

    And here's the bivariate analysis:

    Code for the plot of `Complaint_Code` versus `Target_Churn`, is given here:

    ```
    plt.figure(figsize=(17,10))
    p=sns.countplot(y="Complaint_Code", hue='Target_Churn',
    data=data,palette="Set2")
    legend = p.get_legend()
    legend_txt = legend.texts
    legend_txt[0].set_text("No Churn")
    legend_txt[1].set_text("Churn")
    p.set_title('Customer Complaint Code Distribution')
    ```

    From this plot, you'll observe that call quality and billing problems are the two main reasons for customer churn.

    Cod for the plot of `Acct_Plan_Subtype` versus `Target_Churn` is given here:

    ```
    plt.figure(figsize=(15,4))
    p=sns.countplot(y="Acct_Plan_Subtype", hue='Target_Churn',
    data=data,palette="Set2")
    legend = p.get_legend()
    legend_txt = legend.texts
    legend_txt[0].set_text("No Churn")
    legend_txt[1].set_text("Churn")
    p.set_title('Customer Acct_Plan_Subtype Distribution')
    ```

Code for the plot of **Current_TechSupComplaints** versus **Target_Churn** is given here:

```
plt.figure(figsize=(15,4))
p=sns.countplot(y="Current_TechSupComplaints", hue='Target_Churn',
data=data,palette="Set2")
legend = p.get_legend()
legend_txt = legend.texts
legend_txt[0].set_text("No Churn")
legend_txt[1].set_text("Churn")
p.set_title('Customer Current_TechSupComplaints Distribution')
```

Code for the plot of **Avg_Days_Delinquent** versus **Target_Code** is given here.

```
plt.figure(figsize=(15,4))
ax=sns.kdeplot(data.loc[(data['Target_Code'] == 0),'Avg_Days_Delinquent']
, color=sns.color_palette("Set2")[0],shade=True,label='no churn')
ax=sns.kdeplot(data.loc[(data['Target_Code'] == 1),'Avg_Days_Delinquent']
, color=sns.color_palette("Set2")[1],shade=True, label='churn')
ax.set(xlabel='Average No of Days Deliquent/Defaluted from paying',
ylabel='Frequency')
plt.title('Average No of Days Deliquent/Defaluted from paying - churn vs
no churn')
```

From this plot, you'll observe that if the average number of days delinquent is more than 16 days, customers start to churn.

Code for the plot of **Account_Age** versus **Target_Code** is given here:

```
plt.figure(figsize=(15,4))
ax=sns.kdeplot(data.loc[(data['Target_Code'] == 0),'Account_Age'] ,
color=sns.color_palette("Set2")[0],shade=True,label='no churn')
ax=sns.kdeplot(data.loc[(data['Target_Code'] == 1),'Account_Age'] ,
color=sns.color_palette("Set2")[1],shade=True, label='churn')
ax.set(xlabel='Account_Age', ylabel='Frequency')
plt.title('Account_Age - churn vs no churn')
```

From this plot, you'll observe that during the initial 15-20 days of opening an account, the amount of customer churn increases; however, after 20 days, the churn rate declines.

Code for the plot of **Percent_Increase_MOM** vs **Target_Code** is given here:

```
plt.figure(figsize=(15,4))
ax=sns.kdeplot(data.loc[(data['Target_Code'] == 0),'Percent_Increase_MOM']
, color=sns.color_palette("Set2")[0],shade=True,label='no churn')
ax=sns.kdeplot(data.loc[(data['Target_Code'] == 1),'Percent_Increase_MOM']
, color=sns.color_palette("Set2")[1],shade=True, label='churn')
ax.set(xlabel='Percent_Increase_MOM', ylabel='Frequency')
plt.title('Percent_Increase_MOM- churn vs no churn')
```

From this plot, you will note that customers who have **Percent_Increase_MOM** within a range of –ve% to +ve% have a greater likelihood of churning.

Activity 14: Performing MN of OSEMN

1. Import the **RandomForestClassifier**, **train_test_split**, and **numpy** library:

    ```
    from sklearn.ensemble import RandomForestClassifier
    from sklearn.model_selection import train_test_split
    import numpy as np
    ```

2. Encode the columns:

    ```
    data["Acct_Plan_Subtype"] = data["Acct_Plan_Subtype"].astype('category').
    cat.codes
    data["Complaint_Code"] = data["Complaint_Code"].astype('ca
    tegory').cat.codes
    data[["Acct_Plan_Subtype","Complaint_Code"]].head()
    ```

3. Split the data into a training and testing set:

    ```
    target = 'Target_Code'
    X = data.drop(['Target_Code','Target_Churn'], axis=1)
    y=data[target]
    X_train, X_test, y_train, y_test = train_test_split(X,y,test_size=0.15,
    random_state=123, stratify=y)
    ```

4. Perform feature selection using the random forest classifier:

    ```
    forest=RandomForestClassifier(n_estimators=500,random_state=1)
    forest.fit(X_train,y_train)
    importances=forest.feature_importances_
    features = data.drop(['Target_Code','Target_Churn'],axis=1).columns
    ```

```
indices = np.argsort(importances)[::-1]
plt.figure(figsize=(15,4))
plt.title("Feature importances using Random Forest")
plt.bar(range(X_train.shape[1]), importances[indices],
        color="r",  align="center")
plt.xticks(range(X_train.shape[1]), features[indices],
rotation='vertical',fontsize=15)
plt.xlim([-1, X_train.shape[1]])
plt.show()
```

5. Import **statsmodels**:

```
import statsmodels.api as sm
top7_features = ['Avg_Days_Delinquent','Percent_Increase_MOM','Avg_Calls_
Weekdays','Current_Bill_Amt','Avg_Calls','Complaint_Code','Account_Age']
logReg = sm.Logit(y_train, X_train[top7_features])
logistic_regression = logReg.fit()
```

6. Find out the parameters:

```
logistic_regression.summary
logistic_regression.params
```

7. Create a function to compute the cost function:

```
coef = logistic_regression.params
def y (coef, Avg_Days_Delinquent,Percent_Increase_MOM,Avg_Calls_
Weekdays,Current_Bill_Amt,Avg_Calls,Complaint_Code,Account_Age) :
    final_coef=coef[0]*Avg_Days_Delinquent+ coef[1]*Percent_Increase_
MOM+coef[2]*Avg_Calls_Weekdays+coef[3]*Current_Bill_Amt+ coef[4]*Avg_
Calls+coef[5]*Complaint_Code+coef[6]*Account_Age
    return final_coef
```

8. Input the given attributes of the customer to the function to obtain the output:

```
Avg_Days_Delinquent:40, Percent_Increase_MOM:5, Avg_Calls_Weekdays:39000,
Current_Bill_Amt:12000, Avg_Calls:9000, Complaint_Code:0, Account_Age:17
y1 = y(coef, 40, 5, 39000,12000,9000,0,17)
p = np.exp(y1) / (1+np.exp(y1))
p
```

Chapter 8: Fine-Tuning Classification Algorithms

Activity 15: Implementing Different Classification Algorithms

1. Import the logistic regression library:

    ```
    from sklearn.linear_model import LogisticRegression
    ```

2. Fit the model:

    ```
    clf_logistic = LogisticRegression(random_state=0, solver='lbfgs').fit(X_
    train[top7_features], y_train)
    clf_logistic
    ```

3. Score the model:

    ```
    clf_logistic.score(X_test[top7_features], y_test)
    ```

4. Import the svm library:

    ```
    from sklearn import svm
    ```

5. Fit the model:

    ```
    clf_svm=svm.SVC(kernel='linear', C=1)
    clf_svm.fit(X_train[top7_features],y_train)
    ```

6. Score the model:

    ```
    clf_svm.score(X_test[top7_features], y_test)
    ```

7. Import the decision tree library:

    ```
    from sklearn import tree
    ```

8. Fit the model:

    ```
    clf_decision = tree.DecisionTreeClassifier()
    clf_decision.fit(X_train[top7_features],y_train)
    ```

9. Score the model:

    ```
    clf_decision.score(X_test[top7_features], y_test)
    ```

10. Import a random forest library:

    ```
    from sklearn.ensemble import RandomForestClassifier
    ```

11. Fit the model:

```
clf_random = RandomForestClassifier(n_estimators=20, max_
depth=None,    min_samples_split=7, random_state=0)
clf_random.fit(X_train[top7_features], y_train)
```

12. Score the model.

```
clf_random.score(X_test[top7_features], y_test)
```

From the results, you can conclude that the random forest has outperformed the rest of the algorithms, with the decision tree having the lowest accuracy. In a later section, you will learn why accuracy is not the correct way to find a model's performance.

Activity 16: Tuning and Optimizing the Model

1. Store five out of seven features, that is, **Avg_Calls_Weekdays**, **Current_Bill_Amt**, **Avg_Calls**, **Account_Age**, and **Avg_Days_Delinquent** in a variable **top5_features**. Store the other two features, **Percent_Increase_MOM** and **Complaint_Code**, in a variable **top5_features**.

```
from sklearn import preprocessing
## Features to transform
top5_features=['Avg_Calls_Weekdays', 'Current_Bill_Amt', 'Avg_Calls',
'Account_Age','Avg_Days_Delinquent']
## Features Left
top2_features=['Percent_Increase_MOM','Complaint_Code']
```

2. Use **StandardScalar** to standardize the five features.

```
scaler = preprocessing.StandardScaler().fit(X_train[top5_features])
X_train_scalar=pd.DataFrame(scaler.transform(X_train[top5_
features]),columns = X_train[top5_features].columns)
```

3. Create a variable **X_train_scalar_combined**, combine the standardized five features with the two features (**Percent_Increase_MOM** and **Complaint_Code**), which were not standardized.

```
X_train_scalar_combined=pd.concat([X_train_scalar,  X_train[top2_
features].reset_index(drop=True)], axis=1, sort=False)
```

4. Apply the same scalar standardization to the test data (**X_test_scalar_combined**).

```
X_test_scalar_combined=pd.concat([X_test_scalar,  X_test[top2_features].
reset_index(drop=True)], axis=1, sort=False)
```

5. Fit the random forest model.

```
clf_random.fit(X_train_scalar_combined, y_train)
```

6. Score the random forest model.

```
clf_random.score(X_test_scalar_combined, y_test)
```

7. Import the library for grid search and use the given parameters:

```
from sklearn.model_selection import GridSearchCV
from sklearn.model_selection import StratifiedKFold
parameters = [ {'min_samples_split': [4,5,7,9,10], 'n_
estimators':[10,20,30,40,50,100,150,160,200,250,300],'max_depth':
[2,5,7,10]}]
```

8. Use grid search CV with stratified k-fold to find out the best parameters.

```
clf_random_grid = GridSearchCV(RandomForestClassifier(), parameters, cv =
StratifiedKFold(n_splits = 10))
clf_random_grid.fit(X_train_scalar_combined, y_train)
```

9. Print the best score and best parameters.

```
print('best score train:', clf_random_grid.best_score_)
print('best parameters train: ', clf_random_grid.best_params_)
```

10. Score the model using the test data.

```
clf_random_grid.score(X_test_scalar_combined, y_test)
```

Activity 17: Comparison of the Models

1. Import the required libraries.

```
from sklearn.metrics import classification_report,confusion_
matrix,accuracy_score
from sklearn import metrics
```

2. Fit the random forest classifier with the parameters obtained from grid search.

```
clf_random_grid = RandomForestClassifier(n_estimators=100, max_depth=7,
    min_samples_split=10, random_state=0)
clf_random_grid.fit(X_train_scalar_combined, y_train)
```

3. Predict on the standardized scalar test data X_test_scalar_combined.

```
y_pred=clf_random_grid.predict(X_test_scalar_combined)
```

4. Fit the classification report.

```
target_names = ['No Churn', 'Churn']
print(classification_report(y_test, y_pred, target_names=target_names))
```

5. Plot the confusion matrix.

```
cm = confusion_matrix(y_test, y_pred)
cm_df = pd.DataFrame(cm,
                     index = ['No Churn','Churn'],
                     columns = ['No Churn','Churn'])
plt.figure(figsize=(8,6))
sns.heatmap(cm_df, annot=True,fmt='g',cmap='Blues')
plt.title('Random Forest \nAccuracy:{0:.3f}'.format(accuracy_score(y_test,
y_pred)))
plt.ylabel('True Values')
plt.xlabel('Predicted Values')
plt.show()
```

6. Import the library for auc and roc curve.

```
from sklearn.metrics import roc_curve,auc
```

7. Use the classifiers which were created in our previous activity, that is, clf_logistic, clf_svm, clf_decision, and clf_random_grid. Create a dictionary of all these models.

```
models = [
{
    'label': 'Logistic Regression',
    'model': clf_logistic,
},
{
    'label': 'SVM',
    'model': clf_svm,
},
{
    'label': 'Decision Tree',
    'model': clf_decision,
},
{
    'label': 'Random Forest Grid Search',
    'model': clf_random_grid,
}
]
```

8. Plot the ROC curve.

```
for m in models:
    model = m['model']
    model.fit(X_train_scalar_combined, y_train)
    y_pred=model.predict(X_test_scalar_combined)
    fpr, tpr, thresholds = roc_curve(y_test, y_pred, pos_label=1)
    roc_auc = metrics.auc(fpr, tpr)
    plt.plot(fpr, tpr, label='%s AUC = %0.2f' % (m['label'], roc_auc))
plt.plot([0, 1], [0, 1],'r--')
plt.xlim([0.0, 1.0])
plt.ylim([0.0, 1.05])
plt.ylabel('Sensitivity(True Positive Rate)')
plt.xlabel('1-Specificity(False Positive Rate)')
plt.title('Receiver Operating Characteristic')
plt.legend(loc="lower right")
plt.show()
```

Comparing the AUC result of different algorithms (logistic regression: 0.78; SVM: 0.79, decision tree: 0.77, and random forest: 0.82), we can conclude that random forest is the best performing model with the AUC score of 0.82 and can be chosen for the marketing team to predict customer churn.

Chapter 9: Modeling Customer Choice

Activity 18: Performing Multiclass Classification and Evaluating Performance

1. Import pandas, **numpy**, **randomforestclassifier**, **train_test_split**, **classification_report**, **confusion_matrix**, **accuracy_score**, **metrics**, **seaborn**, **matplotlib**, and **precision_recall_fscore_support**:

```
import pandas as pd
import numpy as np
from sklearn.ensemble import RandomForestClassifier
from sklearn.model_selection import train_test_split
from sklearn.metrics import classification_report,confusion_matrix,accuracy_score
from sklearn import metrics
from sklearn.metrics import precision_recall_fscore_support
import matplotlib.pyplot as plt
import seaborn as sns
```

2. Load the marketing data using pandas:

```
data= pd.read_csv(r'MarketingData.csv')
data.head(5)
```

3. Check the shape, the missing values, and show the summary report of the data:

```
data.shape
```

The shape should be (20000,7). Check for missing values:

```
data.isnull().values.any()
```

This will return **False** as there are no null values in the data. See the summary report of the data using the **describe** function:

```
data.describe()
```

4. Check the target variable, **Channel**, for the number of transactions for each of the channels:

```
data['Channel'].value_counts()
```

5. Split the data into training and testing sets:

```
target = 'Channel'
X = data.drop(['Channel'],axis=1)
y=data[target]
X_train, X_test, y_train, y_test = train_test_split(X.values,y,test_
size=0.20, random_state=123, stratify=y)
```

6. Fit a random forest classifier and store the model in a **clf_random** variable:

```
clf_random = RandomForestClassifier(n_estimators=20, max_depth=None,
    min_samples_split=7, random_state=0)
clf_random.fit(X_train,y_train)
```

7. Predict on the test data and store the predictions in **y_pred**:

```
y_pred=clf_random.predict(X_test)
```

8. Find out the micro- and macro-average report:

```
precision_recall_fscore_support(y_test, y_pred, average='macro')
precision_recall_fscore_support(y_test, y_pred, average='micro')
```

You will get approximately the following values as output for macro- and micro-averages respectively: **0.891, 0.891, 0.891, None** and **0.891, 0.891, 0.891, None**.

9. Print the classification report:

```
target_names = ["Retail","RoadShow","SocialMedia","Televison"]
print(classification_report(y_test, y_pred,target_names=target_names))
```

10. Plot the confusion matrix:

```
cm = confusion_matrix(y_test, y_pred)
cm_df = pd.DataFrame(cm,
                        index = target_names,
                        columns = target_names)
plt.figure(figsize=(8,6))
sns.heatmap(cm_df, annot=True,fmt='g',cmap='Blues')
plt.title('Random Forest \nAccuracy:{0:.3f}'.format(accuracy_score(y_test,
y_pred)))
plt.ylabel('True Values')
plt.xlabel('Predicted Values')
plt.show()
```

From this activity, we can conclude that our random forest model was able to predict the most effective channel for marketing using customers' annual spend data with an accuracy of 89%.

Activity 19: Dealing with Imbalanced Data

1. Import all the necessary libraries.

```
from sklearn.metrics import classification_report,confusion_
matrix,accuracy_score
import numpy as np
import pandas as pd
import matplotlib.pyplot as plt
import seaborn as sns
from sklearn.ensemble import RandomForestClassifier
from sklearn.model_selection import train_test_split
from imblearn.over_sampling import SMOTE
from sklearn.preprocessing import StandardScaler
from collections import Counter
```

2. Read the dataset into a pandas DataFrame named **bank** and look at the first few rows of the data:

```
bank = pd.read_csv('bank.csv', sep = ';')
bank.head()
```

3. Rename the **y** column as **Target**:

```
bank = bank.rename(columns={
                        'y': 'Target'
                        })
```

4. Replace the **no** value with **0** and **yes** with **1**:

```
bank['Target']=bank['Target'].replace({'no': 0, 'yes': 1})
```

5. Check the shape and missing values in the data:

```
bank.shape
bank.isnull().values.any()
```

6. Use the **describe** function to check the continuous and categorical values:

```
bank.describe()
bank.describe(include=['O'])
```

7. Check the count of the class labels present in the target variable:

```
bank['Target'].value_counts(0)
```

8. Use the **cat.codes** function to encode the **job**, **marital**, **default**, **housing**, **loan**, **contact**, and **poutcome** columns:

```
bank["job"] = bank["job"].astype('category').cat.codes
bank["marital"] = bank["marital"].astype('category').cat.codes
bank["default"] = bank["job"].astype('category').cat.codes
bank["housing"] = bank["marital"].astype('category').cat.codes
bank["loan"] = bank["loan"].astype('category').cat.codes
bank["contact"] = bank["contact"].astype('category').cat.codes
bank["poutcome"] = bank["poutcome"].astype('category').cat.codes
```

Since **education** and **month** are ordinal columns, convert them as follows:

```
bank['education']=bank['education'].replace({'primary': 0, 'secondary':
1,'tertiary':2})
bank['month'].replace(['jan', 'feb', 'mar','apr','may','jun','jul','aug','
sep','oct','nov','dec'], [1,2,3,4,5,6,7,8,9,10,11,12], inplace  = True)
bank['education'].replace({'primary': 0, 'secondary': 1,'tertiary':2})
bank['month'].replace(['jan', 'feb', 'mar','apr','may','jun','jul','aug','
sep','oct','nov','dec'], [1,2,3,4,5,6,7,8,9,10,11,12], inplace  = True)
```

9. Check the **bank** data after conversion:

```
bank.head()
```

10. Split the data into training and testing sets using **train_test_split**, as follows:

```
target = 'Target'
X = bank.drop(['Target'], axis=1)
y=bank[target]

X_train, X_test, y_train, y_test = train_test_split(X,y,test_size=0.15,
random_state=123, stratify=y)
```

11. Check the number of classes in **y_train** and **y_test**:

```
print(sorted(Counter(y_train).items()))
print(sorted(Counter(y_test).items()))
```

12. Use the **standard_scalar** function to transform the **X_train** and **X_test** data. Assign it to the **X_train_sc** and **X_test_sc** variables:

```
standard_scalar = StandardScaler()
X_train_sc = standard_scalar.fit_transform(X_train)
X_test_sc = standard_scalar.transform(X_test)
```

13. Call the random forest classifier with parameters **n_estimators=20**, **max_depth=None**, **min_samples_split=7**, and **random_state=0**:

```
clf_random = RandomForestClassifier(n_estimators=20, max_depth=None,
min_samples_split=7, random_state=0)
```

14. Fit the random forest model:

```
clf_random.fit(X_train_sc,y_train)
```

15. Predict on the test data using the random forest model:

```
y_pred=clf_random.predict(X_test_sc)
```

16. Get the classification report:

```
target_names = ['No', 'Yes']
print(classification_report(y_test, y_pred,target_names=target_names))
cm = confusion_matrix(y_test, y_pred)
```

17. Get the confusion matrix:

```
cm_df = pd.DataFrame(cm,
                     index = ['No', 'Yes'],
                     columns = ['No', 'Yes'])
plt.figure(figsize=(8,6))
sns.heatmap(cm_df, annot=True,fmt='g',cmap='Blues')
plt.title('Random Forest \nAccuracy:{0:.3f}'.format(accuracy_score(y_test,
y_pred)))
plt.ylabel('True Values')
plt.xlabel('Predicted Values')
plt.show()
```

18. Use the **smote()** function on **x_train** and **y_train**. Assign it to the **x_resampled** and **y_resampled** variables, respectively:

```
X_resampled, y_resampled = SMOTE().fit_resample(X_train,y_train)
```

19. Use **standard_scalar** to fit on **x_resampled** and **x_test**. Assign it to the **X_train_sc_resampled** and **X_test_sc** variables:

```
standard_scalar = StandardScaler()
X_train_sc_resampled = standard_scalar.fit_transform(X_resampled)
X_test_sc = standard_scalar.transform(X_test)
```

20. Fit the random forest classifier on **X_train_sc_resampled** and **y_resampled**:

```
clf_random.fit(X_train_sc_resampled,y_resampled)
```

21. Predict on **X_test_sc**:

```
y_pred=clf_random.predict(X_test_sc)
```

22. Generate the classification report:

```
target_names = ['No', 'Yes']
print(classification_report(y_test, y_pred,target_names=target_names))
```

23. Plot the confusion matrix:

```
cm = confusion_matrix(y_test, y_pred)

cm_df = pd.DataFrame(cm,
                    index = ['No', 'Yes'],
                    columns = ['No', 'Yes'])
plt.figure(figsize=(8,6))
sns.heatmap(cm_df, annot=True,fmt='g',cmap='Blues')
plt.title('Random Forest \nAccuracy:{0:.3f}'.format(accuracy_score(y_test,
y_pred)))
plt.ylabel('True Values')
plt.xlabel('Predicted Values')
plt.show()
```

In this activity, our bank marketing data was highly imbalanced. We observed that, although without using a sampling technique our model accuracy is around 90%, the recall score and macro-average score was 32% (Yes - Term Deposit) and 65%, respectively. This implies that our model is not able to generalize, and most of the time it misses potential customers who would subscribe to the term deposit.

On the other hand, when we used SMOTE, our model accuracy was around 87%, but the recall score and macro-average score was 61% (Yes - Term Deposit) and 76%, respectively. This implies that our model can generalize and, more than 60% of the time, it detects potential customers who would subscribe to the term deposit.

Index

About

All major keywords used in this book are captured alphabetically in this section. Each one is accompanied by the page number of where they appear.

Printed in Great Britain
by Amazon